European Studies in Social Psychology

Social interaction in individual development

European studies in social psychology

Editorial Board: J. M. F. JASPARS, University of Oxford; WILLEM DOISE, Université de Genève; COLIN FRASER, University of Cambridge; SERGE MOSCOVICI, Ecole des Hautes Etudes en Sciences Sociales; KLAUS R. SCHERER, Justus-Liebig-Universität Giessen; MARIO VON CRANACH, Universität Bern.

The series is jointly published by the Cambridge University Press and the Editions de la Maison des Sciences de l'Homme, in close collaboration with the Laboratoire Européen de Psychologie Sociale of the Maison, as part of the joint publishing agreement established in 1977 between the Fondation de la Maison des Sciences de l'Homme and the Syndics of the Cambridge University Press.

It consists mainly of specially commissioned volumes on specific themes, particularly those linking work in social psychology with other disciplines. It will also include occasional volumes of 'Current Research'.

Cette collection est publiée en co-édition par Cambridge University Press et les Editions de la Maison des Sciences de l'Homme en collaboration étroite avec le Laboratoire Européen de Psychologie Sociale de la Maison. Elle s'intègre dans le programme de co-édition etabli en 1977 par la Fondation de la Maison des Sciences de l'Homme et les Syndics de Cambridge University Press.

Elle comprend essentiellement des ouvrages sur des thèmes spécifiques permettant de mettre en rapport la psychologie sociale et d'autres disciplines, avec à l'occasion des volumes consacrés à des 'recherches en cours'.

Already published:

The analysis of action: recent theoretical and empirical advances, edited by Mario von Cranach and Rom Harré
Current issues in European social psychology, volume 1, edited by Willem Doise and Serge Moscovici
Advances in the social psychology of language, edited by Colin Fraser and Klaus R. Scherer
Social markers in speech, edited by Klaus R. Scherer and Howard Giles
Social identity and intergroup relations, edited by the late Henri Tajfel

Forthcoming:

Social representations, edited by Serge Moscovici and Robert Farr

Social interaction in individual development

Edited by
Willem Doise
Université de Genève

and

Augusto Palmonari
Università di Bologna

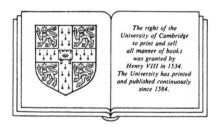

The right of the
University of Cambridge
to print and sell
all manner of books
was granted by
Henry VIII in 1534.
The University has printed
and published continuously
since 1584.

Cambridge University Press
Cambridge
London   New York   New Rochelle
Melbourne   Sydney

Editions de la Maison des Sciences de l'Homme
Paris

CAMBRIDGE UNIVERSITY PRESS
Cambridge, New York, Melbourne, Madrid, Cape Town, Singapore,
São Paulo, Delhi, Dubai, Tokyo, Mexico City

Cambridge University Press
The Edinburgh Building, Cambridge CB2 8RU, UK

Published in the United States of America by Cambridge University Press, New York

www.cambridge.org
Information on this title: www.cambridge.org/9780521154840

First published 1984
First paperback edition 2010

A catalogue record for this publication is available from the British Library

Library of Congress catalogue card number: 83-7697

ISBN 978-0-521-25024-5 Hardback
ISBN 978-0-521-15484-0 Paperback

Contents

Contributors   xii

Acknowledgements   xiv

1 **Introduction: The sociopsychological study of individual development**   1

Willem Doise and Augusto Palmonari

  1 The editors   1

  2 The recognition of the social in studies of development   2

  3 A sociopsychological conception of individual development   9

  4 New approaches to old debates   13

  5 Research implications   18

  6 Content of the volume   19

  References   20

Part I

The ethological and sociological study of interaction patterns   23

2 **Development of early peer interaction**   25

Hubert Montagner, Albert Restoin, Véronique Ullmann, Danilo Rodriguez, Dominique Godard and Mireille Viala

  1 General outline of the method   26

  2 Results   27

  3 Conclusions   37

  References   39

3 **Family way of life and interaction patterns**   42

Martti Takala

  1 Socioecological approach and the concept of the way of life   42

2 Activity structure as revealed by the use of time   46
3 Work, urbanization and interaction patterns   48
4 Work conditions and family interaction   53
5 Family way of life and children's social development   55
6 Final comments   59
   References   60

Part II
Adult control techniques   63

**4 Parental control techniques in the context of socialization
   theory**   65
   H. Rudolph Schaffer
   1 Socialization models   66
   2 Parental control techniques   71
   3 A developmental framework   75
   References   77

**5 Behaviour and goals in adult–child interaction in the day
   nursery**   78
   Francesca Emiliani and Bruna Zani
   1 Introduction   78
   2 Methodology   80
   3 Data analysis   82
   4 Conclusions   89
   References   89

Part III
Language development   91

**6 On the failure of the interactionist paradigm in language
   acquisition: a re-evaluation**   93
   *Luigia Camaioni, Maria F. P. de Castro Campos and Claudia de
   Lemos*
   1 Introduction   93
   2 Towards a new paradigm   96
   3 Empirical evidence   100
   4 Methodological choices   103
   References   105

7 **Coming to understand that referential communication can
   be ambiguous**   107
   Elizabeth J. Robinson and W. Peter Robinson
   1 Introduction   107
   2 What is said and what is meant?   109
   3 Development from Fitok to Nurok   111
   4 Realizing that you do not understand   114
   5 The current state of the problem   117
   6 Summary and discussion   117
   Acknowledgement   122
   References   122

Part IV
Social interaction in cognitive development   125

8 **Social regulations in cognitive development**   127
   Gabriel Mugny, Paola De Paolis and Felice Carugati
   1 A socio-psychological approach to cognitive development   127
   2 Social regulations of socio-cognitive conflict   131
   3 Social marking of cognitive responses   136
   4 Some illustrations of an experimental paradigm   139
   5 Conclusions   143
   Acknowledgment   144
   References   144

9 **The representation of distance in the individual and
   collective drawings of children**   147
   Marie-Danielle Frésard
   1 Introduction   147
   2 Method   149
   3 Results   150
   4 Conclusions   154
   References   156

Part V
Understanding the social environment   157

10 **Some trends in structuring social knowledge.
    A developmental study**   159
    Luciano Arcuri, Rosanna De Negri Trentin, Remo Job and Paola Salmaso
    1 Script theory and the representation of social knowledge   159

2 The research   161
3 Conclusion   168
References   172

**11 Levels of social and logico-mathematical thinking:
their nature and inter-relations**   173
Gustav Jahoda
1 Introduction   173
2 Method   174
3 Results: I. Individual tasks   175
4 Results: II. Inter-relations   182
5 Discussion   185
Acknowledgements   186
References   186

**Part VI
Social construction of adolescent identity**   189

**12 Coordinating the sociological and psychological in adolescent
interactions**   191
Carolyn Wood Sherif
1 Social-psychological bases for changed interactions during
   adolescence   193
2 Effective sociocultural frameworks for studying adolescents 198
3 Formation of 'natural' groups among adolescents   202
4 Intercategory and intergroup differentiations   209
5 Impact of the changing times on adolescent groups   213
6 Conclusion   214
References   214

**13 Social differentiation in adolescence: the case of
North Africans in France**   217
Maryla Zaleska and Hanna Malewska-Peyre
1 Cultural differentiation   217
2 Population studied   219
3 The alternative choice questionnaire   219
4 Results   220
5 Cultural differentiation of the North African boys and girls 221
6 Cultural differentiation of the North African boys in the
   'mineurs de justice' and comparison groups   225

7   Experience of racial discrimination   226
8   Some hypotheses in conclusion   228
References   230

14   Re-socialization processes in institutionalized adolescents   231
Felice Carugati, Francesca Emiliani and Augusto Palmonari
1   Institutional care   231
2   Experiments in re-socialization   234
3   Life in apartment groups   238
4   Conclusions   242
References   245

Part VII
On becoming a worker   247

**15   Social interaction in adolescent development: schools,
sex roles and entry to work**   249
Michael A. West and Peggy Newton
1   Introduction   249
2   The study   250
3   The effects of school organization and ethos 251
4   Sex differences in transition from school to work 253
5   Life changes   257
References   259

**16   Work entry: a critical moment in the occupational
socialization process**   261
Guido Sarchielli
1   Introduction   261
2   Research on the first contact with the world of work 264
3   Two studies in Bologna   268
4   Conclusions   274
References   275

Concluding remarks   279

17   Characteristics of contemporary socialization studies   281
Willem Doise and Augusto Palmonari
1   An assessment by H. R. Schaffer   281
2   Further comments   282

Author index   284

Contributors

LUCIANO ARCURI
Università di Padova, Italy
LUIGIA CAMAIONI
Università di Roma, Italy
FELICE CARUGATI
Università di Urbino, Italy
MARIA F. P. DE CASTRO CAMPOS
State University of Campinas, Brazil
CLAUDIA DE LEMOS
State University of Campinas, Brazil
ROSANNA DE NEGRI TRENTIN
Università di Padova, Italy
PAOLA DE PAOLIS
Université de Genève, Switzerland
FRANCESCA EMILIANI
Università di Bologna, Italy
MARIE-DANIELLE FRÉSARD
Université de Genève, Switzerland
DOMINIQUE GODARD
Université de Besançon, France
GUSTAV JAHODA
University of Strathclyde, Scotland
REMO JOB
Università di Padova, Italy
HANNA MALEWSKA-PEYRE
Centre de Formation et de Recherche de l'Education Surveillée, Vaucresson, France
HUBERT MONTAGNER
Université de Besançon, France
GABRIEL MUGNY
Université de Genève, Switzerland
PEGGY NEWTON
Huddersfield Polytechnic, England
AUGUSTO PALMONARI
Università di Bologna, Italy
ALBERT RESTOIN
Université de Besançon, France

ELIZABETH J. ROBINSON
  University of Bristol, England
W. PETER ROBINSON
  University of Bristol, England
DANILO RODRIGUEZ
  Université de Besançon, France
PAOLA SALMASO
  Università di Padova, Italy
GUIDO SARCHIELLI
  Università di Trento, Italy
H. RUDOLPH SCHAFFER
  University of Strathclyde, Scotland
MARTTI TAKALA
  University of Jyväskylä, Finland
VÉRONIQUE ULLMANN
  Université de Besançon, France
MIREILLE VIALA
  Université de Besançon, France
MICHAEL A. WEST
  Bermuda College, Bermuda
CAROLYN WOOD SHERIF
  The Pennsylvania State University, USA
MARYLA ZALESKA
  Centre National de la Recherche Scientifique, France
BRUNA ZANI
  Università di Bologna, Italy

Acknowledgements

The editors would like to thank the contributors who displayed a great deal of good will in drafting and adapting their chapters to integrate them within the general framework of this book. The Maison des Sciences de l'Homme in Paris, the Carlo Cattaneo Institute in Bologna, and the Universities of Bologna, Geneva and Urbino have between them enabled the organization of several working meetings and a colloquium on 'Social Interaction in Individual Development' (Urbino, 15–20 December 1980) which have made this book possible. Editorial assistance by E. Aeschlimann and P. Carroll is gratefully acknowledged.

1. Introduction: The sociopsychological study of individual development

WILLEM DOISE and AUGUSTO PALMONARI

1. The editors

The two editors of this book met for the first time at a general meeting of the European Association of Experimental Social Psychology at Bielefeld (West Germany) in 1975. Their interest in social psychology had very different origins. After taking a degree in psychology at the Sorbonne, one of the editors then did a doctoral thesis in social psychology and, by 1967, had begun a series of experimental investigations on inter-group relations and group decision making (see Doise, 1978). The other obtained a doctorate in medicine at the University of Bologna and continued a specialization in psychology which he began then in association with the Institute of Psychology at the same university. He became more deeply interested in social psychology during the period when he worked with abandoned and socially maladjusted children, and, more recently, in the course of his work on the social identity of adolescents (Palmonari *et al.*, 1979; Palmonari *et al.*, in press).

Since this first meeting the association between the editors has continued within the frameworks of the European Association and of the Maison des Sciences de l'Homme in Paris and, most recently, within a convention involving their respective faculties at the universities of Bologna and Geneva.

If the editors of this book actively sought to increase their contacts, it was in part because of the increasing convergence of their research interests, which ultimately led to joint research projects involving their respective teams, work to which a chapter in this volume by their colleagues Mugny, De Paolis and Carugati is dedicated. But an equally important reason is that at a more general level their conceptions of the nature and function of social psychology led them to question the implications of the work of psychologists and social psychologists. Thus, while one (Palmonari, 1981, 1982) was engaged in an extensive investigation of psychologists' conceptions of their work, the other (Doise, 1982) was working on an analysis of the explanatory schemes employed by social psychologists. At first sight, these are very different enterprises but in fact they both tackle the problem of articulation between the individual and the collective, whether at the level of practice or at that of theory.

It is precisely this problem of articulation between the individual and the collective which will also be the focus of this volume, because current studies of development pose this question in a quite explicit manner.

2. The recognition of the social in studies of development

One of the most marked characteristics of current studies of the psychological development of the individual is their more and more frequent recourse to explanations of a social nature. The already widespread use of the word 'social' in the designation of different lines of research is one indication of this. Behaviourists refer to social learning (Bandura, 1977) or social behaviourism (Staats, 1975), ethologists to social development (Hinde, 1978), psychologists to the role of social interaction in cognitive development (Perret-Clermont, 1980) or of social cognition (Flavell and Ross, 1981), and psycholinguists to interactional processes in the construction of language (Bruner and Sherwood, 1981). These theoretical approaches seek to move beyond a position of sociological determinism which represents the child as a passive entity modelled through processes of socialization. The emphasis is rather on the manner in which young children actively construct their own competencies in interacting and coping with the social environment. This general trend is particularly evident in current studies of language development, but there are other examples of it that we .will discuss in this general introduction before moving on to the more specific and detailed studies which make up the rest of the volume.

2.1. Socio-ethological studies

The work of Bowlby (1969) on attachment describes how the new-born human is pre-adapted to becoming a social being thanks to contacts established with an individual of its own species, its mother. A series of similar investigations have since enabled us to obtain a more precise picture of the behavioural repertoires possessed by children from the first days, weeks or months of their lives for engaging in social interaction. Dunn (1977) enumerates among these repertoires movements of locating the nipple, sucking, movements towards mother–infant contact, and signal movements such as smiling and crying. To these may be added the perceptual mechanism which induces the infant to fix its gaze on the mother's face and later on her eyes during feeding sessions (Stern, 1977).

Even more significant for our purposes are the theses advanced by Newson (1974) and Schaffer (1977): the early interaction between the baby and the mother (or her substitute) constitutes a context in which the mother attributes 'intentions' and 'meanings' to the gestures, expressions and spontaneous activities of the baby. The mother and other adults around the small child attribute to it capacities for social responsiveness with regard to desire, intentions and feelings communicated to others. It will be within these shared understandings and shared expectations, constructed by the adult with regard to the child, that we must look for the origins of intentionality, self-consciousness and communication.

In this general context one might refer to the work of Trevarthen (1979) who distinguishes two important aspects of the development of latent sociability and intentionality in the new-born. The *primary inter-subjectivity* of the two and three month old is manifested by a highly varied repertoire of expressive behaviours, a ready orientation of gaze towards or away from the mother's face, and immediate responses to her signs of interest and to her speech. Later, between the fourth and eighth months there occurs a period of games and exchanges with the mother during which a form of joint action becomes possible in which the baby is actor or motivator and the mother is a secondary participant in the action. Thus a *secondary inter-subjectivity* is established, characterized by manifestations of the fundamental urge for cooperative understanding. In effect, towards nine months the child becomes conscious of sharing his own world with others and can give his interlocutor an object so that the other will do something in relation to the child's own action.

There remains the problem of determining to what extent this early readiness for social interaction is constructed, as opposed to transmitted as some kind of social instinct. On this subject Trevarthen speaks explicitly of instincts for cooperation, and disagrees with those authors who interpret in terms of learning those phenomena that underlie the genesis of the self. But his polemic is also addressed to the authors mentioned above (Dunn, Newson, Schaffer) who, while acknowledging a predisposition in the child to social interaction, none the less seek in social exchanges the origins of the elaboration of new interactional competencies, of intentionality, and of self-consciousness.

2.2. Social behaviourism and social learning

For the behaviourist the study of psychological development is essentially a study of learning. The environment plays a role of prime importance, but it is not studied as something social. Recently, however, work deriving from behaviourism has come to argue for a more systematic study of the social as such, and thus to recommend linking studies of the laws of learning and analyses derived from social psychology. Thus Staats (1975), following Doob (1947), locates the notion of attitude at the centre of this conception of learning; it is attitudes that determine the reinforcing qualities of behaviour and that direct them. But while stressing the necessity of studying attitudes in order to explain the evolution of specific behaviours, Staats (chapter 7) breaches the conceptual framework of behaviourism by introducing other social psychological notions such as those of the self, reactance, communication, attraction, conformity, prejudice, leadership and impression formation. In the same way, Bandura (1977) emphasizes the importance of studies of social processes in accounting for learning. From birth the social environment in which children develop will model their thought processes. Consciousness of the various characteristics which emerge in their environment as well as the strategies for classifying, elaborating and interpreting information will be deduced principally from observation of the behavioural models around them. It will be likely also that structural aspects of the environment such as mathematical relations will not be grasped directly and intuitively, but that they will be mediated by the manipulations and symbolic actions that others effect upon the environment. It is unlikely that direct learning will take place only on the basis of contacts with physical objects since the individual's resources for sampling environmental characteristics are too limited. Socially mediated experience enormously expands the individual's knowledge.

2.3 The development of social cognition

Though Kohlberg has followed Piaget in pursuing his research on moral development, he nevertheless places much greater emphasis than Piaget on the need specifically to study the social context. Other authors, studying other aspects of social development, also distance themselves from Piaget as is shown for example in the following quotation from Waller (1978, p. 13): 'These remarkable and relatively early attempts by Piaget to integrate aspects of social development within his theoretical and structuralist model of cognitive development characteristically consider social development only as an epiphenomenon of cognitive development.' Damon (1977, p. 320) also considered an exclusively cognitive analysis of social development as insufficient: 'the influence of general structural development upon social knowledge is to a certain extent uneven. A change in one area does not automatically and immediately register across all other areas in the same manner. Parallels between different aspects of social knowledge do not generally hold in transitive or uniform fashion.' He envisages the development of social intelligence as being realized through a dynamic that is specific to itself:

As we have asserted on several occasions, there is never a total, one-to-one relation between any general or partial structure and any social concept. That is, no level of social knowledge in any area can be wholly explained by the use of a child's classification, compensation, or social perspective taking at that level . . . All social concepts are organized according to their own particular principles.

From this derives the attempt to study social development as such. Waller, for example, studies the development of expectations with respect to others' behaviour (*Verhaltenserwartungen*). He demonstrates it is the most obvious social distinctions, with respect to age and sex, that principally determine the behavioural expectations of young children, while various more situational characteristics only later influence expectations. In describing the development of justifications used in a task involving distribution of rewards, Damon (1977) distinguishes three levels, each divided into two sub-stages. At the first level children justify only with reference to their own desires or invoke more objective but variable reasons which serve in practice as *a posteriori* justifications for self-serving decisions. These are justifications of the form: 'I will take three for myself and I will give him two because I want them more' or 'I am taking more because I am bigger/older.' At the first sub-stage of the subsequent level strict rules of equality are applied, while at the second sub-stage children invoke the respective merits of different partners. However, this right to equality, like inequality as a result of merit, is invoked in a rigid and inflexible fashion, all other behaviour being considered as unjust. It is only at the third level that the notion of need intervenes and more complex combinations of the various principles appear. At the end of this phase, equality, merit, and need in effect constitute parameters which can be weighted according to more situational exigencies.

It should be stressed that Kohlberg, Damon and Waller provide only three examples among a great variety of approaches which all have as their object the study of socio-cognitive development in the child. In order to appreciate this variety and the significance of some of the recent work in this area, the reader is invited to turn to Flavell and Ross (1981) and to Butterworth and Light (1982) for exhaustive reviews of the Anglo-Saxon literature, and also to Eckensberger and Silbereisen (1980) who report on several investigations carried out in Germany.

2.4. The socio-genesis of intelligence

We cannot discuss here all the factors that argue for a social definition of intelligence, considering it not simply as a system of coordinations of action schemas, as Piaget does, but rather as essentially a system of social coordinations (see on this subject Doise and Mugny, 1981). But let us present some more specific propositions, integrated within this social definition, which have been illustrated experimentally.

1. It is in coordinating their actions with others that children are led to construct cognitive coordinations which they would not be capable of individually. Hence, it has been shown experimentally that at a certain level in their development, children succeed in accomplishing certain motor coordination or spatial transformation tasks when they can carry these out together, while they would not succeed in the same coordinations or transformations if working on them alone.

2. Childen who have participated in various social coordinations then become capable of executing these coordinations alone. Individual progress resulting from participation in social interaction has been equally well observed after a collective performance of various conservation tests (liquid, length, number) as after participation in spatial transformations or motor coordination tasks.

3. Cognitive operations accomplished with respect to one set of materials and in a specific social situation none the less assume characteristics of stability and generality and are to some degree transposable to other situations and other materials. This effect of generalization accompanying the ability to perform cognitive operations at the individual level as a result of social interactions has been demonstrated primarily using various conservation tests.

4. Social interaction becomes a source of cognitive progress by virtue of

the socio-cognitive conflict it engenders. In accordance with a genetic conception of cognitive development we view this development as the elaboration of a more complex structure which reorganizes and coordinates previous regulations. It is precisely the simultaneous confrontation of different individual perspectives or focuses during social interaction that necessitates and gives rise to their integration within a new structure. Spatial transformation and length conservation tasks in particular have illustrated this effect of socio-cognitive conflict. We should stress that for such conflicts to be a source of development, it is not necessary for the opposing perspective to be cognitively more advanced than the one the child is already capable of; indeed, provided they set up an opposition, children can profit from responses at a similar level or indeed at a level inferior to their own.

5. For a socio-cognitive conflict to occur the participants in an interaction must already have certain cognitive tools at their disposal. The child will only profit from an interaction if he is already able to establish a difference between his own approach and that of the other. This prerequisite competence allows some children to benefit from particular interactions while others, who have not achieved it, will not. Experiments using motor coordination and conservation of liquid tasks have demonstrated the role of such initial competence and, more generally, verified that any interaction is not necessarily profitable for any child.

6. The social regulations that govern a given interaction constitute an important factor in the establishment of new cognitive coordinations in a given situation. A certain correspondence can exist between social regulations and cognitive coordinations enabling resolution of the socio-cognitive conflict. The contribution by Mugny, De Paolis and Carugati in this volume develops this last proposition in more detail.

2.5. The social study of adolescence

There is scarcely one recent book on adolescence that does not view the construction of identity as the central problem faced by the adolescent. It is during this phase that individuals must define themselves both in continuity with what they were as children, despite all the changes that are occurring, and at the same time in synchrony with a central 'core' of self, despite the different ways of representing and presenting self to others in different situations. Even if one acknowledges that social factors are very important in shaping the adolescent's identity, such a proposition remains none the less vague and imprecise. Thus a close reading of the works of Erikson (1950, 1968) reveals that the concept of identity has not been developed in such a way as to link it with the study of those social relations in which the individual is enmeshed. The paradigmatic cases that he presents involve the introduction of an identity concept already elaborated within a psychoanalytic framework, but he does not articulate this concept with a theoretical model of social dynamics.

On the other hand, sociologists had strongly urged the importance of social factors in this phase of the individual's life at a time when many writers on adolescence had not even adopted the concept of identity. They were led to advance the thesis that adolescence only became a subject of discussion when industrial societies were emerging as historical realities. At this time formal instruction was prolonged in order to train the more competent individuals who were necessary to the social organization. On the basis of this thesis and of extensive empirical research, it has been maintained that the social behaviour of adolescents varies substantially from one social class to another (Hollingshead, 1949), that peer groups are an instrument of socialization as important as the family, and assume a role that the family cannot (Eisenstadt, 1956), and that the large amount of time adolescents spend together gives rise to intense and novel exchanges within their groups, thus creating juvenile sub-cultures (Coleman, 1961; Friedenberg, 1963).

However, this and other work (for example that of Elder, 1968, on role conflict) does not explain the active involvement of the individual in the constitution of these peer groups, in the acquisition of a social role, or in the elaboration of a sub-culture by means of which the group defines itself. In other words, it seems that the concepts of self and identity, on which psychologists lay so much stress, are not in themselves sufficient to provide an exhaustive understanding of the phase of development that constitutes adolescence in our society.

The theoretical contributions and research by Muzafer and Carolyn Sherif (1964, 1965) furnish the conceptual tools to link the study of development of the self or social identity with study of the experiences and social positions specific to adolescents. They demonstrate a means of escaping from the epistemological impasse which studies of adolescence have previously faced. These authors show how in effect a relation of interdependence is established between those 'universal' phenomena that occur during the adolescent period and the 'self' system of each individual. The universals to which they refer concern the biological side of personal development (the rapidity of physiological development), the social reactions that these physical changes give rise to and also the changes in responsibility assumed by adolescents in liberating themselves from the tutelage of adults. In their turn, these modifications in the self influence behaviours and attitudes, thus giving rise to a process of rapid change both at the personal level and in social relations. An example of these changes is the increasing interest that adolescents show in relation to their peer groups.

All the elements involved in this complex scenario mutually influence one another and as a result there are therefore reciprocal influences between psychological factors (the self system), social factors (membership in the family, gender relationships, life context, position in the school milieu or entry into work) and social behaviour. Elsewhere, (Palmonari *et al.*, in press), one of us has specified the intimate connection that exists between the self system as defined by Sherif and identity as defined in work in developmental psychology since Erikson. In chapter 12 of this same volume Carolyn Sherif presents in more detail the theoretical concepts that have inspired this work.

These are only some examples of the recognition of the social in studies of development, both at the level of concepts and at that of empirical research paradigms. The present volume is situated in this tradition of research and provides some more specific and detailed examples of this theoretical and empirical socio-developmental enquiry. But before presenting these studies we believe it will be useful to offer a general conception of the links that exist between individual development and social interaction.

3. A sociopsychological conception of individual development

Let us first of all dispel any possible misunderstandings. It is not a matter of presenting here a detailed description of specific mechanisms which intervene in the development of individuals. Given the number of mechanisms of a sociopsychological nature, the models that describe them can only be integrated by employing ideas of a very general kind. When Piaget offers the notions of assimilation and accommodation to account for cognitive development, these general notions alone provide no understanding, even less a precise description, of the processes by which the individual adapts cognitively to his environment while adapting this environment to his own cognitive schemas. Nevertheless, the heuristic role played by such general notions is not any the less important, orienting the investigation of the researcher both at the theoretical level, by allowing him to retain only those models that are compatible with these notions, and at the empirical level, leading him to construct paradigms that are able to induce processes whose descriptions will accord with these general ideas. It is just such a general conception of development that we propose here; it should by itself enable us to integrate very different studies within the same framework and, at the same time, it requires that we elaborate more detailed models with respect to specific empirical studies in order to provide a sufficient account of the sociopsychological mechanisms at work in development.

We should also make it clear at this point, although we return to it later, that our concern to articulate psychological and social explanations does not amount to emphasizing the priority of one of these two types of explanation. As is clearly demonstrated by Piaget's magisterial research on cognitive development, a description of development at a single level can indeed become an explanation when it demonstrates that more complex operational structures result from the integration of more elementary factors. This is certainly an explanation which, if not exhaustive, is nevertheless autonomous. Likewise, a sociologist like Bourdieu also moves towards an explanation, though of course of a very different nature, when he studies the way in which the institutionalized expression of intelligence, in other words educational success, is a function of the dynamics of social differentiation and reproduction. It is true that these two types of explanation, one psychological, the other sociological, have developed independently of one another and are based on dynamics which in each case obey laws that are specific to themselves, and that it is not necessary to study the dynamics of one in order to understand those of the other. However, when one seeks to answer the question why certain of the more complex cognitive operations described by Piaget are manifested by some children in a social situation but not by others one is moving beyond Piaget's theoretical framework. In the same way one has moved outside Bourdieu's framework when one asks whether children of different social backgrounds successfully master the same cognitive operations. Answers to these questions are no less theoretically and socially important, and it would be arbitrary to treat them as secondary to those that rest only on a psychological or on a sociological explanation. They depend on an articulation of both these types of analysis.

It should already be clear from the preceding discussion that for us a socio-psychological explanation of individual development cannot be seen in terms of a reductionist viewpoint, whether psychological or sociological. We do not consider the individual to be the passive outcome of social dynamics any more than we consider social dynamics as simply the accumulated effects of autonomous individuals' actions. The psychological is more than an interjection of the social; the social is more than a projection of the psychological.

Our conception of development is constructivist: it is in acting in and upon the environment that the individual develops. But further than that it is socioconstructivist: it is above all through interacting with others, coordinating his approaches to reality with those of others, that the individual masters new approaches. Together with authors as diverse as Bourdieu (1980), Piaget (1975), Staats (1975) and Trevarthen (1982), we consider the individual as mastering the schemas, the regulations of action, the behavioural repertoires and the motives which enable him to participate in social interaction. In the course of these interactions, individual principles of organization are integrated within complex social regulations which, in conditions to be determined, produce in these individuals more complex capacities for coordination. These new competencies then allow the individual to benefit from more complex social regulations, and so on. Certainly, different authors invoke different processes, such as equilibration (Piaget), attitudinal and directional reinforcement (Staats), interiorization (Bourdieu), cooperative understanding (Trevarthen), to account for these growing structures. Our aim is precisely that of integrating the descriptions of these processes within a more general sociopsychological conception of development.

This conception is based on the notion of a spiral of causality: a given state of the individual (I_n) makes possible participation in given social interactions (S_{n+1}) which gives rise to a new individual state (I_{n+1}). As Figure 1 indicates, individual mechanisms I_0 allow the individual to integrate himself in social regulations at level S_1, leading to a state I_1. Of course, at a certain level of generality it is arbitrary to begin the process with a state I_0 or S_0.

General as these ideas may be, they are not compatible with any and every more specific proposition. Thus with respect to cognitive development, for example, they do not allow one to assume a positive effect of any social interaction at any point in individual development. Only those interactions which give rise to the union of clearly determined individual approaches will result in new regulations; individuals who have not mastered certain minimal schemas or organizations will not be able to profit from social interaction in the same manner as those who have such schemas at their disposal. On the other hand, decisive progress may be precipitated in the course of very different kinds of social interaction involving, for example, the real or symbolic presence of another or perhaps only the presence of socially organized material. This does not necessarily mean that an individual's progress will be manifested during the interaction itself as individual restructuring may extend far beyond the particular interaction.

Let us also recall here that, by definition, our conception is concerned only with development, that not all interaction is necessarily structuring and that there may be destructuring interactions. Just as Piaget (1975) postulates that perturbations of earlier regulations may be necessary to make the elaboration of new, more advanced regulations possible, so one can also postulate that socially produced disorganization will sometimes be necessary to generate new socio-affective or socio-cognitive regulations.

The heuristic value of the general conception sketched here can of course only be tested through its use in theoretical and empirical enquiry.

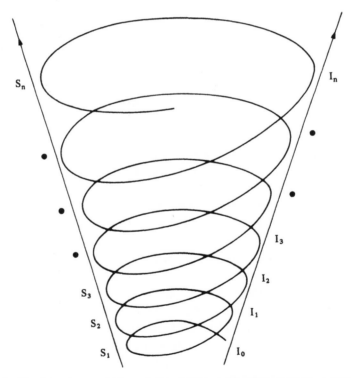

Figure 1. Graphic representation of the sociopsychological dynamics of individual development.

It is precisely this that we hope to achieve through this book, by showing that the socio-psychological approach to individual development can help to resolve many of the debates that perennially involve psychologists.

4. New approaches to old debates

4.1. Individual and society

From the beginnings of modern psychology a distinction has been made between explanations centred on the study of the individual and those centred on collective realities:

All such mental products of a general character presuppose the existence of a mental *community* composed of many individuals, though, of course, their deepest sources are the psychical attributes of the individual. Because of this dependence on the community, in particular on the social community, the whole department of psychological investigation here involved is designated as *social psychology*, and is distinguished from individual psychology, or *experimental* psychology as it may be called because of its predominating method. (Wundt, 1907, p. 26)

This distinction formulated by the founder of the first psychological laboratory very quickly became an opposition. In this respect, we may recall the debate between Allport and McDougall which is still regularly resurrected by different social psychologists, although a detailed study of explanatory approaches (Doise, 1982) shows that the opposition between the individual and the collective is less profound in specific investigations than in general debates. The essence of the task which falls to social psychologists appears to us to be the articulation of explanations of a psychological type with those of a social kind.

Sociologists have also attempted such articulations between levels of analysis, as in the case of Parsons (1964) in his study of the interpenetration of personality systems, family and society. He begins his analysis with a description of the mother-child dyadic system which is predominant at the beginning of the child's life but which must subsequently yield somewhat in the face of constraints within the pre-existing family system where relations between father and mother prevail over it. Abandoning his narrow functional dependence on the mother, the child acquires a functional autonomy that will be useful in the family and enters into a system of authority relations with the father. Up to this point the social development of girls and boys will be identical. Thus, the child will have encountered within the family a bipolarity characterizing the dynamics of much social interaction: the pole of security and solidarity symbolized by the 'paradise' of his inter-dependence with the mother, and the pole of efficacy, an opening to the external world, symbolized by the father who will not only uproot the child from his interdependence with the mother but will also be at the intersection of the family system and the larger social system. Sexual differentiation, which transcends differentiation within the family to link it with general differentiation in society as a whole, is thus directly related to this polarity in which efficacy and universality are contrasted to affectivity and particularism. To summarize, within the family the child learns to manage the relations of authority and bipolarity found in the life of groups. Here will be the essential components of the various social roles that individuals may occupy in different societies. We thus have here an attempt to integrate the study of the development of the child's status within the family with that of its participation in more general social dynamics.

In a study of the characteristics of aesthetic judgments, Bourdieu (1979) argues in favour of a genetic sociology which would be concerned with examining the individual's acquisition of different social taxonomies. In effect, such social classification schemes would be at the basis of aesthetic and value judgments about the social world:

The cognitive structures that social agents employ to understand the social world at a practical level are internalized social structures. Practical knowledge of the social world as assumed by 'rational' behaviour in this world employs classificatory schemas (or, if one prefers, 'forms of classification', 'mental structures', 'symbolic forms', expressions which, if one ignores the connotations, are almost interchangeable), historical schemas of perception and appreciation which are the product of objective divisions into classes (classes of age, sexual classes, social classes) and which operate beyond consciousness and discourse. Being products of the internalization of a society's fundamental structures, these principles of division are common to all agents in this society and make possible the production of a common and sensible world, of a world of common sense. (Bourdieu, 1979, pp. 545f)

This excursion into the domain of sociologists ought to demonstrate that they too are preoccupied with a search within the individual for organizational schemas that are related to social stratifications. However, the two sociologists we have cited have often been criticized for having over-emphasized the impact of society on the individual, and their attempts at articulation should for the moment be considered only as declarations of intent, not as objectives in the process of realization. We will not enter into this debate here, though in terms of our conception of a spiral of development these sociologists can be viewed as limiting themselves to the study of dynamics situated at various points on the S axis, just as psychologists more often focus on different points on the I axis. We hope that this book will demonstrate the possibility of an articulation between these two types of analysis by indicating in a concrete way how participation in certain social regulations structures the individual and how in turn the individual thus structured actively modulates these social regulations.

4.2. The innate and the acquired; the absolute and the contingent

For several days in 1975 Chomsky and Piaget and their followers met to debate the connections between the innate and the acquired, and it might seem ambitious to try and add anything here to the existing accounts of this debate (see Piattelli-Palmarini, 1979). Even if the debate did succeed in making more explicit their different intellectual positions, it would be an exaggeration to suggest that it led to any resolution of the controversy, Chomsky having remained immovable in his position despite some steps in his direction by Piaget. During this debate Piaget attached considerable importance to the contribution of a neuro-physiologist, Changeux (1979), who advanced a hypothesis offering the possibility of a 'biological compromise between Chomsky and Piaget'. The hypothesis advanced concerned a selective stabilization at the level of synaptic connections: activity, and notably learning activity, will at certain critical points in ontogenetic development determine within precise limits the setting up of connections at the level of the central nervous system. In this proposed fusion between neuro-physiological models and models of linguistic and cognitive models we can see an indication of a path that will perhaps one day allow us to escape from this kind of philosophical debate.

The actual terms of the debate, however, do not seem to us to have been sufficiently comprehensive. Indeed, the participants hardly posed the problem except in terms of pre-constructed or neuro-physiological programming versus individual construction. Invoking such a programming of cognitive functioning, transmitted biologically, must in the last analysis take into account the problem of invariance and universality in cognitive functioning.

In our view, neuro-physiological preprogramming is not the only source of generality. The debate between Chomsky and Piaget is in a way only concerned with the I axis of the developmental spiral, for the social is also a source of invariance. Thus, in each culture every individual begins development in a relationship of quasi-absolute dependence, thereafter attaining a relative independence in several areas; every individual participates in elementary social schemas such as giving and receiving, dominating and submitting, questioning and answering, which are viewed by Feffer (1970) as the basis for more complex interactions. Actions between individuals necessitate spatio-temporal systems of coordination such as in front/behind, before/after, above/below which cannot be executed in an arbitrary manner. In our opinion it is indeed the universal participation in such social regulations and coordinations which allows individuals to understand each other, to communicate across different cultural barriers, and finally to translate the essentials of each known language into every other language.

With respect to the phylogenetic explanation of development many authors (see, for example, Stenhouse, 1973) show no hesitation in invoking the regulatory action of the social in the development of the neuro-physiological bases for cognitive functioning. If an interpenetration between the social, the cognitive and the physiological can be postulated with respect to historical development, one should also anticipate such links with respect to development of the individual. Developmental research within the context of the two-component theory of emotional state could open up perspectives in this direction, just as we believe that experiments on the social development of intelligence (Doise and Mugny, 1981) have begun to elucidate the reciprocal links between social and cognitive regulations.

4.3. Sociocultural differences

From its very beginnings the study of psychometrics has served as a caution for racist conceptions (Billig, 1981), and given the social importance of what is at stake one can never overstress the fact that comparisons between different sociocultural groups based on psychometric tests are often poorly managed, above all when their aim is to determine the differences due to the differential genetic potential of the members of these groups. Increasingly, researchers are emphasizing that the possibility of multiple and complex interactions between genetic factors and social environment should be taken into consideration in the mathematical models used (see, for example, Jaspars and de Leeuw, 1980; Ramunni, Matalon and Lemaine, 1979). There is now an extensive endeavour at the level of mathematical models to show that conclusions previously accepted as definitive are not so at all.

Some recent controversies suggest that the same sort of endeavour has not always been made with respect to the collection of empirical data, notably in research aimed at determining the importance of genetic transmission of intelligence (Eysenck and Kamin, 1981). Nevertheless, in this area also the collection of empirical data is no less indispensable than the elaboration of analytic models. Let us develop one example.

We know of the impressive regularity with which in different countries a relationship is found between socio-occupational background and the average IQ of children. In our opinion, this regularity only demonstrates the inequality with which the school culture is diffused in different mileux, but other authors (for example, Eysenck, 1973) derive from it conclusions about genetic differences. How can this debate be advanced? One could certainly raise questions about the validity of statistical and mathematical operations, but one could also look for counter evidence at the empirical level. Without wishing to tackle the issue in terms of genetic potential, Schiff, Duyme, Dumaret, Stewart, Tomkiewicz and Feingold (1978) offer such a counter argument. They studied the school marks and IQ test results of 32 children adopted into professional families whose biological parents were unskilled manual workers, and compared their results with those obtained by school children in the general population. The results for the adopted children matched the level of those obtained by other children from professional backgrounds, while they were far superior to those obtained by the children of unskilled workers living with their biological families. This indisputably argues in favour of an environmental explanation as opposed to an explanation based on biological heredity.

Such research, though, does not yet offer any real articulation between psychological and sociological explanations in accounting for sociocultural differences. Such articulations should demonstrate the mechanisms by which social dynamics impinge upon cognitive dynamics in a school or test situation. Cross-cultural psychologists like Cole and Scribner (1974) have begun to describe certain of these mechanisms. Katz (1973) has done likewise for the test results of black Americans and Lautrey (1980) is trying to do so for certain Piagetian operational tasks. Several investigations inspired by Bernstein's (1973) theory have also opened up perspectives in this direction. In very general terms it can be said that all this research stresses in its own way the need to make analyses of social situations before elucidating the links between competence and performance. Of course, it is not only the characteristics of the immediate social situation involved in taking a test or in a school task that must be taken into consideration but also those more permanent features linked to the specific position of the subject within a set of social relations. Or, returning to our conception of a spiral of causality, a complete analysis of the intervention of the situation S_n in an individual organization I_{n+1} would necessitate an exhaustive knowledge of all the preceding Ss and Is. This will always remain an unattainable limit; one can only proceed from assumptions concerning the dominant sociopsychological characteristics of an individual at a given stage of his development.

5. Research implications

A single exhaustive analysis of the links between social interaction and individual development will not be possible. It is by means of the plurality and the articulation of different approaches that the gaps and limitations of each individual approach, legitimate in its own right, can to some extent be remedied. Developmental investigations that take account of clinical case studies, longitudinal studies, experimental interventions and questionnaire studies have this plurality. But such methodological pluralism should not cause one to lose sight of the ultimate goal, which is to articulate different explanatory models. Different schools of thought currently co-exist without there being many links between them. They have their own methods of investigation as well as their specific theoretical frameworks. There is no doubt that attempts at articulation remain the exception. Inter-, trans- and multi-disciplinary debates have more often served to disguise the imperialist aims of each school in fashionable clothes than to seek articulations of analyses. It is incontestable that as a principal goal each researcher should pursue the greatest possible extension of the explanatory model he advances.

Let us again take the example of the Piagetian enterprise which is limited to a description of the logical development of cognitive operations, while asserting that 'the operational "structure" involved is of a general nature, or "common" and therefore biopsychosociological, and is for this reason logical in its foundations' (Piaget, 1976, p. 226). It is an approach that has been so fruitful heuristically that it would be absurd to contest its legitimacy. However, it cannot explain why under certain conditions and with respect to certain social contexts some individuals apply cognitive operations that others do not apply, just as it cannot explain by what specific processes one can describe a reciprocal causality between physiological and cognitive functioning. It is insufficient to assert that the social and the cognitive are but two aspects of a single development (Piaget, 1965, p. 158) in order to understand how the social intervenes in the cognitive and vice versa; this would be to stop simply at the statement of a correlation.

At the same time, establishing a correlation, just like establishing a local and unilateral causal link, can be an indispensable stage in the search for more complex links. If an investigation procedure constructed *ad hoc* demonstrates the effect of one given variable on another, this should not of course prevent the inverse effect from being envisaged at a theoretical level, or from being elucidated at an empirical level. The nature of a texture of links is revealed just as well by the study of specific links as by their integration within a general framework.

There are, therefore, numerous reasons favouring a pluralism of approaches, more especially because at the methodological level all research is necessarily incomplete. Let us quote on this subject the masters in this matter, Campbell and Stanley (1966, p. 34) who, after enumerating all the criteria which must be satisfied in ideal experimental research, offer this wise advice:

> From the standpoint of the final interpretation of an experiment and the attempt to fit it into the developing science, every experiment is imperfect. What a check list of validity criteria can do is to make an experimenter more aware of the residual imperfections in his design so that on the relevant points he can be aware of competing interpretations of his data. He should, of course, design the very best experiment which the situation makes possible. He should deliberately seek out those artificial and natural laboratories which provide the best opportunities for control. But beyond that he should go ahead with experiment and interpretation, fully aware of the points on which the results are equivocal.

Each investigation reported in this book should therefore be considered as in some respects the formulation of a statement which only derives its overall meaning through its inclusion within a more general discussion. A discussion is only developed by the linking together of statements which are modulated, transformed and indeed mutually opposed. But certain key sentences in a discussion are more important than others. Certain investigations are also more illuminating than others in constructing a vision of the whole. Such are the investigations that we have sought to bring together in this volume.

6. Content of the volume

The research reported in this book should help us to understand better how at different points in development the individual is constituted in and by specific interactions with the social environment. The principal themes examined will be: the study of early interaction patterns from both ethological and sociological points of view; reciprocity and directiveness in early socialization techniques; the development of language as a vehicle of communication in interactional settings; the role of social factors in cognitive development; the growth of social cognitions; the impact of the cultural and social environments on adolescents; the relationship between expectations and first experiences in relation to entry into the world of work.

References

Bandura, A. 1977. *Social learning theory*. Englewood Cliffs, NJ: Prentice-Hall.

Bernstein, B. 1973. *Class, codes and control*. St Albans: Paladin.

Billig, M. 1981. *L'internationale raciste. De la psychologie à la 'science des races'*. Paris: Maspero.

Bourdieu, P. 1979. *La distinction*. Paris: Editions de Minuit.

Bourdieu, P. 1980. *Le sens pratique*. Paris: Editions de Minuit.

Bowlby, J. 1969. *Attachment and loss*. Vol. 1: *Attachment*. London: Hogarth Press.

Bruner, J. and Sherwood, V. 1981. Thought, language and interaction in infancy. In J. P. Forgas (ed.): *Social cognition*. London: Academic Press, pp. 27–52.

Butterworth, G. and Light, P. (eds.) 1982. *Social cognition*. University of Chicago Press.

Campbell, D. T. and Stanley, J. C. 1966. *Experimental and quasi-experimental designs for research*. Chicago: Rand McNally College Publishing.

Changeux, J. P. 1979. Déterminisme génétique et épigenèse des réseaux de neurones: existe-t-il un compromis biologique possible entre Chomsky et Piaget? In M. Piattelli-Palmarini (ed.): *Théories du language, théories de l'apprentissage*. Paris: Editions du Seuil, pp. 276–93.

Cole, M. and Scribner, S. 1974. *Culture and thought*. New York: John Wiley.

Coleman, J. S. 1961 *The adolescent society*. New York: The Free Press.

Damon, W. 1977 *The social world of the child*. San Francisco: Jossey-Bass.

Doise, W. 1978. *Groups and individuals. Explanations in social psychology*. Cambridge University Press.

Doise, W. 1982. *L'explication en psychologie sociale*. Paris: Presses Universitaires de France.

Doise, W. and Mugny, G. 1981. *Le développement social de l'intelligence*. Paris: Interéditions.

Doob, L. W. 1947. The behavior of attitudes. *Psychological Review*, **54**, 135–56.

Dunn, J. 1977. *Distress and comfort*. London: Fontana.

Eckensberger, L. H. and Silbereisen, R. K. (eds.) 1980. *Entwicklung sozialer Kognitionen*. Stuttgart: Klett-Cotta.

Eisenstadt, S. H. 1956. *From generation to generation*. New York: The Free Press.

Elder, G. H. Adolescent socialization and development. 1968. In E. Borgatta and W. Lambert (eds.): *Handbook of personality: Theory and research*. Chicago: Rand McNally.

Erikson, E. H. 1950. *Childhood and society.* New York: Norton. (Pocket: Harmondsworth, Penguin, 1963).

Erikson, E. H. 1968. *Identity, youth and crisis.* London: Faber.

Eysenck, H. J. 1973. *The inequality of man.* London: Temple Smith.

Eysenck, H. J. and Kamin, L. 1981. *Intelligence: The battle for the mind.* London: Pan Books.

Feffer, M. 1970. Developmental analysis of interpersonal behavior. *Psychological Review,* **77,** 197–214.

Flavell, J. H. and Ross, L. (eds.) 1981. *Social cognitive development.* Cambridge University Press.

Friedenberg, E. Z. 1963. *Coming of age in America: Growth and Acquiescence.* New York: Random House.

Hinde, R. A. 1978. Social development: A biographical approach. In J. Bruner and A. Garton (eds.): *Human growth and development.* Oxford: Clarendon Press.

Hollingshead, A. 1949. *Elmtown's youth.* New York: John Wiley.

Jaspars, J. M. F. and de Leeuw, J. A. 1980. Genetic-environment covariation in human behaviour genetics. In L. J. T. Van Der Kamp, W. F. Langerak and D. N. M. de Gruyter (eds.): *Psychometrics for educational debates.* New York: John Wiley.

Katz, I. 1973. Negro performances in interracial situations. In P. Watson (ed.): *Psychology and race.* Harmondsworth: Penguin.

Lautrey, J. 1980. *Classe sociale, milieu familial, intelligence.* Paris: Presses Universitaires de France.

Newson, J. 1974. Towards a theory of infant understanding. *Bulletin of the British Psychological Society,* **27,** 251–7.

Palmonari, A. (ed.) 1981. *Psicologi.* Bologna: Il Mulino.

Palmonari, A. 1982. On becoming a psychologist: A field study in Italy. In J. P. Codol and J. Ph. Leyens (eds.): *Cognitive analysis of social behavior.* The Hague: Nijhoff.

Palmonari, A., Carugati, F., Ricci Bitti, P. and Sarchielli, G. 1979. *Identità imperfette.* Bologna: Il Mulino.

Palmonari, A., Carugati, F., Ricci Bitti, P. and Sarchielli, G. In press. Imperfect identities: A socio-psychological perspective for the study of the problems of adolescence. In H. Tajfel (ed.): *Social dimensions.* Cambridge University Press.

Parsons, T. 1964. *Social structure and personality. New York: The Free Press.*

Perret-Clermont, A. N. 1980. *Social interaction and cognitive development in children.* London: Academic Press.

Piaget, J. 1965. *Etudes sociologiques.* Genève: Droz.

Piaget, J. 1975. *L'équilibration des structures cognitives.* Paris: Presses Universitaires de France.

Piaget, J. 1976. Postface. *Archives de Psychologie,* **44,** 223–8.

Piattelli-Palmarini, M. (ed.) 1979. *Théories du language, théories de l'apprentissage.* Paris: Editions du Seuil.

Ramunni, G., Matalon, B. and Lemaine, G. 1979. Les modèles linéaires et les problèmes de l'intelligence. In P. Delattre and M. Thellier (eds.): *Actes du colloque: Elaboration et justification des modèles. Applications en biologie.* Paris: Maloine, pp. 573–80.

Schaffer, H. R. (ed.) 1977. *Studies in mother–infant interaction.* London: Academic Press.

Schiff, M., Duyme, M., Dumaret, A., Stewart, J., Tomkiewicz, S. and Feingold, T. 1978. Intellectual status of working-class children adopted early into upper middle-class families. *Science*, **200**, 1503–4.

Sherif, M. and Sherif, C. W. 1964. *Reference groups: Exploration into conformity and deviation of adolescents*. New York: Harper and Row.

Sherif, M. and Sherif, C. W. (eds.) 1965. *Problems of youth: Transition to adulthood in a changing world*. Chicago: Aldine.

Staats, A. W. 1975. *Social behaviorism*. Homewood, Ill.: Dorsey Press.

Stenhouse, D. 1973. *The evolution of intelligence*. London: George Allen and Unwin.

Stern, D. 1977. *The first relationship: Infant and mother*. London: Fontana.

Trevarthen, C. 1979. Instincts for human understanding and for cultural cooperation: Their development in infancy. In M. Von Cranach, K. Foppa, W. Lepenies and D. Ploog (eds.): *Human ethology*. Cambridge University Press, pp. 530–71.

Trevarthen, C. 1982. The primary motives for cooperative understanding. In G. Butterworth and P. Light (eds.): *Social cognition*. University of Chicago Press, pp. 77–109.

Waller, M. 1978. *Soziales Lernen und Interaktionskompetenz*. Stuttgart: Klett-Cotta.

Wundt, W. 1907. *Outlines of psychology*. Leipzig: Wilhelm Engelmann.

Part I
The ethological and sociological study of interaction patterns

The first two contributions in this book each summarize the results of a number of investigations but at the same time identify the parameters of the explanatory approaches adopted in the other contributions. The chapter by Montagner and his collaborators concerns interaction among young children and looks at the natural behavioural style of individuals; the chapter by Takala deals with interaction in families as a function of sociological factors. As in his other writings, Montagner gives preference in the study of interaction to those features that characterize different individuals; Takala stresses the impact of sociological factors. Both, however, are able to integrate within their own explanatory models variables that are characteristic of the opposing pole. The style of a child's behaviour changes when the rhythm of the mother's work is modified just as the state of health of the child or its athletic propensities alter interactions within the family. Starting from widely separated positions, these two researchers are none the less able to articulate the study of individual dynamics with that of social dynamics. The inter-penetration of these dynamics is manifested equally in rhythms of hormonal secretions as via the temporal distribution of family activities or conceptions of the parental role.

2. Development of early peer interaction

HUBERT MONTAGNER, ALBERT RESTOIN,
VÉRONIQUE ULLMANN, DANILO RODRIGUEZ,
DOMINIQUE GODARD and MIREILLE VIALA

It was probably the psychoanalyst R. Spitz (1946, 1968) who opened the way to the ethological study of the child. Studying the smile in babies, R. Spitz came to the conclusion that the configuration 'eyes–nose–mouth' in the human species is a releaser of the smile (fixed action pattern) through an innate releasing mechanism (IRM). Spitz's observations, thus, reinforced the innate positions of the Objectivist School which built up around K. Lorenz and N. Tinbergen: we know that, for K. Lorenz in particular, many social behaviours of the human species have been genetically programmed by successive adaptations during evolution. Thirty years after R. Spitz's work, the most characteristic research that is closest to this attitude is that of I. Eibl-Eibesfeldt (1968–79) even if his conclusions are more moderate than those of K. Lorenz. I. Eibl-Eibesfeldt was the founder of the first human ethology institute in Western Germany. Part of his research was devoted to innate baby behaviour (independent of all individual experience).

However, many child ethological studies have developed outside the Objectivist School. This is how N. G. Blurton Jones (1971, 1972), E. C. Grant (1969), W. C. MacGrew (1969, 1972), P. K. Smith (1974), P. K. Smith and M. Green (1975), V. Reynolds and A. Guest (1975), J. C. Rouchouse (1978, 1980), etc. have gone beyond the analogies and models and published systematic studies of children who lived in groups or who evolved with others in situations which did not limit their motor pattern in any way. One of their first objectives was to make an inventory of the behaviour units of children (ethogram), just as animal ethologists do when studying a new species. However, just dissection of behaviour into more or less elementary units does not always enable the worker to usefully approach the child's relational behaviour. As N. G. Blurton Jones began to do in 1972, it is also important to study when and how these units combine to form more and more complex behaviours in relation to age, sex, family and social events, experienced situations, physiological state, etc. This way, functional combinations (or sequences) of behaviour units can be isolated: those that have a communication value, those that regulate leadership, cooperation, aggression, fear, isolation, etc. Consequently, it becomes possible to study how the young child organizes his behavioural responses when confronted with questions posed by various socio-ecological events throughout the day, week and year. This is our research approach since 1970 (Montagner, 1974–83; Montagner *et al.*, 1975–82).

1. General outline of the method

As is often done in ethology, we made a list and quantified the different types of interactions of the child with his peers during continuous periods of observation (during several consecutive hours from one day to the next) within a structure where children in the same class according to their age could have spontaneous interactions and lived in the same physical and social environment away from any direct family influence. In France, the child care centre which receives children under 3 years fulfils these requirements. Observation was often done with a camera and tape recorder (it can be estimated that from 1970 to 1981 information was obtained from more than 12,000 hours of observation and 120 km of film).

The children moved within groups of from 2 to 15 children according to their age and the type of activity. Two study methods were used alternately from one day to the next: (1) Each child was observed during all his movements and interactions by a worker. Two to 4 children can be observed the same day by the same worker when this worker has had about two years' experience with this type of work. Thus, from 10 to 15 children are usually observed daily by the research team; (2) the next day the same children were observed in the same group (except when the children were away due to illness or other reasons) in the same room with the same nurses after a change which brought about competition. In our study we either turned a table upside down on another table (there was competition to occupy the position near the legs of the upturned table), or introduced one or two empty cartons (there was competition to get inside the cartons) or introduced one or several attractive objects on the periphery of the group which was gathered together on a big rug (there was competition to take objects).

The first observations were devoted to observing the 2 to 3 year olds whose locomotor skills, motor coordination and sphincter control were sufficiently developed to enable the children to be relatively autonomous in relation to adults. First of all we made a list of the most characteristic and measurable behaviours which the child had and which brought about characteristic and measurable responses in the target child. We then looked for the correlations between the observed modifications in these behaviours, the responses, and several series of variables (age, sex, physiological, family and other social events such as a new nurse, changes in nurses' behaviour and changes in the group composition). At the same time more and more observations were being made on even younger children (18 to 24 months, 14 to 18 months, 6 to 14 months) and finer and finer analyses (frame by frame, consideration of the time intervals between items during the sequences, spectral analyses of vocalizations using a sonagraph) were being made which enabled us to study systematically the emergence and the evolution of elementary behaviours which then combined to regulate the interactions of the child with his peers.

Research was also done on the interaction systems of children from 2 to 6 years in the kindergarten and from 6 to 11 years in the primary school.

2. Results

2.1. The behavioural repertoire

Table 1 gives the elementary behaviours which were listed and quantified in children from 18 to 36 months at the day care centre and from 2 to 6 years at the kindergarten.

Some of these child behaviours, i.e. linking and appeasement items, have a higher probability of bringing about the responses called linking and appeasement sequences in the target child, i.e. smiling, stroking, non insistent touching of the other's body, offering, stopping crying. The interaction then consists, in more than 80 per cent of the cases, and in all populations under study, of reciprocal imitation, cooperation, verbal or non-verbal exchanges where there is no fear, isolation or agression, even if the target child is usually aggressive, or if there is aggression it is absorbed and not repeated (Montagner, 1978). This way, the correlation coefficients of 0.84 (for children from 8 to 26 months) and 0.96 (children from 18 to 36 months) for the linking and appeasement behaviours and free play activities were obtained (Ullmann, 1981).

Other behaviour often presented at a distance and in any case without bodily contact brings about in more than 70 per cent of the cases a

Table 1. *Categorization of elementary behaviours (or behaviour items) of 1½ to 6 year old children in free play situations at the day centre (18 to 36 month old children) and the kindergarten (2 to 6 year old children)*

Appeasement and linking items	Agonistic items		Fearful and withdrawal items	Isolations
	Threat	Aggression		
Smiling	Wide opening of the mouth	Striking a blow with arm, hand or fist	Enlargement of the uncovered part of cornea	Sucking one's finger
Bending the head on the shoulder	Clenching the wide bare teeth	Kicking	Putting the arms in front of the face (protective gesture)	Sucking toy, cloth, etc.
Bending the chest on one side	High-pitched vocalization	Striking a blow with an object	Withdrawal of the head or the chest	Standing aside
Nodding one's head	Loud vocalization 'Ah'	Scratching	Moving back	Lying down
Waddling	Frowning	Pinching	Running away	Curling up
Swinging	Clenching fists	Biting	Blinking	Sobbing or crying independently of any interaction with other children
Offering	Stretching out the arm with one hand opening downwards	Pulling the other child's clothes by force	Crying after having received a threat or an aggression	
Stretching out the arm with one hand opening upwards	Throwing out the arm in front of oneself	Knocking over		
Light touching	Forefinger pointing to the other child	Shaking the other child		
Taking the other child by the hand	Sudden opening of both arms	Grasping an object in the other child's hand		
Stroking	Sudden bending of the head forward			
Kissing	Sudden bending of the bust forward			
Squatting down	All sudden movements forward			
Jumping	Breaking a blow			
Hopping				
Turning round oneself				
Clapping the hands				
Vocal exchanges with no threatening vocalization				

Note: A behavioural sequence is a combination of two or more items. The frequency of items or sequences is calculated for each child every one, two and three months or every year (see Table 3). This table does not give: items rarely observed; attraction items (the child goes towards or imitates a peer); non-determined items, i.e. those which appeared to have a different meaning or function in a given context (putting his arms around the other and making the other fall over; sitting on another child's back; gently hitting another child's head, etc.); simulation items (for example barking, like a dog) and object manipulation items.

releasing of an object, fear, running away or crying in the target child. Called threatening items, this behaviour appears mainly in conflicts and competition. Quite distinct from aggression both in structure and function, it can however be regrouped with aggressive behaviour under the heading of agonistic behaviour as is often done in ethology (Table 1). Other items are labelled aggressions. By aggression we mean any contact which brings about crying and continued isolation. In the present state of our work, we have not looked at the aggressive content of words, even if we recorded them.

All these communication items and sequences are described in several recent articles and works (Montagner *et al.*, 1975–82; Lombardot, 1977; Godard, 1978).

The regrouping of items and sequences within the categories of Table 1 is justified from the functional and ontogenetic points of view.

The functional point of view
After showing that all the items of each category had a higher probability of bringing about similar responses in the target child our research group looked for the possible negative or positive correlations between the items of each category and between the items of the different categories. The results obtained from the correlation analysis confirmed the conclusions already published (Montagner, 1978). Let us take an example in the category of aggression items: V. Ullman (1981) obtained a correlation coefficient of 0.84 between the grasping acts (see Table 1: Grasping an object in the other child's hand) and the overt aggressive acts that were characteristic of children from 18 to 36 months, i.e. biting, kicking, giving a blow, etc. It was the same for children from 3 to 4½ years in the kindergarten (Viala, 1980; Table 2). It would thus appear to be logical to regroup these two types of behaviour into the category covering aggressive items. However, for all children studied there was no significant correlation between the aggressive items and the linking and appeasement items (Table 2), nor between aggressive items and free play activities (the correlation coefficient between these two last behaviours was of −0.04 with children from 18 to 36 months).

Yet, it is obvious that all observed behaviours could not be regrouped under the headings in Table 1 (see below).

The ontogenetic point of view
The research on the emergence moment(s) of the different kinds of interactions with peers and of the items in Table 1 and responses to these

Table 2. *Correlation coefficients between overt aggressions, grasping, offering and isolation in 8 kindergarten classes receiving children from 3 to 4½ years*

Behaviours / Kindergarten classes	Overt aggressions vs. grasping	Overt aggressions vs. offering	Overt aggressions vs. isolation	Grasping vs. offering	Grasping vs. isolation	Offering vs. isolation
A La Bouloie	.90	−.18	−.24	−.22	−.26	−.41
B Bourgogne–Planoise	.80	.22	−.01	−.06	−.27	−.04
C Rosemont I	.53	.25	−.19	.56	−.29	−.28
D Rosemont II	.49	−.08	−.28	−.15	−.42	.11
E Ile de France–Planoise	.75	−.08	−.01	−.03	−.29	−.11
F Champagne–Planoise	.80	.17	−.31	.25	−.34	−.21
G Les Sapins–St Ferjeux	.81	−.16	.18	−.43	−.13	−.42
H Saône	.84	.09	−.31	.06	−.30	.03

Note: The coefficients were calculated from data collected at the kindergarten every Monday and Friday from September 1976 to June 1977.

behaviours shows that from 6–7 to 14 months according to the child, the young child has already made a distinction between the different categories of items, whether he be the initiator or the target. Then the vocalizations play an important role in the emission and reception of the message. For example, when the offering items are combined with vocalizations they are followed by acceptance by the target child in 76 per cent of cases whereas the silent offering only brings about acceptation in 34 per cent of the cases (Rodriguez, 1983). This is not the case between the age of 2 and 3 years which is a period during which the offering gesture brings about the same percentage of acceptances whether the offering be accompanied or not by vocalizations. Everything takes place as if during the second year the sound reinforcement of the offering becomes less and less necessary for the offering gesture to be recognized as a signal with a minimum of ambiguity. It would appear that it is also the same for many other signals: research is being done to try and confirm this point.

Everything would suggest that among the vocalizations that are emitted by children from 7 to 14 months there is only one that is actually characteristic: the vocalization that is combined with the sudden opening of the mouth, raising of the eyebrows, lifting and then lowering of one of the arms and often the sudden throwing forward of the chest (when the child is standing) and often appears in conflictual and competitive situations between children from 18 to 36 months (Montagner, 1978; Montagner et al., 1982). This vocalization which often brings about the dropping of an object, the turning of the head or chest and/or running away, can be considered as having mainly a threatening function in the ethological meaning of this term. When this vocalization is emitted there is a reduction in the probability of overt (biting, scratching, etc.) aggression resulting both with the emitter and the receiver. When this vocalization is analysed on the sonagraph there is a typical bell shape (Rodriguez, 1983), which cannot be confused with other sound forms. A child from 7 to 14 months is thus able to decode one of the signals which announces the possibility or the beginning of a conflict or a competition between the emitter and himself or another child, for example when he turns his back towards the emitter. It is as if one of the priorities of the young child is to recognize and differentiate from the beginning of his life in a group of peers one of the signals which governs many conflicts and which enables him to participate without overt aggression in competitions enabling him to have access to a limited number of situations and objects. All threat items in Table 1 which do not involve an upright posture are already presented by children aged from 7 to 12 months in the same contexts: when the child tries to keep back an object from another who grasps it; when a child is looking at a child who is sitting very closely to him; when a child is looking at an object held by another or at the holder. However these are often mixed with aggression items. It is during the second year of life that the threatening items become clearly distinct from aggressive items, particularly in competitive situations.

More generally, all the items in Table 1 were expressed by all the children at some time between 6 and 16 months, depending on the child, at the day care centre at Besançon whatever their socio-economic or ethnic background. These items were also observed in all the populations that have been studied either in France or in the Congo (Didillon and Gremillet, in preparation). Most of these have also been described in English and American children (Blurton Jones, 1971, 1972; MacGrew, 1969, 1972; Lewis, 1978).

The different types of responses to linking and appeasement behaviour and to agonistic behaviour such that they have been listed in children from 2 to 3 years (Montagner, 1978) also appear at the end of the first year or at the beginning of the second. This is particularly the case in canalization and redirecting aggressive behaviour.

It is, thus, possible that the behaviour in Table 1 and the responses to this behaviour could be 'universals' in the human species. However, contrary to I. Eibl-Eibesfeldt (1973, 1977, 1979), we cannot infer their genetic programming. We do not know indeed anything of the real influence of the various social influences received after birth, and even before, on the more or less early emergence of these 'universals', their non-emergence or the emergence of unusual behaviour. To do this the children would have to be observed from birth. We have started to do this, but only up until the twelfth day and only in relation to the olfactory and acoustic interactions between the baby and his mother (Schaal *et al.*, 1980, 1981). In any case, it is possible that the non-emergence of these behaviours or the emergence of different behaviours during the children's interactions with their peers can be early indications of an evolution probability towards a pathological behavioural state that is more important than for other children. From other preliminary studies it would appear that children who at 3 or 4 years of age are considered as pre-psychotic or psychotic only have the behaviour items in Table 1 and the responses to these behaviours in rough outline or do not have them at all. For example, the threatening mimicry has just been outlined – the mouth slowly opens, but not completely and there is no vocalization; when one of the children has just undergone aggression he can turn towards a third child with his hands directed as if he was going to hit or push with the beginning of a threatening mimicry. However, the follow-up of the usual sequence does not appear: the movements stop and the child remains still with his head down or with his eyes looking elsewhere.

Research is in progress or planned to show the possible differences of the repertoire of the children considered to be normal from the day care centre, the kindergarten and children received more or less early into institutions (children without parents, taken from their parents, with character disturbances, pre-psychotic children, etc.) and children with sensory disturbances. This way perhaps it will be possible to see which part belongs to internal factors and which belongs to environmental factors in the emergence or non-emergence of the behaviour listed in Table 1.

2.2. The differentiation of behaviour profiles

When the percentages concerning the behaviour categories of Table 1 are established from one month to another and the structure of the behaviour sequences during interaction with peers is analysed, individual behavioural tendencies become clearer and clearer in most children during the second year. Thus, figure 1, based on multi-factorial analysis (Romeder, 1973; Duvernoy, 1976) shows that in the initiator situation some children are differentiated from others: the dark area (see the legend of Figure 1) with the results of the observations made on each of the 10 children from 8 to 26 months goes towards the linking and appeasement behaviour and attraction axes (axes 3 and 4) for the child E, the aggression and non-determined interactions (axes 1 and 2) for children F and J and towards the fear axis (axis 5) for child G. Note the proximity of the non-determined interactions and aggression axes on one hand and the proximity of the linking and appeasement and attraction axes (by attraction we mean the number of times the child goes towards and imitates another child). Thus, everything would seem to indicate that from items of Table 1 and also probably from other behaviours that have not been sufficiently analysed children tend to select certain types of behaviour rather than others during their second year, with some children behaving more and more aggressively, while others behave more and more fearfully. Note in particular that the children who tend to favour aggressive behaviour with peers also have many non-determined interactions, i.e. make an ambiguous mixture of acts which usually have the value of linking and appeasement as well as threats and aggressions. It would appear that these children have a tendency to link their behavioural sequences without taking into account the obtained responses. Following on this their different types of interaction are less ritualized and less diversified than in other children who have a comparable interaction frequency. These differentiations begin to appear clearly when the child starts to walk and are usually reinforced during the third year. Then it is possible to distinguish several behaviour profiles that are more or less marked from three types of parameters (Table 3): (1) the relative proportions of the different categories in Table 1, either from

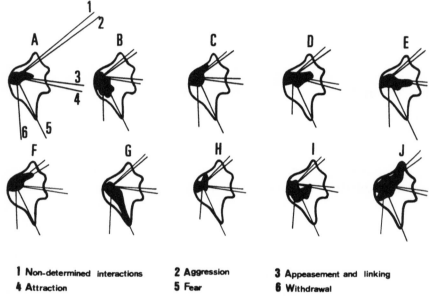

| 1 Non-determined interactions | 2 Aggression | 3 Appeasement and linking |
| 4 Attraction | 5 Fear | 6 Withdrawal |

Figure 1. Graphic representation of the multi-factorial analysis of the different behaviour characteristics which were analysed in each child (A to J) in relation to the same characteristics presented by the total population of peers at the day care centre (n=10). The large area is where all the observations concerning the 10 children are recorded. The dark shaded area is where all the observations concerning each child are recorded. The axes 1 to 6 define the behaviour characteristics of Table 1, except that threatening behaviour and isolation are not represented, fear and withdrawal are analysed separately, and the 'non-determined' interactions and 'attraction' categories have been added. 'Non-determined interactions' mean interactions without any particular meaning or function and 'attraction' means the number of times that the child goes towards or imitates another child. The age of children is from 8 to 26 months (7 girls and 3 boys). Each individually shaded area goes towards the 'favoured' characteristics of the child. Thus, the most marked behavioural tendency or tendencies can be visualized in each of the children from A to J. For example children F and J were the most aggressive ('dominant-aggressive' profile), and children D and E the most linking and appeasing and G the most fearful ('dominated-fearful'). Note the proximity of the non-determined interactions and aggression axes, and the proximity of the linking and appeasement and attraction axes.

Table 3. *Relative proportions of appeasement and linking items and agonistic items (threat and aggression) and fear and withdrawal items in children in the same peer group who were aged from 2 to 3 years at the day care centre in 1977 and were observed in free activities throughout the year (from September to June) (per cent)*

Child	Date of birth	Appeasement and linking items	Agonistic items	Fearful and withdrawal items	Level of participation in competitions	Behaviour profile
Jerome	09.11.75	28.8	7.6	63.4	−	dominated-fearful
Karine C.	30.09.75	48.7	18.4	32.7	−	dominated with leader mechanisms
Frederic	18.07.75	51.9	34.6	13.4	+	dominant-fluctuating
Nicolas	20.06.75	21	7.8	71	−	dominated-fearful
Katia	27.04.75	44.6	17.8	37.5	−	dominated with leader mechanisms
Sebastien	21.04.75	25.9	40.7	33.3	+	dominant-aggressive
Elizabeth	07.04.75	36	26.4	37.3	+	dominant-fluctuating
Damienne	10.03.75	70.4	11.4	18	+	leader
Karine H.	01.03.75	68.9	9.2	21.7	+	leader
Stephanie	28.01.75	68.9	10	20.9	+	leader
Kaouthar	03.07.75	21	34	45	−	dominated-aggressive
Marianne	16.02.75	66.6	20.2	13	+	leader
Gerald	20.12.74	31.2	54.1	14.5	+	dominant-aggressive

Note: + = high level of participation in competitions.
− = low level of participation in competitions.

one month to the next or for one year as in Table 3; (2) the results of successes or failures in competitions (see General outline of the method); (3) the structure of the sequence linking behaviour during interactions (Montagner, 1983).

Seven profiles have been set out: three among the children called dominant, i.e. asserting themselves most often in competitive situations over a time unit of one month (the leader who is very appeasing and attractive; the dominant-aggressive who has more aggression than linking and appeasement items; the dominant-fluctuating who alternates between the leader and the dominant-aggressive); four among the children called dominated, i.e. asserting themselves very little in competitions or not participating at all (the dominated with leader mechanisms: the structure of the sequence linking behaviour is the same as that of a leader; the dominated-fearful who have a relatively high frequency of fear items; the dominated-aggressive who present alternation of fear, isolation and aggression; the dominated who stay apart and who look like solitary children). If most children have these profiles in a marked way, other profiles appear that are intermediary between two profiles.

In any case, the data obtained show that there is no correlation between the level of dominance as we have defined it and the frequency of aggressions as we have listed them. The very dominant leaders are rarely aggressive. However the dominated aggressive child who does not participate much in competitions and does not assert himself when he does participate is more aggressive than leaders and often in a repeated and sustained way. There does not appear to be any significant correlation between attractiveness within the group and on the one hand the frequency of aggressions and on the other hand the level of dominance: for example, the dominated with leader mechanisms are very attractive particularly for the small number of children who follow and imitate them. The leaders are more attractive than the dominant-aggressive profiles even if a group can form around the dominant-aggressive, and the leader's attractiveness is much more lasting (for more details, see Montagner, 1978).

Continuous observation has shown more often a stability or a reinforcement of the behaviour profile from one month to another during the third year and then from the third to the fifth year (Montagner, 1978; Viala, 1980). However, considerable modifications can be observed which sometimes go as far as inverting the profile completely.

The accumulation of growth and physiological data (various illnesses, hormonal dosages in urine, blood pressure, electrocardiogram, body temperature), past and present information concerning family (illnesses, behaviour, life and work rhythms, composition, particular events) and information concerning the present and past way of life of the child (sleep–awake rhythms, characteristics and number of people looking after the child, etc.) have enabled us to distinguish the variables which most clearly influence the differentiation and the modifications of the behaviour profile during the second and third years. Using several methods already described (Montagner, 1978), we have found that there is a close relationship between these phenomena and family behaviour and especially that of the mother with the child. Temporary or long-lasting changes in the mother's behaviour have been related to physiological (illnesses, profound modifications of the ovarian cycle, digestive disorders) and social (especially the work rhythms, but also changes in the composition of the family and to a lesser extent conjugal conflicts) factors. Let us take an example: we have seen children who were leaders at 2 years of age evolve more and more clearly towards a dominant-agressive profile as the mother's behaviour in relation to them changed into acts of impatience, threat and overt aggression. Then when the mother's behaviour became more appeasing and less aggressive (after an improvement in health, a change in work rhythm) the child of less than 4 years of age expressed once again more appeasement items than aggression and linking in behaviour sequences similar to that of children who had remained leaders since the age of 2, yet at the same time he retained some mechanisms of the dominant-aggressive profile. His profile was, thus, intermediary between that of a leader type and that of a dominant-aggressive of the same age who had differentiated his profile since walking age. However, the changes in behavioural profile are not as obvious when the family changes its way of being in relation to the child as from the age of 5 (approximately 10 per cent of the children at the day care centre and at the kindergarten were able to be followed up throughout primary school until the age of 9 or 10). We also found correlations between the child and his mother in the excretion pattern of corticosteroid hormones (Montagner, 1978, 1982; Montagner et al., 1975, 1977) and magnesium (Restoin et al., 1981).

3. Conclusions

Ethology has provided us with its principles and methods for studying the social behaviour of young children with their peers in free activities and in competition situations in the playroom and playground of day care centres and kindergartens. This way we found that it is through all corporal expressions including the functioning of vocal cords (vocalizations and speech) that the young child transmits and decodes appeasement, solicitation, threat, aggression, fearfulness, isolation, etc. in relation to his peers. The listing of behaviour items and sequences allowed us to find the same motor repertoire in all children of the same age classes (2 to 5 years) in all populations of children we observed throughout one or several years either in France or in Africa. All behaviour items which are not dependent on an upright posture were seen to emerge from 6–7 months to 15–16 months according to the child.

However this does not mean that the repertoire belongs necessarily and totally to the genetic background of the human species. Perhaps it is rather or also because of the same environmental influences and, at the same time, the same ontogenetic events that the same behaviour items and sequences are emerging in all children, most often in the second part of the first year. As we are studying the dynamics of interactions between the mother and her infant from birth, we think that we could find some relationships between these early interactions and the emergence or non-emergence of the repertoire used by the toddler with his peers as well as with the emergence of other motor patterns.

Yet we observed that during the second year a second level of organization is put into place. The children combine the items and sequences of the repertoire in different ways. Certain children tend to present most often homogenous linking of items and sequences of items, i.e. belonging to the same functional category, that are connected to the actual situation; at the same time, the frequency of their appeasement and linking items is always higher than the frequency of their agonistic items; their aggression is rarely repeated and sustained. Other children tend to present most often heterogeneous linking of items and sequences of items, i.e. belonging to distinct different categories, whatever the actual situation; at the same time, the frequency of their agonistic items and sequences, and even of their aggressions, is higher than the frequency of their appeasement and linking items and sequences, with one month as a unit of time; etc. This way, children differentiate a more or less marked behavioural profile. We found that the differentiation, the reinforcement or the modifications of the behavioural profile were closely correlated to the behaviour of the family, and especially to that of the mother with the child.

Note in particular that the tendency to favour aggressive acts is accompanied by a tendency to present non-determined interactions (due to the heterogeneity of the behaviour sequences of the initiator and of the responses of the target child it is difficult to put these interactions into a particular category). Everything takes place as if a high frequency of aggressive acts goes against the establishing of ritualized interactions and then restricts the diversity and the frequency of reciprocal imitations, cooperations and free play activities. However the tendency to favour appeasement and linking acts is accompanied by a high tendency to approach other children (what we called attractions) and then by a high probability of reciprocal imitations, cooperations and ludic activities. It can be said that the place a child occupies in a group of the same age class depends mainly on the setting up of the second level of organization of behaviour, i.e. the behavioural profile, whatever the behavioural profile is. This level does not appear to be under genetic influences since it is significantly influenced by the behaviour of the family in relation to the child.

References

Blurton Jones, N. G. 1967. An ethological study of some aspects of social behaviour of children in nursery schools. In D. Morris (ed.): *Primate ethology*. London: Weidenfeld and Nicolson, pp. 347–68.

Blurton Jones, N. G. 1971. Criteria for use in describing facial expressions of children. *Hum. Biol.*, **43**, 365–413.

Blurton Jones, N. G. 1972. *Ethological studies of child behaviour*. London: Cambridge University Press.

Didillon, H. and Gremillet, H. Etude comparative des communications non-verbales chez les jeunes enfants congolais et français. In preparation.

Duvernoy, J. 1976. Optical recognition and clustering: Karhunen-Loeve analysis. *Appl. Opt.*, **15**, 1590–4.

Eibl-Eibesfeldt, I. 1968. Zur Ethologie des menschlichen Grussverhaltens. I. Beobachtungen an Balinesen, Papuas und Samoanern nebst vergleichenden Bemerkungen. *Zeitschrift für Tierpsychologie*, **25**, 727–44.

Eibl-Eibesfeldt, I. 1973. *Der vorprogrammierte Mensch. Das Ererbte als bestimmender Faktor im menschlichen Verhalten*. Vienna: Molden.

Eibl-Eibesfeldt, I. 1974. Les universaux du comportement et leur genèse. In *L'unité de l'homme*. Paris: Editions du Seuil, pp. 233–45.

Eibl-Eibesfeldt, I. 1977. The biological unit of mankind: Human ethology, concepts and implications. *Prospects*, **7**, 163–84.

Eibl-Eibesfeldt, I. 1979. Human ethology: Concepts and implications for the science of man. *The Behavioral and Brain Sciences*, **2**, 1–57.

Godard, D. 1978. Agression et isolement: Approche éthologique. Thèse de Médecine de l'Université de Franche-Comté Besançon.

Grant, E. C. 1969. Human facial expression. *Man*, **4**, 525–36.

Lewis, M. 1978. *The secret language of your child*. London: Souvenir Press.

40   Hubert Montagner *et al.*

Lombardot, M. 1977. Comportement de communication et physiologie surréna-
lienne de l'enfant de 3 à 5 ans. Thèse de Neurobiologie et Biologie du
Comportement de l'Université de Franche-Comté Besançon.

McGrew, W. C. 1969. An ethological study of agonistic behaviour in preschool
children. In C. R. Carpenter (ed.): *Proc. of the Second Intern. Congr. of
Primatology. I. Behavior.* Basle: Karger, pp. 149–59.

McGrew, W. C. 1972. *An ethological study of children's behavior.* London: Academic
Press.

Montagner, H. 1974. Communication non-verbale et discrimination olfactive chez
les jeunes enfants – Approche éthologique. In *L'unité de l'homme.* Paris:
Editions du Seuil, pp. 235–53.

Montagner, H. 1978. *L'enfant et la communication.* Paris: Stock.

Montagner, H. 1979. La genèse du comportement de l'enfant à partir de l'étude
des interactions au sein de groupes à la crèche et à l'école maternelle. In *Petits
Groupes et Grands Systèmes*, **5**, 197–208. AFCET: Editions Hommes et
Techniques.

Montagner, H. 1979. Le temps du jeune enfant. In A. Reinberg *et al.* (eds.):
L'homme malade du temps. Paris: Stock.

Montagner, H. 1983. *Les Rythmes de vie de l'enfant et de l'adolescent.* Paris: Stock.

Montagner, H. 1983. Ethologie humaine. *Encyclopaedia universalis*, 6, 561, Symp.
Paris: Maury (in press).

Montagner, H. and Henry, J. Ch. 1975. Vers une biologie du comportement de
l'enfant. *Revue des Questions Scientifiques*, **146**, 481–529.

Montagner, H., Henry, J. Ch., Lombardot, M., Benedini, M., Restoin, A.,
Bolzoni, D., Moyse, A., Humbert, Y., Burnod, J. and Nicolas, R. M. 1977. Les
variations physiologiques sous l'effet des facteurs sociaux et des changements de rhythme imposés aux organismes. *Vers l'Education Nouvelle*, Special
Issue, 63–126.

Montagner, H., Henry, J. Ch., Lombardot, M., Restoin, A., Bolzoni, D., Durand,
M., Humbert, Y. and Moyse, A. 1978. Behavioural profiles and corticosteroid
excretion rhythms in young children. Part I: Non-verbal communication and
setting up of behavioural profiles in children from 1 to 6 years. In V. Reynolds
and N. G. Blurton Jones (eds.): *Human behaviour and adaptation.* London:
Taylor and Francis, pp. 207–28.

Montagner, H., Henry, J. Ch., Lombardot, M., Burnod, J. and Nicolas, R. M.
1978. Behavioural profiles and corticosteroid excretion rhythms in young
children. Part II: Circadian and weekly rhythms in corticosteroid excretion
levels of children as indicators of adaptation to social context. In V. Reynolds
and N. G. Blurton Jones (eds.): *Human behaviour and adaptation.* London:
Taylor and Francis, pp. 229–65.

Montagner, H., Henry, J. Ch., Lombardot, M., Restoin, A., Benedini, M.,
Godard, D., Boillot, F., Pretet, M. T., Bolzoni, D., Burnod, J. and Nicolas,
R. M. 1979. The ontogeny of communication behaviour and adrenal physiology
in the young child. *Child Abuse and Neglect*, **3**, 19–30.

Montagner, H., Restoin, A., Schaal, B., Rodriguez, D., Ullmann, V., Ladouce, I.,
Guedira, A., Viala, M., Godard, D., Hertling, E., Didillon, H. and Gremillet,
H. 1981. Apport éthologique à l'étude ontogénétique des systèmes de
communication de l'enfant. *Médecine et Hygiène*, **39**, 3906–22.

Montagner, H., Restoin, A. and Henry, J. Ch. 1982. Biological defense rhythms, stress and child communication behavior. In W. Hartup (ed.): *Review of Child Development Research*, **6**, 291–319. Chicago and London: University of Chicago Press.

Restoin, A., Montagner, H., Godard, D., Henry, J. Ch., Henrotte, J. G., Lombardot, M., Benedini, M., Pretet, M. T. and Prouteau, C. 1981. New data on circadian rhythms of corticosteroid hormones and magnesium in the young child in the day care center and in the kindergarten. In A. Reinberg, N. Vieux and P. Andlauer (eds.): *Advances in the Biosciences – Night and Shift Work, Biological and Social Aspects*, **30**, 331–9. Oxford: Pergamon Press.

Reynolds, V. and Guest, A. 1975. An ethological study of 6–7 year old school children. *Biology and Human Affairs*, **41**, 16–29.

Rodriguez, D. 1983. Etude de l'ontogenèse des vocalisations et des séquences motrices sonores chez l'enfant. In preparation.

Romeder, J. M. 1973. *Méthodes et programmations d'analyse discriminante*. Paris: Dunod.

Rouchouse, J. C. 1978. Ethologie humaine. Ethogramme et communication non-verbale entre nourrissons. *Enfance*, **1**, 13–20.

Rouchouse, J. C. 1980. Ethologie de l'enfant et observation des mimiques chez le nourrisson. *Psychiatrie de l'Enfant*, **23**, 203–49.

Schaal, B., Montagner, H., Hertling, E., Bolzoni, D., Moyse, A. and Quichon, R. 1980. Les stimulations olfactives dans les relations entre l'enfant et la mère. *Reprod., Nutr. Develop.*, **20**, 843–58.

Schaal, B., Hertling, E. and Montagner, H. 1981. Existe-t-il une communication olfactive entre la mère et son enfant? In E. Herbinet and M. C. Busnel (eds.): *Les Cahiers du Nouveau-Né*, **5**, 359–77. Paris: Stock.

Smith, P. K. 1974. Aggression in a preschool playgroup: Effects of varying physical resources. In I. de Witt and W. W. Hartup (eds.): *Determinants and origins of aggressive behavior*. La Haye: Mouton, pp. 97–105.

Smith, P. K. and Green, M. 1975. Aggressive behaviour in English nurseries and playgroups: Sex differences and response of adults. *Child Development*, **46**, 211–14.

Spitz, R. 1968. *De la naissance à la parole*. Paris: Presses Universitaires de France.

Spitz, R. and Wolff, K. M. 1946. The smiling response: A contribution to the ontogenesis of social relations. *Genetic Psychology Monographs*, **34**, 57–125.

Ullmann, V. 1981. Contribution à l'étude ontogénétique du comportement et des rythmes biologiques chez le jeune enfant à la crèche. Thèse de Neurobiologie et Biologie du Comportement de l'Université de Franche-Comté Besançon.

Viala, M. 1980. Etude comparative des effets de changements de rythme de vie contrôlés à l'école maternelle chez des enfants de 3 à 5 ans. Thèse de Neurobiologie et Biologie du Comportement de l'Université de Franche-Comté Besançon.

3. Family way of life and interaction patterns

MARTTI TAKALA

1. Socioecological approach and the concept of the way of life

Early research on social development in the family looked for simple relationships. To sum up, the linkages examined in these studies were of the following types (only single examples of each approach are mentioned):

- parental attitudes → personality disturbance of children (Levy, 1930, 1943);
- structure of the principles, rules, attitudes and practices adopted by the parents (Baldwin *et al.*, 1945; Schaefer and Bell, 1958; M. Takala *et al.*, 1960);
- parental attitudes, child rearing practices → personality development in children (Baldwin *et al.*, 1945; Sears *et al.*, 1957);
- socioeconomic group → parental attitudes, value orientation, child rearing practices (Davis and Havighurst, 1946; A. Takala, 1960);
- socioeconomic group → family interaction, children's social behaviour (Bernstein, 1962; Hess and Shipman, 1965);
- environmental stimulation/deprivation → the development of competence (Strodtbeck, 1958; Winterbottom, 1958).

The psychological studies of the socioeconomic conditions of the family were frequently restricted to single background variables. What was regarded as 'social environment' may have consisted of scattered variables or of unsystematic selection of both micro- and macrosocial factors with no theoretical justification.

One could maintain that the *ecological description* of human activity and interaction was largely neglected. What is more important, is that in most studies attitudes and values were isolated from the general living conditions of the family. It has been shown, for instance, that situational and environmental constraints can be more relevant for the description of family life style in large families and in poor families, under insecure living conditions etc. (A. Takala, 1960). Therefore, the abstract attitude dimensions are not always fruitful for an analysis of the differences among the families. The main restriction of purely psychological interpretations may have been in their *ahistorical* nature. They failed to consider such changes of value systems, attitudes, life styles and living conditions within each social class which occur continuously and at a different pace in various countries and which have been examined in sociological interpretations (e.g. Habermas, 1970; Walter, 1973). Several researchers (e.g. Walter, 1973; Holter, 1976; M. Takala, 1977; Schneewind and Lukesch, 1977) have described the process through which the societal and cultural systems are mediated to children. Bronfenbrenner (1979) grouped various psychological and social environments within a systemic framework which has been applied by a great many scholars.

The nature of the processes mediating between macro- and microsocial systems has been analysed more thoroughly in recent research on socialization (Hess, 1970). Kohn (1969) and Holter (1976), for instance, examined the impact of social class and class conflicts, and Kohn and Schooler (1973, 1978) various aspects of work and occupational experience. The results have differed in their relative emphasis on either educational level or occupational status. The interpretations are to some extent interlocking, but it would be extremely difficult to explicate their mutual connections. In any case they indicate different psychological mechanisms which mediate the processes and structures of societal and cultural systems through the microsocial system or 'learning environment' to an individual child.

In a study of children's development in the family one should admit that the three general classes of contributing factors, viz.
- living conditions,
- activity structures and interaction patterns, and
- goals, orientations and various aspects of parental awareness of parenthood,

are intimately interconnected. It may be neither possible nor necessary to isolate the causal connections involved. The network of relationships is both conceptually and empirically far too complicated for an integration of all the levels of description. Causal analysis of the impact of either the parents or children on their reciprocal interaction may be limited to simple situations, while the socioecological conditions for the activity structures and interaction patterns are revealed in complex and naturalistic settings. Both large samples and a longitudinal design are required for closer analyses of the contribution of various factors (e.g. Kohn and Schooler, 1978).

The primary goal of the present theoretical examination is, accordingly, modest. Description of family's activity, goals and living conditions is emphasized. Various levels and spheres of activity are studied simultaneously, within the same samples. Among the conditions of life, *work* is considered most important. Both the significance of work to an individual and the position of the worker in the hierarchy of the organization are directly and indirectly associated with activity outside work (HEW Task Force, 1973). The mutual roles of wife and husband are assumed to determine the external patterning of activity and interaction in the family. The social status of the job and the content of work are revealed in the adaptation to necessities, the identification with work roles, the recognition of class conflicts, and the prospects for the future. The role of work in human life was hardly discussed in the traditional psychology of personality.

The examination of activity in relation to personal goals and living conditions corresponds to the point of view developed in connection with the concept of the way of life or life style. *Way of life* is defined, at the theoretical level, as the system of activities characteristic of people living under certain life conditions (Rutkevich, 1975; Glezerman *et al.*, 1980). Way of life is thus a complex system related to material and non-material conditions, social relations, needs and activities of men. Its application presupposes a study of the relationships among these categories and their expression in various spheres of life. As a more descriptive concept it is concerned with the essential aspects of everyday life of individuals and groups (Gordon and Klopov, 1974). Sociological studies have paid attention to the socioeconomic aspects of the way of life (Zablocki and Kanter, 1976; Ryvkina, 1979). It cannot be separated from educational and life ideals (e.g. Manz, 1974; Rapport du groupe 'Sciences de l'homme. . .', 1976), and is being used for the formulation of minimum conditions for human life in the recommendations and resolutions of international organizations. In the theoretical debates concerning the concept of the way of life one has to cope with the general problems encountered in the comparison of sociological and psychological systems with each other (Bestuzhev-Lada, 1974). On the basis of existing evidence it might be assumed that the concept of the way of life is, heuristically, useful for the description of socialization in the family, provided that the meaning of activity is emphasized (cf. Willmott and Young, 1972; Zetterberg, 1977).

A hierarchic view of activities is necessary. The use of time or the 'time budget' (Szalai, 1972) provides a general framework for understanding the activity structures of family members. The unit of time consumption or the frequency of occurrence corresponds to the notion of the organization of human activity in time and space. It indicates, at least, some boundary conditions of everyday life. Shortage of time necessitates that a person choose between alternative activities, and the choices are directly or indirectly related to the living conditions of the parents, as well as to their goals in life. From the point of view of social development in the family it emphasizes everyday routine activities which have been neglected in the study of parent–child interaction. It also indicates what kinds of activity are totally lacking in children's learning environment.

The activity structure of each person is defined on the basis of the differentiation and the relative significance of various activities. The social change brought about by technological revolution – the location of the unit of production outside home, new division of labour, the development of specialized tasks and jobs – has decreased the links between work and non-work (e.g. Parker, 1971; Kramer, 1975), and the differentiation of the spheres of activity has gradually increased. Children's activity structure can be described in terms of dominant activities, and its development is indicated by differentiation and increased independence. Family coherence can be estimated on the basis of common conversations, and a provisional measure of family integration consists of the amount of common conversation concerning children's independent activities.

The family time budgets also show the time available for being together, as well as the amount of active and passive interaction among parents, children and peers.

The content of communication is indicated by the topics of common discussions and the estimated frequencies of occurrence. Both the participants and initiators can be assessed. The emotional tone of interaction is reflected in the communication climate which corresponds to some aspects of the traditional measures of parental attitudes. A more detailed analysis of family communication requires a systematic observation of interaction sequences.

What does concept of the way of life mean from the point of view of socialization research? The scope proposed involves:
- realistic description of family activity patterns, including daily routines and important or critical incidents;
- construction of a hierarchic view of activities;
- analysis of the parents' awareness of parenthood: both the level of

awareness and the content of their aims, expectations, rules and procedures;

– examination of the relationships among life conditions, family activity and parental goals and, possibly, integration of the description into 'portraits' of theoretically important groups.

The data can also be used for assessing changes of the way of life. Thurnher *et al.* (1974) refer to discussions of the social changes that generate distinctive life styles of any given age cohorts. The time interval necessary to produce changes is estimated to be about 25 to 30 years in Western culture. There has been a marked acceleration of the process at certain periods, although, in general, there is less change than is popularly believed.

2. Activity structure as revealed by the use of time

So far our research in progress has emphasized the activity structure and interaction patterns in the family. Only preliminary results are available concerning the components of the way of life and their relationship with children's social development. They do not cover all the aspects of the way of life mentioned above. The results refer to Finnish samples and no detailed comparisons with data available elsewhere will be presented. The use of time in Finland 1979 has been examined on the basis of a national sample of over 6,000 respondents (Niemi *et al.*, 1981). Our own samples ranged between 80 and 212 families. The impact of educational level and class position was greatly eliminated in some samples by choosing the families to be rather homogeneous in these respects. Only families including both parents and at least one child, representing a fixed age level, were employed. A few studies of extreme groups have also been carried out. Limited data are available concerning the changes of the way of life in Finnish families after a period of forty years.

First, some results will be presented concerning the time budgets of the parents, while main attention is devoted to the *sharing of work and tasks* between wife and husband. In families with school-aged children, the average time used by men for work amounts to ten hours on weekdays, and that used by women is about one hour longer. Work includes both gainful employment and travelling to work as well as domestic work (household work, repairs and maintenance, child care and errands). Due to men's limited participation the difference in daily domestic work is about two hours. Practically all adults estimate at present that they have some leisure time on regular weekdays, while in our study carried out in

1957 only a small percentage of farmer-wives had any leisure at all, except for short periods at weekends. The change is, to some extent, connected with the differentiation of work and non-work.

The difference in the average working load of the spouses is relatively small as compared with earlier data from other countries (Szalai, 1972; Norwegian Central Bureau, 1972), and one could maintain that their contribution is increasingly 'symmetrical' (Willmott and Young, 1972). Such a conclusion is, however, oversimplified and partly incorrect. The dispersions are much wider in the group of wives. More detailed analyses (Lerber *et al.*, 1979; Niemi *et al.*, 1981) indicate that the phase of family cycle and pattern of employment of the family have very little impact on the husband's time consumption, including the amount of domestic work. Married men do about ten minutes more domestic work per day than unmarried men, and children have an effect of increasing it by an additional ten minutes. The total contribution of the husband amounts to 14 vs. 16 hours a week. On the other hand, married women spend one hour more on domestic work daily than other women, and children increase the time by another hour (Niemi *et al.*, 1981). If a wife has a full-time job outside home or is working on a livestock farm, her total working load is still high today in a family with children. If she acts as homemaker, the time devoted to work is, on average, much less than the mean for all mothers, though no sharp distinction can be made between work and non-work under these circumstances. The mother of young children is, in any case, strongly tied to the home.

The results concerning the sharing of domestic work can be summarized as follows. If both spouses in a family with children are employed, the wife does approximately two-thirds of domestic work. The wife running a household does about 75 per cent of the total time used for domestic work. There are strong differences in the nature of participation in domestic work. Men assume main responsibility for home repairs and maintenance. They also participate in shopping and preparing meals. Cleaning and washing up rest mainly on women's shoulders. Great differences occur in child care. In families with small children (0–4 years) the majority of fathers participate daily in some tasks of child care in an urban environment, while the traditional division of labour is strong in farmer families. The fathers do not generally assume active responsibility for child care. They rather tend to accept the role of 'assisting the mother' (Lerber, 1979; M. Takala, 1979; Niemi *et al.*, 1981).

Children's use of time is, at present, rather homogeneous. During the school terms there are minor differences which are directly related to ecological factors. More time is spent for travelling to school in a rural environment. Interaction frequency is lower and the amount of solitary play higher in farmer families. As compared with earlier results, there have been great changes, associated with the development of technology at home as well as with the decreasing size of the family. In 1938 the school-aged children participated in domestic work for 45 minutes on workdays and 1 hour 20 minutes on weekends on average. In 1954 participation had decreased to 30 minutes and in 1975 to 20 minutes on workdays (Koskenniemi, 1980), and today only about 25 per cent of school-aged children assume regular duties. The participation is only slightly higher in the farmer families during the school term (Lerber *et al.*, 1979). In forty years children's active play, social participation, recreation and hobbies have greatly increased. These activities require approximately double the amount of time as compared with the previous results. The participation in passive entertainment has increased correspondingly, though it is considerably less than in, e.g., the USA. School-aged children are watching TV on average 60 to 90 minutes per day.

3. Work, urbanization and interaction patterns

The following data are based on a sample of 184 families including a seven-year-old child. The activities of the other children were not recorded. The impact of occupation and the employment status of the family will be considered. The husbands were chosen from three main divisions of occupation: agriculture (farmers), services (sales personnel), industry (workers in metal industry). The wife's employment status was defined as follows: homemakers; those employed full-time at home (farming, gardening, 'family day-nursery' for a small number of children from the neighbourhood); those employed full-time outside home and in the same occupational area as the husband; wives in irregular or part-time work outside home.

Time available for *being together* in the family on workdays is shown in Table 1.

Potential time for interaction, e.g. when the external conditions for interaction exist, was approximately four hours daily in each occupational group. Potential time for interaction with the child consisted mainly of leisure time and meals. The parents spent about $1\frac{1}{2}$ hours of this time doing their individual tasks or in collective activities which did not include the child. Another $1\frac{1}{2}$ hours was spent being together with no continuous active interaction (passive interaction: TV watching, oc-

Table 1. *Use of time for family interaction on workdays. Average time in minutes; only periods of 15 minutes or longer are recorded*

| | Division according to father's occupation | | | | | |
| | Father–child | | | Mother–child | | |
	Farmers	Salesmen	Workers	Farmers	Salesmen	Workers
Active cooperation	25	32	31	34	42	44
Passive cooperation	117	95	101	152	127	148
Potential time for interaction	215	222	216	293	283	293

| | Division according to mother's employment status | | | | | | | |
| | Father–child | | | | Mother–child | | | |
	Home-maker	Employed at home	Regular work outside home	Irregular work outside home	Home-maker	Employed at home	Regular work outside home	Irregular work outside home
Active cooperation	24	20	43	26	55	34	45	34
Passive cooperation	87	114	94	118	198	163	117	96
Potential time for interaction	212	198	238	233	363	307	269	224

Note: Dispersions and significances are reported in the original studies.

casional conversation, while staying or working in the same space, etc.). Active interaction was defined as an activity guided by the child's aims and interests or by the goals presented by parents for him. Active interaction between the parent(s) and the seven-year-olds was, on average, limited to half an hour per workday. It covered 12 to 15 per cent of the potential time available for interaction. One should, however, consider that brief contacts, which may be important for reciprocal communication, are not included in time budgets. The figures are slightly higher for mothers, and it is obvious that the proportion of short contacts is much higher in the case of mothers who are running the household (Lerber et al., 1979).

It is also shown in the table that the husband's occupation had very little impact on the parents' active or passive interaction with the child. On the other hand, if the wife was running the household or employed full-time at home, the main responsibility of interaction was left to her. If both the parents were employed full-time outside the home, there was much more symmetry in their communication with the child. In general, the fathers of salesman and industrial worker families interacted more actively with children than those of farmer families. It might be mentioned that the basic structure of time use by the population dwelling in urban and rural municipalities is nearly the same (Niemi et al., 1981).

The families of salesmen and industrial workers did not differ greatly regarding their time budget on workdays. The estimate of the total amount of participation of one or both parents in the various activities of the child during the whole week (Table 2) also indicates considerable similarity in their communication and interaction with the seven-year-old child. The table shows, again, the difference in the interaction pattern of rural and urban environment and the close relationship between the employment status of the mother and parent–child interaction. The total time spent on active interaction (excluding TV watching) amounted to 7½ hours a week, and it was less in the farmer families due to their lower participation in outdoor recreation, indoor plays and reading. On the other hand, slightly more time was spent in these families on interaction in domestic work.

Slight differences were found in the *amount of active conversation* with the child, and the relative *importance of topics of discussion* varied, depending on the occupation of the father (Table 3). Work and religion were proportionately more frequent topics of discussion in the farmer families, and the problems of society somewhat more frequent in the families of industrial workers. The table also indicates the most frequent

Table 2. *Total participation of parents in child's activities in a week (average time in minutes)*

	Division according to father's occupation			Division according to mother's employment status			
	Farmers	Salesmen	Workers	Home-maker	Employed at home	Regular work outside home	Irregular work outside home
Outdoor recreation, sports	73	136	134	207	91	98	189
Domestic tasks	110	90	95	48	108	102	98
Reading, drawing	85	140	131	113	92	166	72
Handicraft, manual art	19	26	16	(1)	18	29	22
Indoor play, game	27	53	74	41	42	72	29
Pet care	40	24	(2)	(11)	32	21	(0)
Total of active participation	409	503	483	443	397	516	453
TV, music listening	268	369	383	349	268	398	419

Note: Total of active participation includes unclassified interaction in addition to those listed above. Very low frequencies are in brackets.

Table 3. *Topics of conversation with child (per cent of families)*

| | Regular topics of conversation | | | Principal initiator, if mentioned | | | |
| | Division according to father's occupation | | | | | | |
	Farmers	Salesmen	Workers	Father	Mother	Parents	Child
School	83	91	91	(1)	23	11	25
Work	37	18	17	6	4	19	17
Child's behaviour	36	39	33	4	19	22	22
Child's fears, problems	39	23	40	(0)	11	8	34
Leisure	77	80	80	4	8	15	12
Society	9	8	18	3	(1)	9	40
Religion	21	(0)	13	(0)	6	2	44
Intimate experiences	28	24	22	(2)	9	6	60

initiators of conversation according to the parents' estimation. The father was seldom an initiator in common conversation and his role was concentrated on such topics as work and general social issues. Emotional problems of the child and intimate topics were mostly discussed between mother and child, regardless of the sex of the child.

The families were divided into extreme groups on the basis of overall intensity of verbal communication with children which was used as an indication of family coherence. In a rural environment the families emphasizing verbal communication were generally active and they participated in various kinds of activities at home and in society. The passive families of the countryside also formed a rather homogeneous type of restricted activity and verbal interaction. On the other hand, in an urban environment the intensity of verbal communication with children was unrelated to the other interests of the parents and was, accordingly, a more specific characteristic of family interaction and an indication of family-centredness (Lerber *et al.*, 1979).

The relationship between social class or educational level and the communication and control patterns in the family, discussed by Bernstein (1962, 1971, 1975), has been further examined by several authors (e.g. Robinson, 1972) and various kinds of mediating processes have been suggested. The relative importance of verbal and nonverbal communication has been considered to be an essential factor (Hess and Shipman, 1965). One should, of course, raise the question concerning the particular functions and aspects of nonverbal communication which can be relevant in various contexts.

In one of our experiments concerning parent–child interaction the contribution of school education and sex of both parents and their seven-year-old children was examined during interaction tasks and games in videotaped dyadic situations. It was shown that neither the educational background nor the sex of the parent was decisive for verbal and nonverbal communication with the child in any tasks. There were, however, a few differences: in a game situation the parents with high educational level introduced the task in advance to the child and explained the rules of the game. They also checked that the child had understood the rules and followed them. The parents with less education limited the instruction to a minimum and added information about the procedure as far as needed during the first stages of the game. Accordingly, educational background is not essential for the communication and control codes in ordinary interaction and routine activity (Rasku-Puttonen, 1982). The differences of verbal and nonverbal style and competence are revealed in more complex tasks as well as in intimate emotional interaction.

4. Work conditions and family interaction

A more detailed analysis of the work conditions of the parents and their connection with family interaction was carried out with a sample representing a greater variety of occupations. It was yet relatively homogenous as to educational level. The sample consisted of 212 families with a six-year-old child. The following aspects of the parents' work are examined in the present context:
- outside home/at home
- wife in gainful employment/not employed
- shift-work/regular day-time work
- nature of work: social/not social
- nature of work: independent activity/dependent
- nature of work: in-service training and career-oriented/no in-service training.

These aspects of work are compared with interaction and conversations at home and with children's independent activities (Table 4). The results can be summarized as follows: If the husband and/or wife worked outside home, their interaction with the child was increased and intensified in leisure-time and they had more common topics of conversation. A tendency toward the same direction was also found in the families in which the wife was in gainful employment, as compared

Table 4. *Relationship between working conditions and family interaction. Summary of results*

	Parent–child interaction		Variety of topics of conversation	Child's independent activities	Conversation concerning child's activities
	Amount	Intensity			
Work outside home					
Wife	++	+	++	0	0
Husband	+	+	++	0	0
Wife in gainful employment	(+)	(+)	(+)	+	0
Shift-work					
Wife	– –	0	–	+	–
Husband	– –	0	–	+	–
Nature of work social					
Wife	++	0	0	++	++
Husband	++	+	++	++	++
Nature of work independent					
Wife	++	0	+	0	0
Husband	0	0	++	0	0
In-service training, career					
Wife	++	0	0	0	0
Husband	0	0	0	0	++

with homemakers. On the other hand, when the wife and/or husband was in shift-work, interaction decreased and was limited in regard to content: they had less conversation with the child concerning his or her own activities, and the child's independent activity increased. The social nature of the parents' work was associated with the amount and variety of total interaction and verbal communication, but also the child's own activity increased. Independence at work and the possibility for career were likewise related to increased family interaction. In a previous study it was estimated that the social nature of the parents' work had, at the same level of occupational and educational status, an impact of increasing the amount of active communication with the child approximately one hour a week.

These examples concerning work conditions and family interaction give only a preliminary idea of the network of relationships within the microsocial environment of the child. Within a homogeneous sample they still are significant sources of variance which characterize the family way of life. The difference between the rural and urban life style is, however, more conspicuous, especially as to the differentiation of the main spheres of activity.

5. Family way of life and children's social development

The empirical illustrations have not integrated the parental goals and awareness of parenthood into the description of the family way of life. The Finnish data show that the hierarchic structure of parental principles, expectations, attitudes and procedures has changed in twenty years and, simultaneously, the differences between socioecological environments have decreased in all these components.

In connection with a longitudinal study of adolescents Pulkkinen (1977, 1982) extracted two main dimensions of living conditions and family interaction: stability/insecurity of life; child-centred guidance and active participation/adult-centred treatment with low awareness of parenthood. These dimensions define some basic types of the way of life in the family. She also examined the linkages between various components of the family way of life and adolescent personality and was able to show consistent relationships to, e.g., constructive/aggressive behaviour.

Our comparisons have concentrated on more concrete aspects within the homogeneous samples described above. The network of relation-ships between the *work conditions* of the parents and children's social

Table 5. *Way of life in family and children's social behaviour at age six to*

	Active-constructive	Receptive-constructive Main
Use of Time:		
Father–child, active	Low	Low
Mother–child, active	High	–
Father–child, passive	Low	–
Mother–child, passive	Very low	–
Father–mother, passive	Low	–
Interaction:		
Common activities with parents	High	Very high
Verbal communication: Amount, variety	Rich	Rich
Verbal communication: Central topics	Activities+	–
Communication atmosphere (questionnaire)	·	–
Activities with peers:		
Amount, variety	High, rich	–
Organized social activity	High	–
Alone at home	–	Low
TV watching	–	–
Parental awareness of parenthood:		
Goals	–	Differentiated
Child-centred guidance in conversation	High	High
Rules: amount	–	–
Rules: central topics	Responsibility+ Conduct–	–
Techniques of control	Verbal explanation+	–

behaviour, as displayed in realistic game situations, in school class, and particular small-group tasks, was consistent, although the correlations were low. High amounts of initiative and constructive activity were associated with the following characteristics of the occupation of the parents: independence at work, social character of work, opportunity for advancement. High amount of common conversation, intentional nature of communication and high level of awareness of parenthood seemed to act as mediating processes. It was also shown, as is known on the basis of previous results, that children's previous experience in peer groups correlated with their activeness and basic communication skills.

The use of time for *active interaction* between the parents and children was linked with some characteristics of children's social behaviour, as is *seven in a homogeneous sample*

types of social behaviour			
Adult-Dependent	Shy	Impulsive, conflicts with peers	Aggressive
Very low	High	Very high	Low
Low	–	High	Very low
–	High	Low	Very high
Very low	–	–	Very high
–	Very high	–	–
High (Mother) Low (Father)	Very high	–	Low
Rich	Scarce	–	Scarce
Work+	Intimate+	Intimate+	Intimate–, Society–
Child's activity+	Work, Society–		Child's activity–
Warm (Mother)	–	–	Conflicting
Cold (Father)			atmosphere?
–	Low, scarce	–	Scarce
–	Low	Low	–
Low	Very high	High	High
–	High	–	High
–	Differentiated	–	–
–	–	–	–
Very high	High	Low	Low
Hygiene+, Safety+	Responsibility+	Conduct+, Hygiene+	Responsibility–
Conduct+	Safety+	Responsibility–	
–	Verbal Explanation+	Scolding & Punishment+ Negligence+	Verbal explanation– Scolding & Punishment+ Negligence+

Note: Source: Takala, 1979; Pölkki, 1982.

shown in Figure 1. In these comparisons children were classified separately in each situation according to characteristics revealed in systematic observation or teachers' semistructured descriptions. Withdrawing and destructive children differed most strongly from the other groups.

A summary of the results concerning the *family way of life* and children's social behaviour is given in Table 5 with regard to different components of the way of life. The main types of social behaviour were assessed on the basis of both teachers' description and systematic observation. The description is only preliminary and no detailed comments of the findings are made in the present context. Most of the linkages were, again, weak but the network of relationships was usually consistent. The aggressive

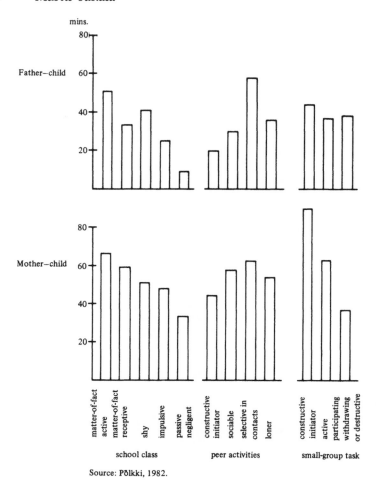

Figure 1. Relationship between the types of social behaviour in three situations and parent–child interaction (active cooperation): sum of time consumption on a weekday and Sunday.

group was clearly distinguished from the others, as can be expected on the basis of previous knowledge. Among the other groups it can be pointed out that the active-constructive children were characterized by lack of passive interaction in the family, by high amount and great variety of verbal communication and activities. On the other hand, emotional topics were not emphasized in conversation and the parents' awareness of parenthood was at the average level. All the components of the way of life were associated with some particular types of children's social behaviour. In the use of time the proportion of active and passive interaction seems to be essential. The amount and content of verbal conversation and the content of rules emphasized by the parents seem to express more about communication atmosphere than a questionnaire-based assessment.

The examples may suffice to indicate how the description of the way of life can be applied in a study of family life and socialization. The theoretical concept of the way of life would, however, require additional integration of data.

6. Final comments

Research on the family way of life and interaction patterns can be continued by applying more qualitative methodology. Extreme groups chosen on the basis of either children's or parents' situation or goals seem to provide a fruitful strategy. Two examples will be briefly mentioned.

The way of life and family adjustment was examined in a sample of 40 children with chronic heart disease (Heiskanen *et al.*, 1981; Myllylä, 1981; Heiskanen and Koskinen, 1982). Both the parents and the child were interviewed and compared with a matched control group. In regard to the use of time most families had developed successful ways of coping with threat and anxiety aroused by the disease. The differences of activity were mainly due to physical restrictions in some children. Social interaction was not seriously affected. On closer inspection, however, there were important changes. Future plans were determined by insecurity. Both parents participated actively in the treatment and indicated their affection more than the control group. In case of changes in the regular life pattern the mother had adjusted to new requirements. The asymmetry in the roles of spouses was marked in emotional and intimate matters: in discussions of the risk involved, in preparation for the hospital, and putting the child to sleep. There were indications of both denial of risks and over-protective attitudes and the spouses differed to some extent from each other in these respects.

The second example is concerned with children and adolescents who were actively engaged in sports (Vanhalakka-Ruoho, 1981). The most extreme group consisted of 15- to 17-year-old boys of ice hockey teams who spent 15 to 19 hours a week for training and matches. In these families the majority of the parents were actively involved in these activities and ice hockey was a common topic of daily conversation. The families had developed time schedules and life styles according to the boys' requirements. The adults' role was that of supporter and helper, and the mother spent a lot of time washing up. The coherence of the family might be considered strong, but it was greatly determined by the interests of the adolescent. The future plans of the most active adolescents were concerned with professional or top-ranking teams.

One might suggest that a systemic description of the life process of families chosen on the basis of theoretical expectations will turn out to be the most promising area for future research.

References

Baldwin, A. L. *et al*. 1945. Patterns of parent behavior. *Psychol. Monog.*, **58**, 268.
Bernstein, B. 1962. Social class, linguistic codes and grammatic elements. *Language and Speech*, **5**, 221–40.
Bernstein, B. 1971. *Class, codes, and control*. Vol. 1: *Theoretical studies towards a sociology of language*. London: Routledge and Kegan Paul.
Bernstein, B. 1975. Language and socialization. In S. Rogers (ed.): *Children and language: Readings in early language and socialization*. London: Oxford University Press.
Bestuzhev-Lada, I. V. 1974. Sotsiologicheskie problemy 'obraza zhizni'. *Sotsiologicheskie issledovania*, **2**, 64–80.
Bronfenbrenner, U. 1979. *The ecology of human development*. Cambridge, Mass.: Harvard University Press.
Davis, A. and Havighurst, R. J. 1946. Social class and color differences in child rearing. *Amer. Sociol. Rev.*, **11**, 698–710.
Glezerman, G. E. *et al.* (eds.) 1980. *Sotsialistichesky obraz zhizni*. Moscow: Politizdat.
Gordon, L. A. and Klopov, E. V. 1974. *Man after work*. Moscow: Progress.
Habermas, J. 1970. Thesen zur Theorie der Sozialisation. In J. Habermas: *Arbeit, Erkenntnis, Fortschritt, Aufsätze 1954/1970*. Amsterdam: Munder.
Heiskanen, M. *et al.* 1981. Child with heart disease: General scope and methods of an empirical study (in Finnish). M. Soc. Sc. thesis. Dept. of Psychology, University of Jyväskylä.
Heiskanen, M. and Koskinen, P.-L. 1982. Child with heart disease: The child's experiences in the hospital, life style, physical and mental development (in Finnish). M. Soc. Sc. thesis, Dept. of Psychology, University of Jyväskylä.
Hess, R. D. 1970. Class and ethnic influences upon socialization. In P. H. Mussen (ed.): *Carmichael's manual of child psychology*. New York: Wiley, 3rd edition.
Hess, R. D. and Shipman, V. C. 1965. Early experience and the socialization of cognitive modes in children. *Child Dev.*, **34**, 869–86.
HEW Task Force 1973. *Work in America: Report of a special Task Force to the Secretary of Health, Education, and Welfare*. Cambridge, Mass.: MIT Press.
Holter, H. *et al.* 1976. *Familjen i klassamhället*. Malmö: Bonniers.
Kohn, M. 1969. *Class and conformity*. Homewood, Ill.: Dorsey.
Kohn, M. and Schooler, C. 1973. Occupational experience and psychological functioning: An assessment of reciprocal effects. *Amer. Sociol. Rev.*, **38**, 97–118.
Kohn, M. and Schooler, C. 1978. The reciprocal effects of substitutive complexity

of work and intellectual flexibility: A longitudinal assessment. *Amer. J. Sociol.*, **84**, 24–52.

Koskenniemi, M. 1980. The day circle of school-children (in Finnish). Rep. No. 84, Dept. of Education, University of Helsinki.

Kramer, D. 1975. Freizeit und die Reproduktion der Arbeitskraft. Cologne: Pahl-Rugenstein.

Lerber, E.-L. *et al.* 1979. Family's life style, described in terms of activities and time consumption: Comparisons between farmers, salesmen and industrial workers (in Finnish). Rep. No. 216, Dept. of Psychology, University of Jyväskylä.

Levy, D. M. 1930. Paper on maternal overprotection. *Amer. J. Orthopsychiat.*, **9**, 900–4.

Levy, D. M. 1943. *Maternal overprotection*. New York: Columbia University Press.

Manz, G. 1974. Way of life and leisure time use. *Society and Leisure*, **6**, 75–86.

Myllylä, M. 1981. Child with heart disease: The adjustment of the parents to chronic disease (in Finnish). M. Soc. Sc. thesis, Dept. of Psychology, University of Jyväskylä.

Niemi, I. *et al.* 1981. *Use of time in Finland 1979.* Central Statistical Office in Finland, Study No. 65.

Norwegian Central Bureau of Statistics 1972. *Time studies.* Oslo.

Parker, S. 1971. *The future of work and leisure.* Glencoe, Ill.: Free Press.

Pölkki, P. 1982. Children's communication and interaction skills at the age of six and seven (in Finnish). In preparation.

Pulkkinen, L. 1977. Psychology of home education (in Finnish). Jyväskylä: Gummerus.

Pulkkinen, L. 1982. Self-control and continuity from childhood to late adolescence. In P. B. Baltes and O. G. Brim (eds.): *Life span development and behavior.* New York: Academic Press, vol. 4, pp. 64–105.

Rapport du groupe 'Sciences de l'homme et aménagements à la commission de la recherche de VIIe Plan'. 1976. *Le progrès scientifique*, **182**, 3–40.

Rasku-Puttonen, H. 1982. Dyadic verbal and nonverbal communication between parent and child in families with different educational background. To be published in the *Scandinavian Journal of Psychology*.

Robinson, W. 1972. *Language and social behaviour.* Harmondsworth: Penguin.

Rutkevich, M. N. 1975. Sotsialistichesky obraz zhizni i ego razvitie. *Voprosy Filos.*, **11**, 46–58.

Ryvkina, R. V. 1979. *Obraz zhizni sel'skogo naselenia.* Novosibirsk: Nauka.

Schaefer, E. S. and Bell, R. Q. 1958. Development of a parental attitude research instrument. *Child Dev.*, **29**, 339–61.

Schneewind, K. and Lukesch, H. (eds.) 1977. *Familiäre Sozialisation.* Stuttgart: Klett-Cotta.

Sears, R. R. *et al.* 1957. *Patterns of child rearing.* Evanston, Ill.: Row and Peterson.

Strodtbeck, F. L. 1958. Family interaction, values, and achievement. In D. C. McClelland *et al.* (eds.): *Talent and society.* Princeton: Van Nostrand.

Szalai, A. 1972. *The use of time.* The Hague: Mouton.

Takala, A. 1960. Parental attitudes and child rearing practices. *Acta Acad. Paed. Jyväskylä*, **19**, 2.

Takala, M. *et al.* 1960. Parental attitudes and child-rearing practices. *Acta Acad. Paed. Jyväskylä*, **19**, 1.

Takala, M. 1977. Way of life and personality (in Finnish). *Psykologia*, **12**, 26–38.

Takala, M. 1979. Family's way of life, parental awareness of parenthood, and children's social development (in Finnish). Rep. No. 219, Dept. of Psychology, University of Jyväskylä.

Thurnher, M. *et al*. 1974. Value confluence and behavioral conflict in inter-generational relations. *J. Marriage and the Family*, **36**, 308–19.

Vanhalakka-Ruoho, M. 1981. Family and sporting child (in Finnish). Rep. No. 123, Dept. of Psychology, University of Tampere.

Walter, H. 1973. Einleitung oder auf der Suche nach einem sozialisationstheoretischen Konzept. In H. Walter (ed.): *Sozialisationsforschung I*. Stuttgart: Frommann-Holzboog.

Willmott, P. and Young, M. 1972. *The symmetrical family*. Harmondsworth: Penguin.

Winterbottom, M. R. 1958. The relation of need for achievement to learning experiences in independence and mastery. In J. W. Atkinson (ed.): *Motives in fantasy, action and society*. Princeton: Van Nostrand.

Zablocki, B. D. and Kanter, R. M. 1976. The differentiation of life-styles. *Ann. Rev. Sociol.*, **2**, 269–98.

Zetterberg, H. L. 1977. *Arbete, livsstil och motivation*. Stockholm: SAF.

Part II
Adult control techniques

How do children succeed in behaving in a proficient and adapted manner with regard to the social world? Studies on socialization have frequently tried to answer this question by invoking the existence of a control activity on the part of the adult that relies on a system of sanctions and punishments. Elsewhere this behaviourist terminology has been replaced by the apparently more subtle and sophisticated language of psychoanalysis. Still other studies assume that the child participates to varying degrees in processes of modelling and training that constitute its socialization. Finally, mention might be made of the anthropologists and sociologists who have not been slow to introduce to the study of socialization numerous and often very ambitious contributions of their own.

It is, however, the recent adoption of methods of systematic observation, derived from ethology, that has allowed movement beyond these somewhat imprecise considerations, revealing how children from the first moments of their lives actively intervene in interaction with adults and thus construct their own social competencies.

The two contributions to this Part are concerned in particular with the techniques of control used by adults in relation to children less than four years old. Schaffer, in some laboratory-based research, demonstrates the importance of reciprocity in the exchanges observed between mothers and children, while Emiliani and Zani show with the help of a case study how institutions, via the concepts of education that prevail within them, differentially influence the behaviour of educational personnel towards children attending creches.

When we consider the active and early intervention of children in their own socialization, we begin to see the importance of such studies for detecting the conditions which will be most effective in enabling children to maximize their own potential.

4. Parental control techniques in the context of socialization theory

H. RUDOLPH SCHAFFER

Children change as a result of interacting with other people, in particular during the early years and in the context of their family. They learn to sleep at night rather than during the day, they acquire particular food preferences and ways of eating such food, they come to communicate by means comprehensible to those around them, they develop ideas as to what behaviour is acceptable or not in their particular society, they learn skills such as reading and writing – the list of such acquisitions could go on for a long time yet, for virtually every facet of a child's behaviour is transformed as a result of coming into contact with other people. These changes are, of course, far from haphazard, for they tend closely to reflect the specific set of values and mores of the particular society into which the child is born. That society ensures, by means of a variety of both explicit and subtle pressures which are brought to bear on the child, that he comes increasingly to conform to the norms prevalent in his social group, for the smooth operation of the group is to a large extent dependent on consensus among its members as to the proper ways of behaving. Thus the child's behaviour becomes channelled into certain directions with a view to making him a fit member of his society.

A considerable amount of descriptive material has gradually accumulated documenting the nature of this process. The socialization literature is indeed a vast one; it is also, however, in many respects diverse and even confusing. In part this confusion stems from the sheer size of the problem: for instance, a great many different aspects of child behaviour are implicated, and there is no *a priori* reason to believe that the processes that explain, say, language acquisition are identical to those that are responsible for the development of sex roles. It cannot simply be taken for granted that developmental principles hold across all functions in identical fashion: each needs to be examined in its own right if we are to determine what part environmental forces play in shaping its course. In addition, methodological problems have contributed to the confusion, for how to obtain reliable evidence on the way children's behaviour is directed into particular socially approved channels has been a topic over which social scientists have agonized a great deal in recent years. On the one hand, parental interview and questionnaire data have come to be viewed with great caution; and on the other hand, the use of experimental studies designed to model the socialization process has also lately met with scepticism on grounds of artificiality and failure to spill over into the child rearing literature (see, for instance, the account by Walters and Grusec (1977) of the way in which experimental studies of punishment have yielded results of a very disparate nature compared to those obtained from socialization studies).

The greatest source of difficulty, however, is of a conceptual nature. It refers to the assumptions which we make regarding the nature of the parental task in bringing up a child, and even to the preconceptions we hold as to the basic nature of the child itself. Let us look at these more closely.

1. Socialization models

An extraordinary variety of definitions have been attached to the term 'socialization'. LeVine (1969), for example, distinguishes three views of the process, namely socialization as enculturation, as the acquisition of impulse control, and as role training. The three views are said to correspond roughly to the orientation of cultural anthropology, psychology and sociology respectively.

Yet even within any one of these disciplines, with particular reference to psychology, there is by no means unanimity. Some writers concentrate primarily on *outcome* characteristics, whereas others emphasize *processes* rather than products. Again, there are those that look at it primarily in terms of what the *adult* has to do, whereas others prefer to put the stress on the *child's* task. There is, of course, no real disagreement as to the ultimate function of socialization, namely to produce individuals fit to participate in the life of their particular society. There is, however, still considerable ignorance as to the way in which this occurs. How do parents bring about change in their children's behaviour?

In the past, two principal models of the socialization process have been prevalent, each linked to a particular set of assumptions about the nature of the child to be socialized. They have dominated most of the research on child rearing in the last two decades, yet it is now becoming increasingly apparent that both are inadequate.

The first model is indeed now generally recognized as unsatisfactory. It views socialization as a *clay-moulding process*: the child, that is, arrives in the world as a formless lump of clay and society, as represented by mothers, fathers, teachers and other authority figures, proceeds to mould him into whatever shape it desires. The end product is then wholly explicable in terms of the external forces which the child has encountered, and it follows that all attempts to understand how socialization comes about must involve an analysis of the behaviour of the adults with whom the child is in contact. The child's own part is confined merely to passively observing, retaining and reproducing whatever occurs in front of him. The research based on this model tended therefore to concentrate exclusively on parental activities: on the way feeds are scheduled, toilet training provided, punishment administered, desirable activities modelled, and so forth. The child's development was then regarded as wholly accounted for by these external forces to which he was exposed.

Such a view has received much criticism in recent years (Bell and Harper, 1977). The concept of the child to which it is linked is that of a passive being, and the relationship with the parent is thus a wholly unidirectional one. There are many reasons now for discarding this view (see Schaffer, 1977a, for a more extended discussion). Even the youngest infant is far from inert: for one thing, experimental research with newborns has pointed to the considerable degree of psychological competence and organization that is present from the beginning; for another, the presence of marked individual differences even in young infants has highlighted the extent to which the characteristics of the child force the adult to adopt appropriate responses; and above all Piaget's constructivist view has made us acknowledge the fact that even in the early weeks of life the child brings to any encounter with objects (social as well as inanimate) certain psychological structures by means of which he can act on the environment and which enable him to influence others as well as be influenced by them. Moreover, far from being a passive being the infant interacts spontaneously with his surroundings; he is capable of initiating interactions with others and is by no means merely an inert being waiting to be stirred into action by his caretakers. A bi-directional approach to social encounters is therefore required, and much of the recent literature on mother–infant interaction reflects this orientation (Schaffer, 1977b).

The second model of the socialization process, unlike the first, is still widely prevalent. Let us refer to it as a *conflict model*, for it views parent and child as engaged in a struggle in which each pursues mutually incompatible objectives. The parent, on the one hand, acts as the representative of society and as such must ensure that the child's destructive impulses (his aggression, his sexuality, and so forth) are not allowed free expression but are contained, inhibited or diverted into socially more acceptable channels. The child, on the other hand, is determined to give free rein to his primitive nature and to act in a totally egocentric fashion, with no awareness of and consideration for the social consequences of his actions. The task of child rearing therefore takes place in the context of a continuing conflict – one that the parent, by virtue of his superior power, generally wins, though at the cost of repression and neurotic conflict as far as the consequences for the child are concerned.

The concept of the child which this model implies is that of an innately depraved and evil being. Such a view can be traced back many centuries (Shorter, 1976): it regards man as conceived in sin, childhood as the period for curbing and eradicating the evil in him, and obedience and submission to authority as the eventual aims of all child rearing practices. The parent commands, the child obeys – but not until a great deal of effort has gone into the task of bringing the recalcitrant child to heel and subduing his self-will by means of strict moral training. The needs and wishes of child and parent are thus antithetical; it is the function of child rearing to preserve the integrity of social life by subduing the child's egoistic and undesirable tendencies. Man is basically an anti-social being, and many years of training and discipline are needed to force him to adopt more acceptable modes of conduct.

Though of long standing, this view has gained modern acceptability through Freudian theory. Freud (1963) too saw the child as a basically selfish being, solely concerned with the immediate gratification of his impulses and unable to tolerate delay and frustration. Yet the maintenance of the social order cannot permit such gratifications, and a clash is therefore inevitable. The Freudian account of socialization is thus based on a conflict model; it is addressed to the problem of how the child learns to restrain his inborn anti-social impulses, and suggests that this comes about only because of the child's fear of the parents' disapproval and of losing their love. Freudian theory thus concentrates on the negative side of the parent–child relationship: on the prohibitiveness of the parent, on the consequent frustrations of the child, and on the incompatibility which Freud alleges to exist, initially at any rate, between them. Development is forced on the reluctant child by the commands, threats, exhortations and prohibitions of his parents, and when conformity to their sanctions does occur in due course it is at the cost of the individual's own nature. Only coercion through rewards and punishment will bring about acceptance of society's rules and customs and ensure that the child eventually adopts behaviour patterns that originally were at variance with his natural inclinations.

There can be little doubt about the influence of this view on research into child rearing. For a long time even those writers not closely identified with psychoanalysis saw socialization in 'potty-training' terms: concerned, that is, with preventing the child from doing what is natural and forcing him to comply with some quite arbitrary requests by powerful adults for new and strange behaviour. Thus much of the socialization literature is concerned with sanctions and with the way in which socially desirable behaviour is reinforced and undesirable behaviour is punished. Investigations focussed mainly on the problem of impulse control, especially as applied to oral, excretory, sexual and aggressive tendencies. Concentrating on these areas (at any rate in the context of Western culture and during less tolerant decades than the present one) may indeed give some support to the conflict model. Yet, as Zigler and Child (1973) have put it so well, if socialization research had instead been focussed on, say, the acquisition of language a much more positive view of child rearing would have emerged. As it is, the conflict model still prevails; it is, for example, evident in the concept of the 'discipline encounter' which Hoffman (1977) puts forward as the typical context within which socialization occurs. The discipline encounter is based on a clash of wills: parent and child have different aims and the task of the parent is to interrupt the child's activity and, by virtue of being more powerful, to impose his wishes on the unwilling and resentful child.

There is, of course, no denying that such situations occur (what parent cannot tell heart-rending tales about them!). Yet on its own the conflict model gives a misleadingly one-sided account; it neglects (as Stayton, Hogan and Ainsworth, 1971, have also pointed out) the basic mutuality that exists between parent and child and to which so much of the recent literature on early social interaction points with great emphasis. Far from starting off as an anti-social being that must be coerced into sociability there is much to suggest that the infant is preadapted for social interaction; far from seeing the parent–child relationship as a never-ending battle research workers have characterized it in terms such as 'smooth', 'synchronized', 'reciprocal' and so forth. What is more, a picture emerges of mothers commonly allowing the child to set the pace of the interaction, frequently letting him determine the topic, showing great sensitivity to the cues that he provides, sensitively fitting in their behaviour to his, and carefully adapting their stimulus input to the child's ability to comprehend and meaningfully absorb it. In other words, for the mother to bring about a 'successful' interaction she cannot arbitrarily impose demands on the child but must take account of his particular state and condition at the time and must adjust her own behaviour accordingly.

This *mutuality* model appears to be at variance with the other two models which we have described. Unlike the clay-moulding model it sees the child as an active participant in social encounters and not just at the mercy of adult wills and whims; unlike the conflict model it regards parent and child as mutually compatible. Let us, however, acknowledge the fact that the picture of mutuality has emerged almost entirely from studies that have placed mother and child in one particular kind of context, namely in situations that are unstructured and unconstrained – face-to-face situations, in which the mother is merely told to amuse the child, or free play situations, in which the two partners can do as they wish with whatever toy material is available. The goal of the interactants in such a context is the interaction itself: their aim is simply to enjoy each other's company and have fun together. Studies based on such situations thereby maximize the possibility for the infant to take the initiative, confining the mother to following his lead and adapting to his particular requirements. But what of those situations where mothers do have to take the initiative, where they do have purposes and goals and needs of their own which they wish to convey to the child and with which the child has to fit in? When the mother does have a particular end-result in mind which she wishes to convey to the child, is the picture of mutuality no longer applicable and does the relationship then revert to a unidirectional one? These are the situations, of course, that relate closely to the socialization issue, in that the mother sets about redirecting and changing the child's ongoing behaviour. It is perhaps ironic that, despite the vast volume of socialization literature, we still have extraordinarily little directly obtained information as to how parents actually set about their directive task – in part because until recently global entities (such as nurturance, hostility, dependence and so forth) formed investigators' building blocks rather than the much more specific behavioural units now found in observational studies; in part because data were mostly obtained by indirect means such as interviews and questionnaires and not by direct observation; and in part also because considerable time gaps between antecedent parental practices and consequent child characteristics were often inserted. The advent of ethological approaches has changed all this: behaviour is defined in much more precise terms; there is a great reliance on observational methods; and we are becoming much less ambitious with regard to large-scale, long-term consequences for the child and content instead to analyse interactive situations in the here-and-now. It is in this spirit that we have started a programme of research devoted to learning how parents exert control over their children's behaviour and produce compliance with their wishes (Schaffer and Crook, 1978, 1979, 1980).

2. Parental control techniques

Let us first of all emphasize that the term 'control techniques', as used here, is not to be understood in a purely negative fashion, denoting force, inhibition, punishment and so on. Rather, control techniques refer to all those behaviours employed by one person to change the ongoing course of another's activity. Their function is to channel behaviour in certain directions, inhibiting some tendencies and enhancing others. They are all those communications from one individual to another that are designed to 'impel, inhibit, direct, guide, shape or otherwise influence the recipient's behaviour' (Flavell, 1977). Although they can be found in the interaction of any two or more individuals, their significance is particularly marked in the encounters of parent and child and especially so in the preschool years.

For the study of control techniques we adopted the same microanalytic methods that we previously employed (Schaffer, 1977b) for the study of unstructured mother–infant interactions. Our initial aim was to arrive at a useful taxonomy that would enable us to describe the sort of methods mothers use for manipulating their children towards short-term goals in particular situations. Accordingly we began by inviting children from two groups, aged 15 and 24 months, one at a time together with the mother, to a playroom in our laboratory. Each mother was told that we were interested in observing children's play at various ages. However, to ensure that she took an active role in the interaction she was instructed to make quite certain that the child played with all the toys available, not to let him spend all his time with just one or two toys, and actively to intervene in order to direct the child's play accordingly. The sessions lasted eight minutes and were recorded from different angles by two cameras stationed behind a one-way mirror. A fine-grained analysis of these social encounters was then carried out.

Controls can either be administered through the medium of language or they may take a nonverbal form. As to verbal controls, their large number found in the transcripts of the mother's speech attests to the fact that the mothers did indeed interpret their task in this situation as a directive one. Nearly half of all verbal utterances (47.3 per cent in the 15-month group and 44.4 per cent in the 24-month group) had a control function. This means that such controls rained down on the children at the average rate of one every 9 seconds. Had these been of the forceful, authoritarian nature so commonly described in the psychological literature on parental socializing practices the children would have been utterly overwhelmed. Impressionistically, this clearly did not happen: in every instance the mother appeared to accomplish her task in an atmosphere of harmony.

There are several reasons for this outcome. The first is that the controls used by the mothers were often of an indirect and highly subtle nature. For instance, very few prohibitives were found (3.3 and 5.9 per cent of utterances in the younger and the older group respectively were overtly concerned with preventing or terminating behaviour); when the mothers wanted to put a stop to a particular activity they relied more on distraction than on direct negative command. And in addition, almost half of all control utterances were expressed in a grammatical form other than the imperative (see Table 1). As writers on speech act theory (Austin, 1962; Searle, 1969) have stressed, the act indicated by a sentence is separable from the precise linguistic form: a request expressed in the interrogative form may have the same illocutionary force as an order expressed as an imperative. The lack of correspondence between purpose and syntactic form in adult conversation is now widely recognized (Ervin-Tripp, 1976); it appears, however, that even speech to children who are only just beginning to comprehend language can also take this indirect and (in a sense) unclear form. As both Shatz (1978) and our own work (Schaffer and Crook, 1980) has shown, the syntactic form of the control utterance has little effect on the likelihood of obtaining the child's compliance – one can get children to do things just as easily by asking them questions as by issuing commands. The use of the former does, however, serve to reduce the emotional intensity of the interaction that would otherwise be created by showering the child with a succession of explicit commands.

The other reason why children were apparently not overwhelmed by the barrage of controls refers to the way in which the mothers timed their interventions. Controls, that is, rarely descended in bolt-out-of-the-blue fashion on the child but were carefully timed by the mother to ensure that

Table 1. *Percentage of grammatical types of control utterances in the two age groups*

	Imperatives	Interrogatives	Declaratives	Moodless
15 months	51	32	8	9
24 months	46	29	12	13

Table 2. *Percentage of attention and action controls according to age*

	Attention controls	Action controls
15 months	43.0	57.0
24 months	25.2	74.8

the child's attention was appropriately focussed on a toy before some action on that toy was requested. Mothers tended to employ sequential strategies, whereby attention-directing devices (nonverbal as well as verbal) were used as a preliminary to action directives. The distinction between attention controls and action controls is thus a most fruitful one to make in any attempt to understand how mothers set about getting the child to perform some task. As shown in Table 2, attention controls were particularly prevalent among mothers of the younger children, whose lesser mobility and spontaneity meant that they were more frequently 'stuck' on any one particular toy. On the whole the mothers preferred to let the child take the initiative in choosing a new toy to play with, and they would then issue an action directive only when they had ensured that the child showed interest in that toy. When this did not happen, however (and this was rather more likely in the younger group) the mother herself would set about manipulating the child's attention by appropriate means, and only when she had succeeded in weaning him from the previous toy and leading him to the new one would action controls be used to indicate some desirable activity to be performed on that toy. Thus mothers rarely leapt in with an action control without first establishing a mutual focus of attention, and the adoption of such a sequential strategy may well have been a further and important contribution to the over-all harmony that prevailed in these sessions. Maternal sensitivity rather than maternal authoritarianism appears to be the central characteristic found in this particular situation.

The same sensitivity can be seen in other respects too, such as the way in which controls were adapted to the age of the children. Let us for this purpose look at the nonverbal controls applied by the mothers. In the younger group significantly more nonverbal controls were found than in the older group, but as shown in Table 3 this difference was largely a function of two of the categories into which we classified these controls. Mothers of younger children made more use of techniques concerned with 'manipulating accessibility', largely because the more limited motor abilities of these children made it more necessary for the mothers to move toys within the child's reach, present them to him, or in some other way alter the physical distance between child and toy. The age difference for the category referring to 'eliciting or prohibiting action' also reflects the greater helplessness of the younger children, as a result of which mothers more frequently began an activity that invited the child to complete it. They were more likely, for example, to prompt the child to act by holding out a stick for rings to be put on, or wait with hands outstretched to receive a toy. By such means, therefore, these mothers were playing a more active role in maintaining the momentum of their children's play. Nonverbal controls were, of course, frequently used in close association with the mothers' verbal controls: taking temporal overlap as our criterion we find such association in something over a third of instances. In this respect, however, there was no age difference.

The over-all picture that emerges from these observations is very different from the conflict situation that is usually conjured up in this respect. Let me emphasize again that I do not wish to deny that such situations do occur: of that there can be no doubt. Nor are we in a position to make normative statements regarding the frequency of any type of encounter, though it is worth noting that the extensive home observations by White and Watts (1973) suggest a view of mother–child interaction closer to ours than, for example, to Hoffman's. I do wish to suggest, however, that when parents set out to change their children's behaviour a clash of wills need not always and necessarily be involved. Parents have at their disposal a wide variety of techniques whereby they can convey a purpose to the child with which they want him to comply. Subtle and indirect means as well as more forceful methods are included in this range and need to be considered in any full descriptive account of parental controls. I thus agree with Stayton et al. (1971) that to regard the socialization process in terms of the basic opposition of parent and child is

Table 3. *Mean numbers of nonverbal controls according*
to control category and age of child

Category	15 months	24 months
1. Attention to speaker	0.3	0.0
2. Attention to surroundings	8.5	8.4
3. Manipulating accessibility	7.4	3.1
4. Eliciting/prohibiting action	5.7	2.5
5. Modelling action	3.6	2.6
6. Guiding action	1.2	1.2

misleading, though unlike these authors I would put the onus for the prevailing harmony primarily on the mother's action rather than postulate such a vague and unidentifiable concept as a disposition in the infant towards obedience. It is the sensitivity of parents with regard to both the nature and the timing of their control techniques that should be seen as the principal basis on which socialization takes place.

3. A developmental framework

It is frequently asserted (e.g. by Hoffman, 1977) that the issue of control arises only when the child becomes mobile and increasingly active, usually in the course of the second year, and that during the first year he receives nothing but nurturance and indulgence. This seems to me much too sharp a dichotomy: socialization pressures are imposed on the child from the moment he is born, and though the motoric competence of the toddler does seem to elicit rather more assertive behaviour on the part of his parents the infant is by no means immune from direction, regulation and restriction. Whether there is a quantitative difference I am in no position to say; it seems likely, however, that there are qualitative differences when compared with controls observed later on. This is suggested by some preliminary observations of mothers whom we videotaped at home in feeding, bathing, dressing and play sessions with their young infants. Examining the transcripts of the mothers' speech, for instance, makes it very apparent that many of their utterances do have a control function: they request particular actions ('lift your legs'), provide instructions on just how he should behave ('now let's have a really loud burp'), and prohibit certain kinds of action ('don't put that in your mouth'). However, when one then proceeds to examine the videotape the difference becomes clear: as the mother is saying it she herself is carrying out the instruction on behalf of the child. After all, she knows perfectly well that the four-month-old infant is quite incapable as yet of lifting his legs to enable the mother to put on his nappy, yet a great many of her activities are accompanied by verbalizations as though the child were already an independent actor.

This brings us to the sort of developmental framework within which we can place the use of controls. Vygotsky (1962) regarded the emergence of self-regulative capacities during the early years as one of the central aspects of childhood. Let us make the assumption that the function of parental control is not so much that the *parent* can regulate the child's behaviour but rather that the *child* should do so – eventually. In interactive development generally there is an enormous amount of redundancy: consider all the speech addressed to the child from birth on, even though he may not become capable of comprehending or using speech himself for another year or so. Similarly with controls: parents verbalize them in the full knowledge that the infant cannot possibly comply with them as yet, having neither the ability to comprehend the parent's demands nor the motor or cognitive skills to carry them out. In due course he does develop these abilities, and then (thanks to the parent's frequently repeated demonstrations in the past as to which actions are to follow particular controls) he quickly becomes capable of appropriate compliance. Finally, of course, external controls will no longer be required, the child having become capable of regulating his own behaviour.

A three-stage developmental sequence can thus serve for summary purposes:

(1) Controls are provided by the adult, but with no expectation of the infant complying. Instead, the parent carries out the required action on the infant's behalf.

(2) In due course the child does become able to carry out the activities demanded by the parent, and true compliance can now be observed.

(3) Eventually, controls are internalized and the child is no longer dependent on constant parental regulation of his behaviour. He has progressed (to use Vygotsky's terminology) from other-direction to self-direction.

This sequence may be a considerable over-simplification – if for no other reason than none of us totally leaves behind even the earliest stage. It may nevertheless serve to give an overview of the operation of some aspects of the socialization process during a child's early years.

Parental control techniques　77

References

Austin, J. L. 1962. How to do things with words. London: Oxford University Press.
Bell, R. Q. and Harper, L. V. 1977. Child effects on adults. Hillsdale, NJ: Lawrence Erlbaum.
Ervin-Tripp, S. 1976. Is Sybil there? The structure of some American English directives. Language and Society, 5, 25–66.
Flavell, J. H. 1977. Cognitive development. Englewood Cliffs, NJ: Prentice-Hall.
Freud, S. 1963. Civilisation and its Discontents. London: Hogarth Press.
Hoffman, M. L. 1977. Moral internalisation: Current theory and research. In L. Berkowitz (ed.): Advances in experimental social psychology, vol. 10, New York: Academic Press.
LeVine, R. 1969. Culture, personality and socialization: An evolutionary view. In D. A. Goslin (ed.): Handbook of socialization theory and research. Chicago: Rand-McNally.
Schaffer, H. R. 1977a. Mothering. London: Open Books/Fontana. Cambridge, Mass.: Harvard University Press.
Schaffer, H. R. (ed.) 1977b. Studies in mother–infant interaction. London: Academic Press.
Schaffer, H. R. and Crook, C. K. 1978. The role of the mother in early social development. In H. McGurk (ed.): Issues in childhood social development. London: Methuen.
Schaffer, H. R. and Crook, C. K. 1979. Maternal control techniques in a directed play situation. Child Development, 50, 989–98.
Schaffer, H. R. and Crook, C. K. 1980. Child compliance and maternal control techniques. Developmental Psychology, 16, 54–61.
Searle, J. R. 1969. Speech acts: An essay in the philosophy of language. Cambridge University Press.
Shatz, M. 1978. Children's comprehension of their mothers' question-directives. Journal of Child Language, 5, 39–46.
Shorter, E. 1976. The making of the modern family. Glasgow: Collins.
Stayton, D. J., Hogan, R. and Ainsworth, M. D. S. 1971. Infant obedience and maternal behavior: The origins of socialization reconsidered. Child Development, 42, 1057–69.
Vygotsky, L. S. 1962. Thought and language. Cambridge, Mass.: MIT Press.
Walters, G. C. and Grusec. J. E. 1977. Punishment. San Francisco: W. H. Freeman.
White, B. L. and Watts, J. C. 1973. Experience and environment: Major influences on the development of the young child, vol. 1. Englewood Cliffs, NJ: Prentice-Hall.
Zigler, E. F. and Child, I. L. (eds.) 1973. Socialization and personality development. Reading, Mass.: Addison-Wesley.

5. Behaviour and goals in adult–child interaction in the day nursery

FRANCESCA EMILIANI AND BRUNA ZANI

1. Introduction

Psychological theory has recently affirmed the tendency to conceive of and study individual human behaviour in terms of goal directed actions (Castelfranchi and Parisi, 1980; Von Cranach et al., 1980).

A perspective of this kind does not necessarily imply that goals are always consciously conceived: it can be noted how a great many of the routines of daily life, which themselves have specific goals, come to be carried out in an almost automatic way. If, however, people subsequently ask themselves about the meaning they attached to their actions and the goals they intended to pursue, they are usually capable of making this reconstruction. Therefore goals are an important part of behavioural analysis also because knowledge of them allows us to evaluate the adequacy of actions: the adequacy of any act is, in fact, always relative to a given goal and to the conditions in which it must be pursued (Harré and Secord, 1972; Castelfranchi and Parisi, 1980).

If immediate and concrete goals constitute the direct causes of actions, then they are often only a means for realizing a further and higher goal: that is, they come to be selected by the individual and ordered according to a hierarchy, the organizing principle of which is constituted by the individual's system of values. The study of social interaction, particularly that between adult and child, requires not only the detailed observation of manifest behaviour (as indeed characterizes the majority of studies on this theme) but also knowledge of the values and goals the individual intends to pursue.

Having assumed this approach as our basic framework, we conducted a preliminary research on the control techniques adopted by nursery educators in organizing children's play sessions, utilizing the same method elaborated by Schaffer and Crook (1978, 1979) for studying the control techniques used by mothers (Emiliani, Zani and Carugati, 1981).

From a first comparison of the results, the most striking difference that emerged was that which highlighted the more directive conduct displayed by the educators.

After subjecting the imperative controls directing action to an analysis which classified them according to goals, it emerged, however, that the majority of such controls were designed to teach the children the use of the play material in a correct manner.

In this case, therefore, it turned out that the use of direct instruction by the educators was adequate behaviour both in terms of the goal they intended to pursue and of the play situation in which they were pursuing it.

Convinced of the importance of analysing the goals and justifications in the study of adult–child interaction, we conducted a case study in two day nurseries both of which were characterized by their differences in educational orientation.

This difference in educational orientation had previously been verified by a questionnaire submitted in 11 of the 44 day nurseries in Bologna, for a total of 85 educators. It investigated the rules, the goal-values and the images that each member of staff had of their nursery.

We chose two nurseries that presented significantly opposed scores on the 'institution oriented' or 'child oriented' scale both in terms of rules and goal-values while, at the same time, *not* displaying any divergence regarding the image of what a day nursery should be, considered as it was, a psycho-pedagogic service for early infancy. It seemed to us interesting to choose two nurseries with these characteristics, as it would allow us to corroborate differences at the level of manifest behaviour and to reconstruct, through analysis of the goals and legitimations attributed by educators to their own behaviour, a differentiated and more precise articulation of this image.

Our predictions regarding the nursery which is more institution oriented were that one should find:

(a) a greater number of controls and interventions, in absolute terms, with the purpose of organizing the children's behaviour;

(b) teaching behaviour which is characterized by the issuing of commands containing instructions rather than by providing or asking for descriptions;

(c) a considerably smaller amount of empathetic behaviour on the verbal level and of physical contact and expressions of affection on the non-verbal level;

(d) less recourse to the use of conversation to establish and maintain interaction with the children.

Moreover, we hypothesized that when the educators were confronted with these exchanges with the children (on the video play-backs) they would claim that they wanted to achieve different goals – depending on which nursery they worked in – in such a way as to legitimate their behaviour.

2. Methodology

The two nurseries in which the research was conducted are situated in the same neighbourhood (not very far from each other) and therefore appeal to the same catchment area.

All the educators were involved in this research, 5 per nursery, all of whom were responsible for the children who, during the period in which these observations took place, were between two to three years of age. (The observations concern 9 educators out of 10 because of the prolonged absence due to illness of a member of staff in Nursery 2.)

Each adult was observed while interacting with the children during three time periods (moments) of the day at the nursery: the arrival of the children at the nursery (arrival time), time spent on personal hygiene (bathroom time) and play time.

Each observation, which was of 5 minutes' duration for every moment, was video-recorded for a total of 15 minutes for each adult.

The recordings were transcribed in full and a functional analysis was carried out on the adults' speech.

The language of the adults was subdivided into sentences, each of which was classified on the basis of the functional meaning that was being emitted in the conversation (keeping in mind both the transcripts and the video play-backs).

We identified four fundamental areas of adult verbal behaviour, each of which, in its turn, was divided into more detailed categories:

Area 1 – The *organization* of the children's behaviour

(1) Action controls (ACT) and
(2) Attention controls (ATT):

These are sentences whose potential function is to modify the children's behaviour (see Schaffer and Crook, 1979) in terms of both action and attention. As in statements of the type: 'Turn over the page,' or 'Look at the light!'

(3) Declarations of intention (INT):	The adult tells the children what she intends to do with them. For example: 'Now, I'll put your bib on you.'

Area 2 – Teaching

(4) Giving descriptions (GD):	Descriptions are provided of objects, people or events presented in context. For example: 'Look, the doggie is crying' (pointing to a picture of a dog in a book).
(5) Asking for descriptions (AD):	Descriptions are requested of objects, people or events presented in context. For example: 'What is the doggie doing?' (pointing to the picture of the dog in the book).

These two categories group together all those sentences expressed by the adults whose precise function is to teach something to the children, in the sense of increasing their knowledge (Wood, McMahon and Cranstoun, 1980).

Area 3 – Conversation

(6) Asking for information (AI):	Information of news is requested regarding objects, people, events *not* presented in context. For example: 'What did you do at your granny's yesterday?'
(7) Giving information (GI):	Information or news is provided regarding objects, people, events *not* presented in context. For example: 'We played football yesterday.'
(8) Commenting (COM):	The adult expresses judgements or observations on objects, facts or people. For example: 'What a lot of sand there is here!'

These three categories essentially fulfil the role of intitiating or maintaining interaction with the children rather than of controlling their knowledge; this is evidenced when the adult allows the children to speak without correcting them, in situations in which there is a conversational atmosphere of telling stories (Wood *et al.*, 1980).

Area 4 – Empathy
    (9) Empathetic repetition (REP):   The adult repeats what the child has said.

    (10) Confirmation (CONF):   The adult expresses support for what the child has said or done. For example: 'How clever, you've done it!'

We also carried out an analysis of non-verbal behaviour, strictly limiting our study to *physical contact*, which we considered an important indicator for defining the quality of the relationship between educator and child. To this end, we divided physical contact into two categories: *functional* and *affective*, attributing to the former a meaning limited to the simple performance of an activity (e.g. undressing or washing a child) and to the latter, instead, expressions of affection, protection and reassurance.

The codification was filled in by two independent judges and agreement greater than 78 per cent was reached for all categories.

In the second phase of the research, we conducted individual interviews with each adult in a situation of *self-confrontation*: that is, we let each educator re-examine the video recordings that related to her and asked her to comment on the images by answering the following questions: 'What goal had you set yourself here?' and 'Why did you act like this at this point?' (Von Cranach *et al.*, 1980).

3. Data analysis

3.1. Behaviour

The most significant data that emerged from our analysis was the confirmation of the difference in behaviour between the staffs of the two nurseries: in the nursery that was more institution oriented (Nursery 1) all the members of the staff prevalently adopted, in each moment of the daily routine taken into consideration, a pattern of behaviour whose aim was to *organize* the child's activities. However, in the nursery that was more child oriented (Nursery 2) a greater reliance was placed on *conversation* for establishing and maintaining interaction with the children.

In fact, we discover from the regression analysis (see Table 1) that the 'Nursery 2' variable has greater discriminative power in explaining the 'GI' variance: that is, the 'Giving Information' category turns out to be strongly associated with the 'Nursery 2' variable. A tendency of the same kind also discerned for the 'Comment' category.

Anova confirms these data, stating that the difference between the two nurseries for the two conversation categories is statistically significant: for the 'GI' category at arrival time ($F(1.8) = 5.23$, $p<0.6$) and play time ($F(1.8) = 12.42$, $p<0.01$) and for the 'COM' category at bathroom time ($F(1.8) = 7.23$, $p<0.03$).

Continuing with the regression analysis we find that the 'Nursery 1' variable turns out to be associated with the organization categories and in particular 'Action Controls' and 'Declarations of Intention'.

This means that the personnel of this day nursery control the actions of the children with greater frequency, using both direct commands and sentences which explicitly state what the educator intends to do: 'Come here, I'll change your clothes now.'

Anova confirms this result, granting a statistically significant value to the difference between the two nurseries at bathroom time for all three categories in the 'organization area' (area 1): ATT, $F(1.8) = 3.89$, $p<0.09$; ACT, $F(1.8) = 15.64$, $p<0.01$; INT, $F(1.8) = 6.25$, $p<0.04$.

As far as the 'teaching area' (area 2) is concerned, only the 'asking for a description' category turns out to be significant for Nursery 2. However we have found that if we submit all the action controls to an analysis that classifies them according to their function, then a distinctly higher percentage of instruction is given in Nursery 1. That is, the action controls have the precise function of teaching something to the children. This occurs above all at bathroom time and play time.

Looking at Table 2 one can see that instruction accounts for 41 per cent of all action controls in Nursery 1, while the figure for Nursery 2 is only 7 per cent. Moreover, this analysis shows that while action controls designed to promote interaction between the children or with the adults (e.g. 'Give the game to M.' or 'Let your friend see your drawing') are practically non-existent in Nursery 1 (1 per cent), they take up 13 per cent of all control activities in Nursery 2. On the other hand, while the category 'suggestion of an opportunity for action' (e.g. 'Let's do a nice drawing'), which is an indirect way of guiding the children's behaviour, displays a higher percentage of occurrence in Nursery 2, the category

Table 1. *Multiple regression analysis*

	Dependent variable	Significant independent variables		df	p	r Pearson	R^2
Conversation	Giving information	Nursery 2(n = 12)	11.04	1,25	0.01	0.55	31%
	Commenting	Nursery 2(n = 12)	3.82	1,25	0.10	0.36	14%
Empathy	Empathetic repetition	Arrival (n = 9)	3.87	1,25	0.10	-0.37	14%
Organization	Attention control	Arrival (n = 9)	7.13	1,25	0.01	-0.47	22%
	Action controls	Arrival (n = 9)	6.98	1,25	0.05	-0.47	31%
		Nursery 1(n = 15)	3.19	2,24	0.10	0.30	
	Declarations of intentions	Bath time (n = 9)	11.04	1,25	0.01	0.55	50%
		Nursery 1(n = 15)	9.15	2,24	0.01	0.44	
Teaching	Giving description	Play time (n = 9)	10.10	1,25	0.01	0.54	29%
	Asking for descriptions	Nursery 2(n = 12)	18.22	1,25	0.001	0.65	42%

Note: Categories 'Asking for information' and 'Confirmation' are not statistically significant.

Table 2. *Percentage of action controls according to their functions*

	Nursery 1	Nursery 2
Giving instructions	41	7
Promoting social interaction	1	13
Suggesting an opportunity of action	10	35
Limiting the activities of children	10	–
Simple controls	38	45
Total of action controls	100	100

'limiting the activities of the children' (e.g. 'Sit down') only appears in Nursery 1.

The 'simple controls' category, which includes direct commands (e.g. 'Come here,' 'Hold this,' 'Take that'), and to which it is not possible to attribute a function different from that inherent in the command itself, is consistently present in both nurseries.

When considering the area of 'empathy' (area 4), we find that there are no statistically significant differences at the level of verbal behaviour (see Table 1), even if both categories (confirmation and empathetic repetition) tend to occur with greater frequency in Nursery 2 at arrival time. The analysis of non-verbal behaviour however, demonstrates that there are consistent differences between the educators in the two nurseries, above all in the time devoted to affective physical contact (see Table 3).

This difference is particularly evident at arrival time and play time. This result is further confirmed by analysis of another indicator and that is, the average duration of individual physical contacts. In Nursery 2, not only did the educators devote more time overall to expressions of affection with the children but each individual contact was longer than that of Nursery 1. This happened, above all, at arrival time (in which each contact lasted 38 seconds on average in Nursery 2 versus 3 seconds in Nursery 1) and at play time (average duration 51 seconds in Nursery 2 versus 5 seconds in Nursery 1).

As far as functional physical contact is concerned we discovered instead that a homogeneity of behaviour exists between the staff of the two nurseries taking into account both overall duration and the duration of each single contact.

Table 3. *Average time in seconds dedicated by the educators to physical contact with the children*

	Functional physical contact		Affective physical contact	
	Nursery 1	Nursery 2	Nursery 1	Nursery 2
Arrival time	24	18	9	248
Bathroom time	225	238	7	21
Play time	50	57	3	128

3.2. Goals and legitimations

We asked each educator individually, in a situation of self-confrontation, to express the goal that she intended to pursue and the legitimations she ascribed to her behaviour. We conducted a content analysis of these interviews with the aim of identifying *immediate and concrete goals*, relative, that is, to the execution of each concrete action. We proceeded to classify these goals into categories and it was possible to do so using the four areas previously utilized for the analysis of behaviour, that is (a) organization, (b) teaching, (c) conversation and (d) empathy (see Table 4).

For each category, we have indicated whether it was mentioned or not in the educator's report, if it was explicitly emphasized or denied and if an explanation was provided.

One clearly notes an almost symmetrical distribution of goals: the staff of Nursery 1 affirm that they desire to pursue above all those goals which have been classified in the categories of types (a) and (b), while the goals mentioned by the staff of Nursery 2 belong essentially to the categories of types (c) and (d). Within this configuration we again find that some goals clearly delineate the two nurseries. There are some goals which are explicitly mentioned only by the educators of one of the nurseries while no reference is made to them in the other: for example, 'to enforce the rules and the timetable' and 'to teach specific notions' appear only in Nursery 1; 'to promote dialogue between the children' and 'to stimulate the children to freely express themselves' characterize Nursery 2 alone.

However, there are other concrete goals which are mentioned by the staff of both nurseries, even if they are not equally present at the same moments of the day: two examples in this vein are 'to carry out the activities in an orderly fashion' and 'to interpret the wishes of the children'.

We then submitted to analysis the legitimations provided by the educators for their explicitly mentioned (++) or denied (−−) goals. It

Table 4. *Concrete goals of the behaviour*

	Nursery 1			Nursery 2		
Concrete goals	Arri-val	Bath	Play	Arri-val	Bath	Play
(a) Organization						
– to enforce the rules and the timetable	++	++	–	– –	–	–
– to keep the children in order	–	+	+	–	–	–
– to respect the routines of daily life	+	+	+	–	–	–
– to perform the activities in an orderly way	–	++	++	–	–	+
– to organize the space as well as the activities within the nursery	–	+	+	–	–	+
(b) Teaching						
– to teach specific notions	–	–	++	–	–	– –
– to teach appropriate behaviour	+	+	+	–	–	–
– to teach new words	–	–	++	–	–	+
(c) Conversation						
– to converse with the children in order to maintain interaction	+	–	+	+	+	++
– to encourage the children to freely express themselves	–	–	–	–	–	++
– to promote dialogue between the children	–	–	–	+	–	++
(d) Empathy						
– to give security to the children	+	–	–	++	+	+
– to protect the smaller ones	–	–	–	+	–	+
– to interpret the wishes of the children	–	+	+	+	+	+
– to maintain closeness with physical contact	+	–	–	++	++	++

Note: Legend: + goal mentioned
  ++ goal mentioned and justified
  – goal not mentioned
  – – goal clearly denied

emerged from their accounts that concrete goals, in their turn, are considered as means for realizing higher goals or *over-goals*. In Nursery 1 the educators single out two over-goals, the first of which is expressed in terms of 'to organize and regulate the daily life of the institution' and the second is 'to increase the corpus of notions possessed by the child'. In Nursery 2 all the concrete goals, even those classified in the areas of teaching or organization, are submitted to two overriding goals indicated in 'to maintain a warm and reassuring relationship with the child' and in 'to respond to the needs of the child'.

If we consider, for example, the concrete goal of 'to have the rules and timetable respected' we find that in Nursery 1 it is always posed in relation to 'ensuring the efficient performance of the activities during the day' and is justified for arrival time with the following affirmation: 'We have put those rules which must be respected on to signs in the hallway.

We don't want the children to bring toys or sweets into the nursery, otherwise they start to argue.' The same goal for bathroom time is justified in the following way: 'We go into the bathroom to change the children only in the last quarter of an hour [before lunch], otherwise the children start to get tired and make noise . . . we change them using a pre-programmed system which enables us to do it quickly.'

This very same goal is explicitly denied by the staff of Nursery 2 who affirm that 'We have no precise rules nor strict timetables and the parents can even enter the nursery after the scheduled time because such restrictions seem unfair to us given that the morning separation is such a delicate moment and that the most important thing for us is the peace of mind of the child and responding to its needs.' And also: 'If a child brings a toy or indeed any object to the nursery, I try to find out how intensely the child is attached to the object and if it is a lasting attachment or not: to see if by presenting the novelty of a new toy whether the need to always have the object present becomes of secondary importance.'

From this complex of legitimations it emerges that the crucial factor which determines differences in educational orientation lies in the image that the members of staff have of the child who attends a nursery.

In Nursery 1 explicit references to the needs of two to three year old children are very rare and anyway they are almost always viewed in relation to the problems of the workings of the institution. Frequent references are made to the competence that the child must have and the notions he must be taught so that he can fit into the institution without problems: the child is talked about in terms of the things that he must learn (parts of the body, colours) and of the behaviour that he must adopt to win greater independence and personal autonomy. There is portrayed the image of the child who is 'being prepared for further schooling', borrowed as it is from other scholastic experiences (nursery or elementary school) which, in the absence of more specific knowledge on the subject, come to be assumed, by way of analogy, as basic reference points.

In Nursery 2 the staff focus attention on the specific needs of the little child in order to justify their behaviour, and in particular the needs of attachment, protection and affective security. Specific requests are not made to the children in terms of learning or adaptation to the institution but rather the first priority is reserved to the image of the child that requires warm and involving relationships.

4. Conclusions

This research demonstrates that the understanding of the staff interactive behaviour derives not only from the information obtained by direct observation but also from the interpretation of the goals and legitimations provided by the individuals themselves. The identification of concrete goals, their articulation into over-goals and the analysis of the legitimations adopted by the adults in the nursery have, in fact, provided the basic framework in which to insert the results obtained from the observations of their behaviour.

In Nursery 1, where the educators mainly resorted to behaviour designed to control the children's activities and containing less expression of empathy at the level of physical contact, there emerged the over-goals which related to the good working of the institution and a system of legitimations that took into scarce consideration the specific and developing needs of children of two to three years of age.

In Nursery 2, the staff behaviour mainly revolved around initiating and maintaining direct interaction with the children by means of conversational exchange rich in affective expressions. The staff aimed for over-goals which emphasize the importance of such exchanges, focusing on the image of a child who has a great need for attention and protection.

References

Castelfranchi, C. and Parisi, D. 1980. *Linguaggio, conoscenza e scopi*. Bologna: Il Mulino.
Emiliani, F., Zani, B. and Carugati, F. 1981. From interaction strategies to social representations of adults in a day-nursery. In W. P. Robinson (ed.): *Communication in development*. London: Academic Press.
Harré, R. and Secord, P. F. 1972. *The explanation of social behaviour*. Oxford: Blackwell.
Schaffer, H. R. and Crook, C. K. 1978. The role of the mother in early social development. In H. McGurk (ed.): *Issues in childhood social development*. London: Methuen.
Schaffer, H. R. and Crook, C. K. 1979. Maternal control techniques in a directed play situation. *Child Development*, **50**, 989–98.
Von Cranach, M., Kalbermatten, U., Indermuehle, K. and Gugler, B. 1980. *Zielgerichtetes Handeln*. Berne: Hans Huber.
Wood, D., McMahon, L. and Cranstoun, Y. 1980. *Working with under fives*. London: Grant McIntyre.

Part III
Language development

Within the Piagetian tradition, language development has for a long time been considered simply as an aspect of cognitive development in general. The acquisition of language capacities has been treated as a particular manifestation of the development of the symbolic function while the communicative aspects of language have hardly been studied. We are now witnessing a reversal in these perspectives; the development of cognitive capacities, as well as those that are more specifically language-related, are being studied as the outcomes of pre-linguistic interaction and communication patterns.

Though employing highly divergent methods of investigation, the two contributions in this Part are located within this new perspective. Camaioni and her co-authors use an observational approach to situate the first language expressions in their interactional context; Robinson and Robinson construct experimental situations to study referential communication at a later age. But it is in the dynamics of social interaction that the authors of these two contributions look for the origins of the development of linguistic capacities. If the same general thesis is thus illustrated by very different methodological approaches it is because the study of more specific processes does necessitate recourse to investigation procedures that are both appropriate and consistent with the age of the children studied. Thus it is evident that the Robinsons would not have been able to obtain their extremely rich results if they had been confined to the single alternative of systematic observation, while Camaioni and her colleagues would have had difficulty obtaining their illuminating data via the medium of systematic experimentation.

6. On the failure of the interactionist paradigm in language acquisition: a re-evaluation

LUIGIA CAMAIONI, MARIA F. P. DE CASTRO CAMPOS
and CLAUDIA DE LEMOS

This work has been carried out partially with the aid of grant 76/1384 from the Fundacao de Amparo à Pesguisa do Estado de Sao Paolo (FAPESP) to the Research Project on Child Language Acquisition of the Department of Linguistics, IEL, State University of Campinas, where both Claudia de Lemos and Maria Fausta de Castro Campos have been developing their research. Luigia Camaioni was also supported by FAPESP grant 79/1858 which allowed her to participate in the activities of the Project as a Visiting Professor.

1. Introduction

During the past decade there has been a great flowering of research dedicated to analyzing adult–infant social interaction; in particular, there has been an attempt to show evidence for a *significant* relationship between initial mastery of the rules governing social interaction and the subsequent emergence of language. The assumption of a *structural* continuity between an infant's prelinguistic and linguistic development led researchers to postulate an interpretative paradigm that quickly proved itself as unproductive as it was captivating. In fact, in recent years we find explicit statements in the literature about the *failure* of the research inspired by this paradigm. For example Kaye, synthesizing the results of a five-year-long research project, states: 'We certainly cannot say that our contingent and interactive measures added anything to our ability to predict outcomes in the children's cognitive language or social development at age 2½, beyond what we could predict from socioeconomic status and an observation of the mother's behavior alone' (1979, p. 2).

Analogously Richards, subsequent to a thorough analysis of the results of a longitudinal study conducted at Cambridge on a sample of 77 mothers and their children during the first five years of life (Dunn and Richards, 1977; Dunn, 1977), concluded:

From results such as I have described it is tempting to conclude, contrary to some other claims (e.g. Ainsworth, Bell and Stayton, 1974), that the kinds of measures that are usually examined within the attachment rubric in the first year have little to do with subsequent cognitive and linguistic development. *That, of course, would not rule out an integral relation but would suggest that it does not exist along this particular dimension.* (Richards, 1977, p. 203)

We have underlined this last phrase as signalling the awareness – present in Richards but not in Kaye – that the failure of the research in question does not necessarily imply the failure of the theoretical paradigm which they say inspired it. Actually, our position is even more radical; we hold that in *no case* could this type of research have provided a verification of a postulate of continuity between the child's prelinguistic and linguistic development. We will now attempt to explain why this is so.

In the first place, these studies try to correlate individual differences observed in the interaction between mother and prelinguistic child with those possibly present in several linguistic measures relative to the same children in a subsequent phase of development. It is rather easy to see that such an approach can at most identify the factors – or some of the factors – responsible for the differences in the rhythm of language acquisition and explain, in this way, how individual variation emerges. However, nothing insures that the factors associated with individual variability in the rhythm of acquisition are the same, or at least associated with, those implied in the *process* of language acquisition. Thus, the latter remains practically unexplored in these studies.

Secondly, the methodological choice reflected in both the interactional and linguistic measures used in the correlational analysis shows a certain weakness. We find in fact that those studies are attempts to correlate measures relative to the face-to-face communication between mother and infant at six months of age, such as: 'Attention to mother's face', 'Mother's greeting when baby attends', 'Mother's response to baby's greeting', 'Baby's facial activity' (from Kaye and Fogel, 1980) with measures relative to mother–child conversation in the same pairs at $2\frac{1}{2}$ years of age, such as: 'Mother's words per turn', 'Mother's mands' 'Child's turns linked to mother's' (from Kaye and Charney, 1981). Just on a common sense level one would ask oneself why such disparate types of behavior exhibited by mothers and children in chronologically distant moments, should be linked together or should exhibit predictive value (the first with respect to the second).

In the absence of any theoretical justification in the choice of behavior categories used to demonstrate the continuity between prelinguistic and linguistic development, it is not surprising to discover that rarely do such categories show any correlation and, in the few cases where this occurs, the correlational pattern appears confused and difficult to interpret. At both the theoretical and methodological levels, the critical points which we have underlined thus far in the studies in question make practically inevitable the conclusion that: 'The interactionist approach has been singularly unsuccessful in producing any theoretical advance' (Richards, 1977, p. 188). In particular (as we have noted previously) these studies show the impossibility of deriving any hypothesis about the processes responsible for the transition from prelinguistic to linguistic communication, restricted as they are to searching for the origin of individual differences which may emerge in the course of these processes. In our view this is due to the fact that social interaction and language – the two terms between which a structural continuity should be shown as well as at least a partial derivation of the second from the first – are seen as already given entities and not as the result of formation processes. In other words, we are facing a sort of 'reification' of the social and the linguistic seen in categorial rather than in process terms. Furthermore, the cognitive domain and, more precisely, the cognitive function of language, i.e. its ability to construct reality as an object of knowledge, are placed completely between parentheses.

A more promising attempt to analyze the transition between pre-language and language can be found in Bruner (1975), who individuates the origin of the attention/action structures present in language in routines of joint attention and joint activity, which are characteristic of mother–child interaction in the second half of the first year of life. The critical point in this approach (probably responsible for its non-pursuance) is that, whereas 'interactional formats' represent adequate interactional categories, the same cannot be said of the linguistic categories (agent-action, action-object, possession, etc.) derived by Bruner from Case Grammar. It is in fact rather difficult to find in the nature of these linguistic categories the *mutuality* of action and attention used to define the interactional formats. Consequently in more recent works (cf. Ninio and Bruner, 1978) Bruner practically abandons the aim of showing a structural continuity in the transition from prelinguistic to linguistic communication and adopts a 'weak' version of the interactionist approach, limiting himself to showing that certain contexts of mother–child interaction (for example, looking at a picture book together) function as special *loci* for the learning of certain linguistic forms on the part of the child (for example, labelling).

2. Towards a new paradigm

The above considerations can be seen as introductory to our view on how an interactionist paradigm on language acquisition and development should be built up so that it would not lead to necessarily negative or irrelevant results. Initially, the conditions could be specified as follows:

(1) The paradigm should look at social interaction and language as constitutive processes and not as rules operating on already given categories, since only in this way can a hypothesis on their continuity and on their being derived from one another be verified or falsified.

(2) It should look at language as a particular modality for structuring reality (interrelated with other modalities such as action, perception, etc.). The peculiarity of the linguistic modality is based on its cognitive or constitutive function being determined by a social or communicative function. In other words, language must be seen as operating on reality to constitute it, its structuring role being dependent on the fact that linguistic activities are, right from the start, intersubjective processes.

(3) It should adopt linguistic models whose basic unit of analysis is not the single utterance but the *dialogue*, i.e. a structure of at least two utterances. In this direction it is worthwhile to point out proposals such as that by Ochs *et al.* (1979) and by de Lemos (1981) which take the child's ability in providing complementary turns in dialogues as early and basic steps in utterance-construction. Both of those proposals and Scollon's view (1979) on 'horizontal constructions' being derived from 'vertical constructions' seem to allow for the conclusion that intersubjective processes involved in dialogue construction play a definite role in the intrasubjective process of building up utterances.

A rather brief look at developmental phenomena related to naming and to the construction of causal expressions will provide us with some empirical basis upon which we can argue for such a socio-interactionist position.

With respect to early naming behavior, it is important to start by emphasizing that the controversial nature of the relationships between object reference and naming, which is traditional within the philosophical literature, has been hardly dealt with in developmental psycholinguistics. In fact, different approaches to the early use of nouns in the presence of their possible referents usually neglect reference as a communicative problem and concentrate on issues concerning the relationships between the so called semantic content of nouns in adult language and the perceptual and/or functional aspects of the objects 'named'. However, neglecting the problem of how reference can be established and shared or, from a developmental point of view, of how the child becomes able to take the perspective imposed on the world by the adult's use of a word in a particular situation, has strong theoretical implications. Indeed, it would imply either that naming is a labelling activity on objects already given or previously constituted or that, right from the start, adult and child share an internal language or a formal set of conditions for mapping linguistic entities into the world. (This is, by the way, Fodor's (1975) proposal. For an enlightened discussion of it, see De Gelder (1981).)

Such implications seem to hold also for cognitivist approaches which put the weight of the explanation of concept–formation seen as a private relation between the child and the natural world via action and/or perception and consequently, as parallel to language. Indeed, the mapping processes which have been suggested as a sort of one-way bridge from private meaning to linguistic or public meaning stem out of the need for breaking this parallelism (cf. Brown, 1973, and Slobin, 1973, among others). It is also worth pointing out that even psycholinguistic accounts of early naming behavior which assign to language a cognitive function, or in other words, which recognize it as a form of categorizing reality, leave out of consideration the basic communicative nature of reference.

That such an attitude seems to underlie methodological decisions concerning data selection and interpretation in those studies, is clear both in Nelson (1978) and Bates *et al.* (In press). From data on the use of nouns in non-communicative contexts, Nelson concludes that naming, as well as most of the child's early language, can be said to have 'a private cognitive rather than a public communicative function' (p. 14). (Non-communicative contexts are generally defined either by the absence of an empirical interlocutor or by the absence of a child's behavior which can be taken as indicative of his having the interlocutor's response as a communicative goal). Bates *et al.*, whose aim is 'to defend a definition of naming *as a process which occurs outside of communication*' (p. 4, our italics) give explicit recognition of their methodological decision by commenting on the fact that 'once the child does begin to use names, *we immediately find them being used inside and outside of a communicative framework*' (p. 8, our italics).

However, such methodological choice does not avoid considering that the validity of interpreting the use of nouns in non-communicative contexts as private acts of cognition is dependent on explaining their use in communicative situations or, in De Gelder's terminology (1981), on explaining 'cognitive transactions'. Or, obversely, on how cognitive transactions are to be related with private acts of cognition. That is precisely what we will attempt to do in order to set up a preliminary basis for socio-interactionist proposals on language acquisition.

The interactional or dialogical structure of reference establishment seems to be already represented in the prelinguistic period by routines for assuring joint-attention. Indeed, Collis and Schaffer's data (1975) on the mother's tendency to follow the infant's line of regard and to comment upon what is thought to be isolated by the child's attention are to be related to Scaife and Bruner's findings (1975) on the child's ability around his fourth month of age to follow the mother's line of regard. As put forward by Bruner (1975) and by Camaioni (1977), these joint-attention procedures can be seen as precursors of naming behaviors: the fact that adults tend to interpret the child's behavior in both phases as a request for a name and that, later on, the child himself will produce his own act of 'naming' in similar interactional sequences, justifies it. Atkinson's paper on pre-requisites for reference (1979) also points towards the functional continuity of these types of behavior. According to him, since making a statement is a speech act which has as its pre-requisite establishing and securing the interlocutor's attention on the entity upon which something will be subsequently predicated, the manipulation of the addressee's attention is a basic step in the child's linguistic development, manifesting itself in early linguistic behavior such as the use of nouns in communicative contexts.

However, non-linguistic intersubjective processes of constituting 'shared objects', i.e. of framing or singling objects out of the flux of reality, differ from establishing perspectives on situations through the use of nouns in the sense that nouns can be said to have already meaning or to encapsulate shared perspectives on the world. Accordingly, the possibility of assigning to joint-attention procedures the 'status' of precursors of naming behaviors depends on demonstrating that inter-subjective processes determine the way children learn to objectify the world via the use of nouns.

Until now, few authors have paid due attention to the fact that among children's first words one finds segments of the adult discourse which are, both from a semantic and from a morphosyntactic point of view, unanalyzable wholes or, in Guillaume's words (1927), 'indifferentiated protoplasms'. Those segments, which have been described by Piaget (1945) as the first verbal schemes, are not used to refer to particular objects, but to the whole or to aspects of the interactional situations where the adult utterance, from which they have been extracted, was produced. R. Clark's study (1977) on imitation shows that even at later stages children incorporate longer segments of adult discourse which are semantically related, as a whole, with their interactional history.

If, on the one hand, these data point to the need for revising most interpretations of the early use of nouns as instantiations of object reference, on the other hand they allow us to look at interactional units as the *basic* frames the child operates with or as his first segmentation of the natural world by means of language. Consequently, the question of how the child goes from such a use of language to the discovery that particular words or segments can be related to particular objects or aspects of situations cannot be answered by attributing to the child a previous – perceptual or functional – knowledge of objects. One should, instead, look at the properties of interactional units or dialogues in an attempt to explain such a trajectory.

It is a constitutive property of dialogue that each contribution to it should have as its structuring basis the speaker's interpretation of his interlocutor's preceding utterance, such an interpretation being a projection on the entire discourse situation (including assumptions on the interlocutor's knowledge and beliefs) of the utterance's meaning potentials. (For a view on semantic competence as the competence for actualizing meaning potentials, see Rommetveit (1974) and Francesconi (1981). Cf. also a recent work by Vogt (1981), who states that the semantic value of a sentence is a set of instructions concerning the strategies to be used in order to decodify the utterance of such a sentence.) In this sense, one could say that every utterance contains and re-interprets the preceding one.

Accordingly, it could be hypothesized that the adult's responses to the child's behavior – either non-linguistic, as in joint-attention formats, or linguistic, as in early naming behaviors – making available to the child the effects of his own behavior on the discourse situation, allow the child to incorporate such effects into his behavioral structure. Although those dialogue processes, both on the part of the child and on the part of the adult, could be subsumed to Piaget's assimilation and accommodation processes, the view on the child's gradual mastery of using language to objectify reality we have put forward, should be related to Vygotsky's claim (1962) on intrapsychic functioning as derived from interpsychic functioning.

3. Empirical evidence

Within such a framework, solitary or non-communicative naming behaviors can be seen as transition phenomena, the intersubjective nature of them being represented in the fact that the perspectives imposed on the world by the child result from the processes hypothesized above. Empirical evidence favouring such an interpretation is found in data such as those presented by Camaioni (1977), which show dialogical structures or dialogue traces in children's 'egocentric' speech. An example of it is:

C. = *Questo? Cane*   (picking up different toy animals)
This? Dog.   C. = 1; 4.5

The development of causal expressions is another type of evidence for our proposal on the determinative role of dialogical activity in the child's mastering of linguistic processes. As shown in de Castro Campos (1981) and de Castro Campos and de Lemos (1979), data on the emergence and development of *porque*-utterances (correspondent to English *why*-questions and *because*-statements) in two Brazilian children (2;7 to 3;0 and 3;2 to 5;0) point towards the need for considering those utterances as intersubjective constructions. They seem, indeed, to result from the conjunction of two distinct speech acts; order, request, prohibition or refusal to comply with a request plus a justification of it. One of the basic properties of *porque*-interrogative utterances represented in the corpora analyzed is that they are means of requiring the interlocutor to provide a justification for his/her request, prohibition or refusal to comply with the child's request, in the same way as *porque*-assertions are used by the child as justification for his/her own requests, prohibitions or refusals to comply with his/her interlocutor's request. The reconstitution of such complementary activity would not only render explicit the intersubjective processes underlying the construction of these utterance-types, but would also unravel traces of previous and distinct stages of the relationship of the child to his basic interlocutor(s). These stages could be seen as comprising the sequence to be presented below.

A more primitive activity, whose structure is basically determined by the interlocutor's preceding utterance, characterizes the first phase. A large number of *porque*-interrogative utterances produced by the two children can be seen as linguistic behavior responsive to adult utterances. They are, in general, simple *Porque?* or result from the strategy of incorporating the interlocutor's previous turn.

These and other forms of *porque*-response appear either as topic-maintenance devices or in more clearly definable situations as requests for justifications of orders, requests, prohibitions and refusals which have been left unexplained or unjustified.

The main characteristic of the second phase lies in the child's explicitly assuming both the role of the one who asks for explanations and that of the one who is put into the position of giving them, being consequently capable of a partial role reversal, namely asking for justification of his/her own behavior. In any case what seems relevant in this phase is role-taking practice which can display a higher degree of complexity, as illustrated in (1):

(1) (Daniela pinches her sister)
  D: *Mae, por que que eu tô batendo nela? Porque ela ta mexendo.*
  (D: Mommy, why am I pinching her? Because she is messing about.)

(D.2; 7.20)

In the example above, the presence of the interlocutor may obscure a phenomenon which seems crucial for the construction of complex *porque*-utterances: the process of the solitary construction of both complementary roles in dialogue structure which becomes observable in overt soliloquy and symbolic play, as in (2):

(2) (D. in a pretend-dialogue with her doll)
  D: *Você sola pa i na casa do Maicelo?*
    Porque?
    Porque sim?
    Fala dileito.
  (D: Do you cry to go to Marcelo's house?
    Why?
    Just because?
    Say it right.)

(D. 2; 10.21)

What characterizes the third phase is the child's ability to build up utterances whose degree of structural complexity is basically determined by the assumption of the interlocutor's point of view or perspective. Although the interlocutor's role or perspective is not explicitly assumed in this phase as was the case for the second phase, it can be recovered through the presuppositions carried by those utterances.

From their analysis it is possible to isolate some of the elements which interact in such a process of representation of the interlocutor. Those elements could be considered as possible structuring principles in the production of complex *porque*-utterances.

Only two of those principles or perspectives will be mentioned here. The first is represented by the fact that a large number of justifications of requests, prohibitions and refusals are structured on the basis of a presupposed shared knowledge (social norms, physical laws, etc.), as illustrated by (3):

(3) V: *Da un beijo no meu oculu.*
    (V: Give a kiss to my glasses.)
    (Mother kisses Veronica's glasses.)
    V: *E porque ele vai dormi.*
    (V: It's because they're going to sleep.)

(V. 3; 4. 19)

The second structuring principle is a complex one, resulting from two perspectives or points of view interacting in utterance-construction. As one can see in (4), the negative clause represents the product of a pragmatic device operating on the immediately preceding situation (cf. Volterra and Antinucci, 1979, for a pragmatic view on negation and its development). It is also apparent that the justifying clause which follows *porque* in (4) is built up on a social norm which excludes mother's behavior.

(4) (Mother undoes a pile of small notebooks.)
    D: *Não, você não. Eu que dimanso porque eu sô fessola . . . só fessola que desmansa.*
    (D: No, not you. I do it because I'm the teacher . . . only teachers do this.)

(D. 3; 0.29)

On the other hand, if (4) presents a negative clause operating on an immediately preceding situation, (5) illustrates a still more complex activity.

(5) (Lunch-time)
    V: *Manhe, eu num vou tomá limonada não, porque eu bebi agora e ardeu agui.*

(V: Mommy, I am not going to drink the lemonade because I've
drunk it just now and it burnt here (pointing to her throat).)

(V. 4; 11.1)

The child seems to be constructing her explicative *porque*-utterances, at
this stage, not only on her mother's previous turn or preceding action,
but on an implicit or presupposed request. Notice that, as in (5), most of
the instances of this type of explicative utterance have as a first clause a
negative sentence by which the child states her refusal to comply with an
action her mother wants and expects her to do, such as drinking the
lemonade. Thus, the adult's discourse is still present in her explicative
sentences, but now as a presupposition.

4. Methodological choices

Finally, we would like to underline just how the type of theoretical
approach which we have sustained until now and which the preceding
analyses have evidenced as being productive, calls for the adoption of
precise *methodological choices*. The first methodological choice regards the
rigidly *longitudinal* character of data collection. Since the aim is not that of
gathering the most ample and detailed linguistic corpus but to trace the
development of prelinguistic interactional formats to the point where
they become linguistic exchanges, data collection should document
analytically a rather large age span, stretching from the halfway mark of
the first year of life until at least half, or better yet the end, of the second.
As shown here, the research conducted until now tends to be
concentrated on the analysis of prelinguistic communication until about
12–13 months-of-age, or else dedicates itself to the study of linguistic
development, beginning data collection at about 16–18 months-of-age. In
this way, what we can consider the crucial phase for verifying the
continuity between prelinguistic and linguistic development, i.e. the first
half of the second year of life, remains unexplored.

The second methodological choice regards the necessity of having
fine-grained analysis for episodes and for interaction contexts between the
child and the people who constitute his daily social environment,
analysis which is possible only through the use of audio-video-tapes
rather than simple audio-tape-recordings.

Further aspects to keep under control during data collection have to do
with the fact that the adult interlocutor is familiar or unfamiliar to the
child (for example, a parent versus the experimenter at the first

observation, when this is not preceded by a familiarization period with the child), and the fact that the observation takes place in the child's home, i.e. in an environment which is extremely familiar to him, or in a new and unfamiliar environment such as a play room in the laboratory. For example, two studies which analyze longitudinally a certain age span of the same child, can succeed in outlining a rather diversified picture of his socio-communicative-linguistic development according to whether the child is observed in interaction with the mother or with an experimenter. In this sense diary-type studies satisfy to a large extent the methodological choices outlined above, and, in fact, it is necessary to recognize that our knowledge of linguistic development has improved during the past few years, above all thanks to several longitudinal studies carried out by psycholinguist parents on their own children (cf. Clark, 1974; Halliday, 1975).

Starting off from these methodological choices we are carrying out a longitudinal study of three mother–child pairs, homogeneous as regards social class (middle-upper), mother's educational level (high school or college) and children's birth order (first-born only children). The pairs were followed longitudinally from the child's sixth to eighteenth month of life. Audio- and video-recordings were carried out every 20 days on the average during a free play situation in the family environment. The aim of the research was to investigate the development of mother–child social games and their relationship with the child's subsequent communicative and linguistic development.

In more detail, the research sets out to answer the following three questions:

(1) What is the development undergone during this age-range by mother–child games, especially in terms of transition from mainly non-conventional games to mainly conventional games?

(2) How is the child's participation in the game characterized and how does it change as a function of age and/or type of game?

(3) When the child begins to utter his first words, to what extent are they linked to games episodes and do they, wholly or partly, correspond to the linguistic expressions used by the mother to mark roles and/or actions characteristic of a given game?

Preliminary results (see Camaioni, 1982) afford an initial verification of the hypothesis that it is the *conventional* social game – which we define as an interaction episode characterized by a set of culturally defined and agreed-upon rules and by unique form-function relationships – and not social interaction *per se* (i.e. the mastery of its structural characteristics:

turn-taking, role differentiation, etc.), that can act as a suitable precursor for later linguistic development.

Obviously these studies do not represent the only possible direction to follow: but, in any case, we must be very cautious in applying methods of statistical analysis that imply the manipulation of individual differences before having carried out a sufficient quantity of descriptive and explanatory work on the *processes* of development with which we are concerned.

References

Ainsworth, M. D. S., Bell, S. M. and Stayton, D. J. 1974. Infant–mother attachment and social development. In M. P. M. Richards (ed.): *The integration of a child into a social world*. London: Cambridge University Press.

Atkinson, M. 1979. Prerequisites for reference. In E. Ochs and B. B. Schieffelin (eds.): *Developmental pragmatics*. New York: Academic Press.

Bates, E., Bretherton, L., Shore, C. and McNew, S. In press. Names, gestures and objects: The role of context in the emergence of symbols. In K. Nelson (ed.): *Children's language*, vol. 4.

Brown, R. 1973. *A first language: The early stages*. Cambridge, Mass.: Harvard University Press.

Bruner, J. S. 1975. The ontogenesis of speech acts. *Journal of Child Language*, **2**, 1–9.

Camaioni, L. 1977. How the child 'assumes' the world through language. *Italian Journal of Psychology*, **4**, 77–99.

Camaioni, L. 1982. From pre-verbal interaction schemata to language acquisition: Which continuity? Paper presented at the 10th World Congress of Sociology, Sociolinguistic Section, Mexico City, August.

Clark, R. 1974. Performing without competence. *Journal of Child Language*, **1**, 1–10.

Clark, R. 1977. What's the use of imitation? *Journal of Child Language*, **4**, 341–59.

Collis, G. M. and Schaffer, H. R. 1975. Synchronisation of visual attention in mother–infant pairs. *Journal of Child Psychology and Psychiatry*, **16**, 315–20.

de Castro Campos, M. F. P. 1981. On conditionals as dialogue constructs. Paper presented at the International Encounter in the Philosophy of Language, Campinas.

de Castro Campos, M. F. P. and de Lemos, C. T. G. 1979. Pragmatic routes and the development of causal expressions. Child Language Seminar, Netherlands Institute for Advanced Study in the Humanities and Social Sciences, Wassenaar.

De Gelder, B. 1981. Cognitive transactions and the form of beliefs. Paper presented at the CNRS Conference on Knowledge and Belief, Albi.

de Lemos, C. T. G. 1981. Interactional processes in the child's construction of language. In W. Deutsch (ed.): *The child's construction of language*. New York: Academic Press.

Dunn, J. F. 1977. Patterns of early interaction: Continuities and consequences. In H. R. Schaffer (ed.): *Studies in mother–infant interaction*. London: Academic Press.

Dunn, J. F. and Richards, M. P. M. 1977. Observations on the developing relationship between mother and baby in the neonatal period. In H. R. Schaffer (ed.): *Studies in mother–infant interaction*. London: Academic Press.

Fodor, J. A. 1975. *The language of thought*. New York: Thomas Y. Crowell.

Francesconi, C. 1981. The position of the adjective in the nominal phrase in Italian. Unpublished Ph.D thesis, University of Edinburgh.

Guillaume, P. 1927. Le début de la phrase dans le langage de l'enfant. *Journal de Psychologie*, **24**, 1–25.

Halliday, M. 1975. *Learning how to mean*. London: Edward Arnold.

Kaye, K. 1979. *The social context of infant development*. Final report to the Spencer Foundation, June–November.

Kaye, K. and Charney, R. 1981. Conversational asymmetry between mothers and children. *Journal of Child Language*, **8**, 35–49.

Kaye, K. and Fogel, A. 1980. The temporal structure of face-to-face communication between mothers and infants. *Developmental Psychology*, **16**, 454–64.

Nelson, K. 1978. The role of language in infant development. In M. Bornstein and W. Kessen (eds.): *Psychological development from infancy*. Hillsdale, NJ: Lawrence Earlbaum.

Ninio, A. and Bruner, J. S. 1978. The achievement and antecedents of labelling. *Journal of Child Language*, **5**, 1–15.

Ochs, E., Schieffelin, B. B. and Platt, M. L. 1979. Propositions across utterances and speakers. In E. Ochs and B. B. Schieffelin (eds.): *Developmental pragmatics*. New York: Academic Press.

Piaget, J. 1945. *La formation du symbole chez l'enfant*. Paris: Delachaux et Niestlé.

Richards, M. P. M. 1977. Interaction and the concept of development: The biological and the social revisited. In M. Lewis and L. A. Rosenblum (eds.): *Interaction, conversation and the development of language*. New York: J. Wiley, pp. 187–206.

Rommetveit, R. 1974. *On message structure: A framework for the study of language and communication*. New York: John Wiley.

Scaife, M. and Bruner, J. S. 1975. The capacity for joint visual attention in the infant. *Nature*. **253**, 5789, 265–6.

Scollon, R. 1979. A real early stage: An unzippered condensation of a dissertation on child language. In E. Ochs and B. B. Schieffelin (eds.): *Developmental pragmatics*. New York: Academic Press.

Slobin, D. J. 1973. Cognitive prerequisites for the development of grammar. In C. Ferguson and D. Slobin (eds.): *Studies of child language development*. New York: Holt, Rinehart and Winston.

Vogt, C. 1981. *Linguagem, pragmática e ideologia*. Sao Paulo: Hucitec.

Volterra, V. and Antinucci, F. 1979. Negation in child language: A pragmatic study. In E. Ochs and B. B. Schieffelin (eds.): *Developmental pragmatics*. New York: Academic Press.

Vygotsky, L. S. 1962. *Thought and language*. Cambridge, Mass.: MIT Press.

7. Coming to understand that referential communication can be ambiguous

ELIZABETH J. ROBINSON and W. PETER ROBINSON

1. Introduction

From birth the child is interacting with people as well as with the non social environment; child and others, particularly his caretakers, act upon and react to each other. This reciprocal exchange of information involves mutual learning as well as performance *per se*, in relation both to each other and to the immediate environment. Soft vocalization by baby and caretaker is included in mutual gaze contacts from the earliest days (Bullowa, 1979). Communicative motor activities appear to be added to direction of gaze as an indicator of interest; these activities then become differentiated (e.g. pointing separates from reaching) and potentially detachable from visual signalling. Vocalization by the participants exhibits contingently related properties including turn-taking, especially during mutual gaze, and appears also to serve as a complement to pointing and reaching in acts of reference. Eventually the soundings become detachable from these gestures. Carter (1978) offers a case study illustrating the linkages between gestures and sounds on the one hand and goals and schemes on the other.

It would appear to be the case that in the first instance the features added to the repertoire are involuntary accretions that are only subsequently subordinated to willed direction by the infant; the instrumental potential of these acts for regulating the behaviour and states of others and self being utilized by the infants only after they have observed the consequences of their enactment. Pointing may be singled out as clearly referential.

The earliest soundings associated with pointing may be composites which condense a whole demand into a single sounding. If Halliday (1975) is correct, these proto-verbalizations can already differentiate between the specific and the general (e.g. bø – 'Give me my bird'; nã –

'Give me that'). Such differentiation continues as the child begins to develop a mastery of the lexico-grammar of language. His powers of reference allow the possibility of achieving unique reference either via direct naming or via deixis plus gesture for immediately perceptible objects. The latter can only fail to identify an intended referent uniquely if the speaker's pointing is inaccurate or the listener fails to follow the direction of gaze and pointing of the speaker.

Direct naming can be ambiguous from the outset – 'Give me my bird' presumes the existence of only one toy fitting the label. Hence, while direct naming of referents enables speaker and listener to transcend the here and now, this increased power is achieved at the cost of greater likelihood of misunderstanding occurring. However, that it is the potential multiple reference of words which are not 'proper names' which can occasion misunderstanding is an idea of which the child can remain ignorant for a long time for a number of reasons.

One of these is that caretakers are likely to be proficient in compensating for ambiguity in the child's utterances. In so far as the caretakers make accurate or acceptable inferences on the basis of ambiguous speech by the child, they are shielding the child from the problem. In so far as any unaccepted inferences are followed only by actions that focus upon achieving an acceptable solution to the problem in hand (rather than the reasons for its occurrence), the child will also be insulated from learning about ambiguity of references. The empirical evidence we have (Robinson and Robinson, 1981) is consistent with both these propositions; registered misunderstandings appear to be rare, and maternal ways of handling them are for the most part geared to solving the immediate pragmatic problem.

However, our most frequently used technique has been to arrange for communication to fail because the message referred to more than one referent and to ask children a number of questions about these failures and the reasons for their occurrence. Having established a game in which speaker and listener encode and decode respectively and then show each other the card each has selected, we would arrange for communication failures to occur. The cards used only criterial attributes within the lexical-semantic competence of the children and were pre-tested to be complex enough in terms of differentiating attributes to lead to the child sending messages that referred to more than one card (ambiguous messages). The experimenter could send ambiguous messages deliberately. When failure occurred, as shown by the mismatch of the cards selected, the following interrogatory was used:

'Oh! We've got different cards. We went wrong that time. Whose fault was that – mine, yours? Why? Did I/you tell you/me enough to pick the right card?' (If the child answered 'No,' 'What should I/you have said?') 'Whose fault was it we went wrong? Why?'

It is common among 7- and 8-year-olds for them to say that the speaker had not said enough and to attribute the blame for the failure to the speaker (Robinson and Robinson, 1976a, 1976b). Such children can identify in which respects the message was ambiguous. They know that it is the message that has to be improved to avoid subsequent failures. The principle these children appear to be following and that their accounts render explicit will be referred to as the *Nurok* principle (message *N*eeds *U*nique *R*eference to be *OK*; otherwise it is inadequate).

In contrast, among 5-year-olds it is common for their judgements to state that the speaker had said enough and that it was the listener's fault things went wrong: the listener chose the wrong card. When asked about avoiding failure on subsequent trials they suggest that the listener should listen harder, try harder to think more; they make no comment about the message. These children appear to be guided by the *Fitok* principle (if message *FIT*s card it is *OK*; if it does not fit, it is inadequate). They appear to be following a rule that obliges them to judge a message inadequate only if it is positively inconsistent with the referent, but not if it is ambiguous and refers to the referent and one or more other cards. Hence, Fitok following children will blame the speaker when the message is 'A blue flower' and a red one is then displayed; they will not do so if the message is 'A flower', even if this fits all six members of the set (Robinson and Robinson, 1978). Age differences have been robust. If the children observe dolls sending messages, their evaluations are the same as when they participate. They do not change their judgements when given counter suggestions (Robinson and Robinson, 1978). Similar results are found with inkblots and representations of life-like communication failures (Robinson and Robinson, 1976a, 1977).

Is the Fitok principle mentioned indeed the best description of the behaviour of these younger children? Can their judgements be changed? What provokes them to change in everyday life? How are these changes to be interpreted?

2. What is said and what is meant?

It could be argued that the principle of 'If it fits, the message is OK' is an example of a lack of distinction between what is said and what is meant.

Do Fitok dominated children distinguish between what is said and what is intended? Do they realize that their message may not refer uniquely to the card they have in mind? If they do not, then it should be possible to expose this. Say, in the referential communication task, the child sends an ambiguous message, then as the experimenter reveals the mismatch, she could check what the child had said by commenting, 'Oh, we haven't got the same cards. "A man with a red flower". Is that what you said?' If that is what the child has said, he should agree. If she were to ask if the child had said, 'A man with a blue flower', he should deny it because it does not fit. If the experimenter were to pose 'A man with a big red flower' or 'A man with a flower' a Fitok-child should agree. Both the disambiguated and the further degraded message fit the card. By contrast, Nurok followers should reject any amendment of what they said. If the only difference between the two lies in the Fitok followers accepting altered but fitting messages, then differential forgetting cannot be what is important. What should a Fitok follower remember about a card he has chosen? He should remember that he uttered a message that was intended to refer to the card and if he is offered a variant that achieves this he should be contented. Olson and Hildyard (see Olson, 1981) have elsewhere distinguished between the sense of what is said and the verbatim (literal) forms used to realize the sense. They have argued that, *ceteris paribus*, adults are more normally disposed to code for sense rather than form. In many circumstances we do not ordinarily remember the lexico-grammatical details of utterances, but their semantic and/or pragmatic significance. Perhaps Fitok followers have not yet grasped the distinction between the semantics and pragmatics of messages, but for the present all we have to consider is that they do not see any dissociative possibilities between what is said and what is meant, where the latter conjunction compounds semantics and pragmatics.

Experiments were conducted independently in Canada and England to see which of the three varieties of reaction by the experimenter were accepted by children echoing what they had said. In England only 6 of 27 Nurok followers failed to distinguish between what was said and what was meant; whereas 11 out of 12 Fitok followers accepted regraded fitting messages as being what they had said. No Fitok or Nurok followers accepted non-fitting messages. All accepted what they had indeed said. For the Fitok following children not to 'remember' what they had just said seems to us to be a strong test of our hypothesis about their beliefs about message adequacy.

Coming to distinguish between what is said and what is meant is not the only necessary condition that has to be grasped for a Fitok follower to become a Nurok follower. Some, but not all Fitok following children, do not see the need to make exhaustive comparisons among the array when encoding or evaluating messages; as Whitehurst and Sonnenschein (1978) express the issue, younger children do not see that it is crucial to attend to differences. In our original studies we found that judgements of message adequacy were closely linked to the role blamed for communication failure (1976a, 1976b), but subsequently we discovered small numbers of children who judged messages to be inadequate and yet did not blame the speaker for the failure. Our suspicion was and is that children may come to appreciate that messages can be ambiguous before they associate this ambiguity with the speaker's power over its character, although we have not conducted a natural longitudinal study to check this. (If the change from being a Fitok follower to becoming a Nurok follower typically takes place over a matter of days or weeks rather than months, and simply testing children can cause them to think about the matter (see the training experiment below), then checking for understanding even on a weekly basis might be insufficient to examine this possibility.) We did however examine the hypothesis that understanding that causes can be distal as well as proximal is necessary to link the wrong choice of the listener, via the message, to the speaker's control over the formulation of the message. We were able to show that 45 per cent of a small sample of Fitok followers did not refer to distal causes whereas 100 per cent of Nurok followers did in accounting for unintended and unwanted outcomes in narrative stories (Robinson and Robinson, 1978). While who is blamed and why are both integral components of children's understanding about effectiveness of verbal referential communication, this facet can perhaps be analysed separately from their achievement of understanding that messages can be ambiguous.

3. Development from Fitok to Nurok

If Fitok followers do not appreciate that messages have to be unique in their reference can they be provided with opportunities to learn this principle? What kind of treatment will facilitate such learning? Two series of experiments point to the feasibility of such control. Whitehurst and Sonnenschein (1978) take the child's comparison activities as a point of departure. They showed that 5-year-olds would send relatively unambiguous messages when attributes on cards were salient and constant over trials, but that the messages became more inadequate when irrelevant attributes were introduced and when the critical variables were switched from trial-to-trial. Subsequent experiments (Whitehurst and Sonnenschein, 1978) compared the efficacy of different kinds of instructions to the children as to what they were to do. In the first experiment requests to tell about differences gave rise to better messages than requests to 'Tell me about . . . so that I will know . . .' However these latter instructions were abbreviated after the fifth of the 30 trials to 'Tell me about it,' and it appears from the account of the procedure that children did not observe whether or not their instructions could be followed successfully. Within any limitations that these procedures may have set, the difference treatment elicited less ambiguous utterances. Subsequent experiments showed that maximal performance was achieved when advice *to attend to differences* was integrated into the instructions for a communication task and the messages were followed by *feedback* about the nature of any ambiguity left unresolved. While Whitehurst and Sonnenschein (1978) did not establish the entering state of understanding of their 5-year-olds, we can be reasonably confident that most would have been Fitok followers. Whether they became Nurok followers or had simply learned to apply a 'Describe the difference' rule without understanding why it was efficacious to do so cannot be inferred from the performance measures made.

We (Robinson and Robinson, 1981) have published one small-scale learning study. Diagnosed Fitoks were exposed to one of three kinds of reaction while sending instructions about six items of clothing (2 values each of 3 attributes), which they were using to 'dress' a boy doll. Over 90 per cent of their messages were ambiguous. For one third of the Fitoks the experimenter guessed as best she could which garment the child's message was referring to. For a further third she asked, 'Which one?', and then guessed after the child had responded. For the final third she said, for example, 'Well, there are four like that. I don't know whether it's got long sleeves or short sleeves and I don't know whether it's got stripes or checks (squares).' In this third condition the nature of the listener's problem of choice is made explicit. A post-experience test using the 'whose fault' technique in the dressing of a girl doll was used to assess understanding. Performance on the training trials was classified as high or low in ambiguity on the basis of the number of garments any message referred to.

All 9 of the Fitoks exposed to the third treatment made low ambiguity scores: 2 of 11 in the guessing condition and 1 of the 8 in the 'Which one?' treatment made low ambiguity scores ($p < 0.002$). Were the treatments associated with changes in understanding? Seven of the 9 children exposed to the explicit treatment had ceased to be Fitok followers; 2 of the 9 and 3 of 6 in the other two conditions had changed (3 children in these groups failed to provide judgements). While the superiority of the explicit treatment is statistically significant (p = 0.03), it may also be noted that 5 of the 15 other children made progress in understanding, suggesting that these experiences too may have provided weaker opportunities to learn. Certainly there was no indication that any deep-rooted general cognitive egocentrism was preventing development of the relevant understanding.

The role of explicit statements of non-understanding by others in the everyday lives of children has also been examined by Robinson and Robinson (1981). Wells (1981) had collected periodic samples of speech in the homes of young children from the time they were 1 year 9 months old until they were 5 years and 3 months old. These data yielded over 4 hours of possible conversation per child. We were able to test 36 of these children within one month of their 6th birthday to find out whether they were Fitoks or Nuroks. We were also able to examine the transcripts collected over the previous 4 years to search for, classify and count instances of interruptions in the flow of discourse occasioned by a breakdown of some kind. The most common occurrence was the utterance of 'Pardon?' or 'What?' Nine other tactics were identified, which likewise appeared to be immediately directed towards the solution of the pragmatic problem in hand. Only the eleventh category drew explicit attention to non-understanding (by the mother in all cases), e.g. 'What do you mean?'

None of the first ten categories either individually or in combination, discriminated between Fitok followers and Nurok followers. Explicit registration of non-understanding did. None of the 10 Fitoks had mothers who had employed such a tactic, 16 of the 26 Nuroks had such mothers ($\chi^2=9.35$, p. < 0.01). Ten Nuroks had achieved this status via means about which the data available were uninformative. Perhaps their mothers, fathers, siblings, peers or other persons had registered explicit non-understanding of these children's requests, instructions or statements at times other than those recorded. Perhaps the children had observed non-understanding occurring between other people and had reflected upon this, constructing appropriate explanations for that non-understanding. Perhaps they had constructed such explanations from their wondering about the conditions of successful communication. That this last is likely to be rare, but not impossible is suggested by two sets of studies.

4. Realizing that you do not understand

We have found that Fitok followers do attribute the success of uniquely referring messages to the quality of these messages before they judge that ambiguous messages can be responsible for communication failures (Robinson and Robinson, 1978). Karabenick and Miller (1977) found young children to be more accurate in judging 'good' questions as good than in judging 'bad' questions as bad. Asher (1976) found that appraisal of good messages was more accurate than appraisal of bad messages in a 'Password' game. It would only be a hypothetico-deductive mind that insisted that if a person can see that messages can be good, there must be a correlative appreciation that they can be bad; logical implication is not the same as psychological realization. Even if this were so, the possibility remains open that a Fitok follower might not be able to give a detailed account of the qualities of 'goodness'. Their understanding of such 'goodness' remains to be studied.

The reason that this appreciation is unlikely to be the immediate and direct point of departure for learning about the importance of uniqueness of reference is the hypothesized rarity of occasions upon which adults or other children comment upon the reasons for successful communication being a function of message quality. In approximately 175 hours of recordings in home and pre-school we heard only 5 instances of communication failure being registered by explicit statements of non-understanding, and no instances of success being discussed. Why should adults discuss and analyse such success? Only if they deliberately decided to inform a child about quality of message-sending and its consequences might they do so. Hence while analysis of successful messages could logically serve for learning, there is no evidence to suggest that this is in fact used by the vast majority of parents or teachers. Likewise there is no evidence that communication failures are commonly utilized for teaching about the importance of uniqueness of reference. However failures do occasionally evoke 'I don't know what you mean' and will occasionally result in clear discrepancies between what was wanted and what was received.

If communication failure is the more likely point of departure this implies that outcome may have a role to play as the event which can register the failure. As a listener to ambiguous messages the child may find himself unable to choose between two or more referents each of which fits the message and that may cause him to reflect upon the problem, but it is perhaps more likely that he chooses wrongly, as defined by the speaker, and that such wrong choices are subsequently thought about. He ought eventually to realize that 'listening harder' is not the solution. He might begin to reflect upon the quality of the message. As a speaker the child's own ambiguous messages may lead to incorrect outcomes or be challenged by statements of non-understanding, among other possibilities. Are different types of adult response differentially associated with the young child's realization that his message has not been understood?

We carried out an investigation to see how children did interpret the common adult ways of dealing with communication failure. If a child says, 'Have you seen my cardigan?' and the adult says, 'Which one?' does the child realize that the adult's reply has defined his request as ambiguous? To find out, we constructed six snatches of dialogue between imaginary children and their mothers. In each case, the imaginary child had lost an article of clothing (jumper, scarf, etc.) and asked his mother for help. Each imaginary child was represented by a cardboard cutout doll, and the lost object was represented by a picture which was attached in a 'thought bubble' near the doll's head as the dialogue was presented. Each of the dolls said, 'Mum, have you seen my jumper/hat/trousers, etc. please?' and each of the imagined mothers gave a different reply. One of the 'mothers' did know where the lost article of clothing was, another one said she did not know, and the others gave more or less explicit indicators of not understanding what was wanted. The least explicit was 'Which gloves?' and the most explicit was 'I don't know which cardigan you want. You've got two cardigans. You should tell me which one.' Following each snatch of dialogue we asked the child-subject whether the imaginary mother had understood just what was wanted, and whether the imaginary child had said enough about what she wanted.

We found that wrong guesses by the imagined mother were more likely than correct guesses to be judged by children as indicative of the mother not understanding the request. (We also found that our child-subjects (aged between 5 and 6½ years) found it easier to identify the mother's non-understanding if she made her problem explicit ('I don't know which cardigan you want . . .') rather than just asking for the missing information ('Which one?').)

This provides some weak evidence that the child at some stage may be following the rule 'Incorrect listener choice means listener did not understand.'

In a further investigation, we (Robinson and Robinson, 1977) used the 'whose fault?' technique to explore children's assessments of (1) 'unambiguous message – correct listener choice', (2) 'ambiguous message – incorrect listener choice', (3) 'ambiguous message – correct listener choice' and (4) 'unambiguous message – incorrect listener choice'. The interrogations were not sufficiently probing to allow firm conclusions as to the sequence of mastery of understanding the four varieties, but the sequence that would be easiest to defend would be: 1, 2, 3, 4.

What the child has to achieve are several linkages and then coordinate them: (i) listener wrong choice to listener non-understanding, (ii) listener non-understanding to ambiguous message, (iii) ambiguous message – speaker's inadequate formulation. While our experiments suggest that (iii) is the last link to be established, they have not teased out the relations between (i) and (ii). Neither do they indicate whether the child first links listener wrong choice to ambiguous messages, and then perceives the listener's non-understanding as the mediating factor, leading to a simultaneous differentiation of (i) and (ii).

If the Fitok's rule for message assessment is first juxtaposed with the two rules 'If the outcome is incorrect, the message is inadequate' and 'If the outcome is correct, the message is adequate,' these combinations will *not* provoke conflicts of judgement when inadequate messages lead to correct outcomes or incorrect outcomes follow adequate messages; the relation of implication is not the same as one of equivalence. They might come to be seen as equivalent and that could generate a potentially facilitatory conflict, but in reality both types of combination are likely to be very rare occurrences and, if they are, they would be unlikely to serve as a frequent route of development. We would expect it to be more common for children to wonder how messages could be inadequate, having been alerted to this possibility by 'incorrect outcomes'.

Clearly there are pieces missing from the dynamic jigsaw, but at least we can see possible routes of development and some of the principles and coordinations that the child needs to make if he is to become a Nurok follower. It is perhaps appropriate to mention yet one other dangling issue that may need to be incorporated into the final story. Flavell, Speer, Green and August (1981) required kindergarten and second-grade children to listen to and attempt to carry out instructions for making buildings and subsequently they were asked whether their building corresponded to the instructor's and whether they thought the instructions were good or bad. As a comment on the kindergarten children's replies to the second question, the authors state: 'The younger children do not realise the meaning, significance, and implications of the transitory feelings of puzzlement, uncertainty, etc. that they may experience during the building period.' Why should they connect these feelings either with their not understanding or with the inadequacy of the instructions? This would add further linkages and coordinations to be established for Fitok followers to become Nurok followers.

5. The current state of the problem

One reason why the research task may be doubly difficult in this particular field appears to be a matter of unfortunate but exciting coincidence. The child is not only mastering an important phase in the development of his understanding about the requirements of effective referential communication. He also appears to be developing concurrently an appreciation of the difference between understanding and non-understanding. Although the word 'understand' may have been in his productive and receptive vocabulary for some time and used appropriately as far as its universe of discourse is concerned, the child may not have grasped what its negative pole means – that is the meaning may be contrastive with cognate terms such as 'see', 'feel', 'mean', even 'know', but not with 'not understanding'. This may be only an artefact of the particular studies conducted. Those, like ourselves, who have been focussing upon 'understanding about' have all been working with 'messages' (or instructions) where unique reference is important (e.g. Markman, 1977; Flavell *et al.*, 1981; Patterson and Kister, 1981; Whitehurst and Sonnenschein, 1981). We need to know whether the difference between understanding and not understanding emerges earlier in respect of other metalinguistic propositions. If it has, then the research problems in this area are less messy than the opening sentences of this section suggest they may be.

6. Summary and discussion

At the risk of being charged with over-simplification and over-condensation, much of the thinking and evidence can be incorporated into a single table (see Table 1). This chart leaves many questions unanswered and locates many possibilities for investigation as yet unexploited. Since this is a discussion chapter it is perhaps appropriate to conclude with some of the smaller and more grandiose loose ends.

(1) Interpretations of the empirical studies reported have relied most commonly on the analyses of the propositional qualities of messages themselves and on children's commentaries about these qualities.

Table 1. *Awareness in relation to development of understanding that messages can be ambiguous*

Phase 1	Phase 2	Phase 3
Origins of performance 1. Observational learning, including imitation. 2. Associative learning (including operant conditioning). 3. Action schemes and rules constructed from 1 and 2.	1. Direct explanations for failure/success from others, to be integrated into own active analysis in response to failure as S or L, or perceived failures by others similarly analysed. 2. As yet unknown.	Practice with corrective feedback (self-monitored or from others) will lead to semi-automated behaviour in familiar situations.
Characteristics of performance Either fast, fluent and decisive or long latencies – ballistic. Errors not perceived. Weak generalization/transfer.	Slow, considered, tentative responses with monitoring continuous, easily overloaded by task difficulty or listener oddity. (Stronger as L than S?)	In familiar situations either fast, fluent and decisive; in unfamiliar considered but then not tentative. Errors corrected spontaneously. Monitoring intermittent. Ordering, etc. designed to meet L needs. Checks for L following.
Responses to trouble Complexity or subtlety: unable to diagnose isolated critical features.	Complexity or subtlety: may fail to cope, but will try to analyse problem.	Reflective analysis followed by successful adaptation or admission of incompetence and diagnosis of reasons.
Response to failure Switch to another rule or persist with maladaptive behaviour.	Will try to analyse problem.	Reflective analysis followed by success or admission of incompetence and diagnosis of reasons.
Analysis of communication problem As S, ignore off-focus features. Describe the reference 'fully', and as L, choose first referent seen that fits.		As S, scans total array before giving uniquely discriminating message and takes L into account. As L, scans total array before choosing. Questions multiple reference.
Quality of accounts As S for success: ? As S for failure: L not listening. Bad luck. As L for success: L chose correctly. As L for failure: L chose wrongly. No reference to message or understanding. Can't appreciate correct explanation. Unaware.	(L blamer – didn't tell properly – comes to coordinate message/failure link). Explains success before failure. Most difficulty with good message wrong choice. Can locate failure in message when task simple, but liable to overload. Can agree with correct explanation. Aware.	Explains success and failure in terms of message attributes. Finally includes S and L in total evaluation. No overloading problem. Can become aware.

Non-verbal components such as latency of responses have not been ignored entirely (see Patterson and Kister, 1981) but much more could be done. Latency in production and choice is but one variable. Paralinguistic components of messages are another. Facial expressions and hand and eye movements are also available for measurement. Accurate specification of what children actually look at could certainly serve to eliminate some hypotheses about comparison activity, for example.

(2) So far no one has provided pairs of children with sets of cards, a screen, a table and two chairs and then watched to find out what kinds of referential communication games they might construct, and how they would resolve disputes that might arise in such games. Patterson and her colleagues (see Patterson and Kister, 1981) devised conditions in which younger children became willing to ask some questions about ambiguous messages, but did not find such questioning in their standard situation; it is not yet clear why this was so. Similarly in our work it is not known to what extent Fitok followers would resist choosing cards in response to ambiguous messages if the game were not defined as it is. Would choices be deferred and questions asked in situations where Fitok following children had devised their own game? Would disputes arise that changed judgements and performance?

(3) While our own work has made one attempt to examine how development may occur in the natural course of events, the many laboratory studies are as yet not complemented by observations of the manner in which the relevant features of children's behaviour appear and are embedded in activities outside the laboratory. What does happen is as interesting as what can happen, and detailed observation of children in their everyday lives must be seen as a high priority in the near future.

(4) Perhaps the highest priority should be accorded to theory construction. Data are being accumulated. Limited hypotheses are being tested. We are beginning to express and systematize some of the principles which seem to be regulating the behaviour of children. However more general theory of learning and development is not prominent. Table 1 includes associative principles of learning as having potential relevance to some aspects of development. The chapter itself, as well as Table 1, refers to possible roles for observational learning. More generally implicit is a model of the child as an active creature trying to make sense of the way referential communication works – a neo-Piagetian child. Perhaps the most promising approach for specifying the details of development will come from the application of the approach

that has been unfortunately named 'artificial intelligence' (AI) (see Boden, 1977). At least two features of the approach are particularly attractive. One is the requirement that the rules or principles guiding behaviour be written with exactness and exhaustiveness. Logically (and computers are ruthlessly logical) it is necessarily true that both the messages and the reasoning associated with these messages of Fitok and Nurok followers can be expressed in terms of rules. Our problem is to invent rules that might be guiding the children's thinking. If we invent correctly then we should be able to generate both the important aspects of data already obtained and new predictions for investigation. Where programmes fail to generate the data we shall be obliged to examine the assumptions that we may have unwittingly incorporated and attributed wrongly to the child. While AI may not be able to expose which coordinations or principles we have taken for granted, it should at least help to locate points at which our presuppositions may have been wrong. An infallible machine does exert a discipline that our human minds can evade, and its rigour can only be helpful to us.

The second feature lies in the possibilities of devising programmes that are both self-organizing at given moments of time and self-developing through time. The AI approach enables programmes to generate new programmes in response to their own inadequacies, but this can only occur if the details of both the programmes and the data they are to process are specified in detail. Thereby, they afford the possibility of simulating (modelling) development changes with a precision that abstract concepts like 'equilibration' and 'cognitive conflict' lack. That they may also require that the Piagetian algebraic formulations of schemes and operational structures be superseded is a challenge to be faced rather than a fact to be regretted.

Meanwhile notions of cognitive conflict providing an impetus to intellectual development have been revitalized in their birthplace. As long ago as 1926, Piaget argued for the importance of quarrelling with peers as a stimulus for cognitive development. He argued then that parents were too proficient in guessing what children meant for them to encourage children to say explicitly just what it was they intended; that their reactions were likely to maintain their children's egocentrism. Peers would not. While we could endorse the general tenor of this suggestion, our evidence is that at least some parents do occasionally confront their children with the inadequacy of their verbal formulations.

The Genevan group (see Mugny, Giroud and Doise, 1978–9; Doise and Mugny, 1979; Perret-Clermont, 1980; Perret-Clermont and Schubauer-Leoni, 1981) has taken Piaget's suggestion as a point of departure for their work on conservation and seriation and has concentrated on confrontation with peers. This group has demonstrated the developmental efficacy of procedures that present the child with conflicts of rules for obtaining answers to cognitive problems. They insist on describing these as '*socio*-cognitive conflicts' to emphasize the social interactive nature of the contexts of dispute. We would not only endorse this emphasis, but would have to say that for the development of understanding about language, this socio-cognitive basis must be essential.

Where adaptive problems involve interaction with the physical material environment, such as object identity, seriation or conservations, the child has means of testing the validity of his schemas or principles. While the acts of conjecture necessary for solving such problems are or can be in a very important sense the child's own inventions, the 'verification' procedures to probe these can be operated on events and objects that are independent of other persons and their activities. The child's beliefs can be tested through his own interactions with that physical world. Cognitive development might be much slower if there were no contributions from other people, but in principle it is possible (see Peill, 1975).

With language this is not so. While this is an obvious general truth in that language is a cultural product with its conventional basis being culturally defined, it is perhaps less obviously true of communicative acts. It has been suggested that the child may have little need to develop communicative competence through language because his communicative system will at any one time be adequate to his needs and purposes. This is a very dangerous as well as a false generalization to make. We suspect that metacognitive analysis applied to language constitutes a very important developmental achievement and that this would not take place without the interventions of other people. How would the child ever come to learn the distinction between saying and meaning? How would he ever come to realize that what he meant was not necessarily what he said? The Fitok rules treat sense and reference as equivalent. We can see no reason why the child should ever come to consider the problem as existing if it were not for other people contesting his behaviour as either speaker or listener. He has no internal criterion against which he can check the effectiveness of his own utterances or wonder about the adequacy of those of other people. It is only through conflicts defined by other people that the child could become aware that there is a problem of distinguishing between sense and reference, between what is meant and what is said. Hence the need to emphasize the 'socio' in socio-cognitive conflict.

Acknowledgement

We are pleased to acknowledge the financial support of the Social Science Research Council of Great Britain.

References

Asher, S. R. 1976. Children's ability to appraise their own and another person's communication performance. *Developmental Psychology*, **12**, 24–32.

Boden, M. 1977. *Artificial intelligence and natural man*. Hassocks: Harvester Press.

Bullowa, M. 1979. Infants as conversational partners. In T. Myers (ed.): *The development of conversation and discourse*. Edinburgh University Press.

Carter, A. L. 1978. The development of systematic vocalisations prior to words: A case study. In N. Waterson and C. Snow (eds.): *The development of communication*. Chichester: Wiley.

Doise, W. and Mugny, G. 1979. Individual and collective conflicts of centration in cognitive development. *European Journal of Social Psychology*, **9**, 105–8.

Flavell, J. M., Speer, J. R., Green, F. L. and August, D. L. 1981. The development of comprehension monitoring and knowledge about communication. *Monographs of the Society for Research in Child Development*, **47**, 181.

Halliday, M. A. K. 1975. *Learning how to mean*. London: Edward Arnold.

Karabenick, J. D. and Miller, S. A. 1977. The effects of age, sex and listener feedback on grade school children's referential communication. *Child Development*, **48**, 478–83.

Markman, E. M. 1977. Realizing that you don't understand a preliminary investigation. *Child Development*, **48**, 986–92.

Mugny, G., Giroud, J.-C., and Doise, W. 1978–9. Conflit de centrations et progrès cognitif, II: Nouvelles illustrations expérimentales. *Bulletin de Psychologie*, **32**, 979–85.

Olson, D. R. 1981. Assent and compliance in children's language comprehension. In W. P. Dickson (ed.): *Children's oral communication skills*. New York: Academic Press.

Patterson, C. J. and Kister, M. C. 1981. The development of listener skills for referential communication. In W. P. Dickson (ed.): *Children's oral communication skills*. New York: Academic Press.

Peill, E. J. 1975. *The invention and discovery of reality*. Chichester: Wiley.

Perret-Clermont, A.-N. 1980. *Social interaction and cognitive development in children*. London: Academic Press.

Perret-Clermont, A.-N. and Schubauer-Leoni, M.-L. 1981. Conflict and cooperation as opportunities for learning. In W. P. Robinson (ed.): *Communication in development*. London: Academic Press.

Piaget, J. 1926. *Language and thought of the child*. London: Routledge and Kegan Paul.

Robinson, E. J. and Robinson, W. P. 1976a. Developmental changes in the child's explanation of communication failure. *Australian Journal of Psychology*, **28**, 155–65.

Robinson, E. J. and Robinson, W. P. 1976b. The young child's understanding of communication. *Developmental Psychology*, **12**, 328–33.

Robinson, E. J. and Robinson, W. P. 1977. Development in the understanding of causes of success and failure in verbal communication. *Cognition*, **5**, 363–78.

Robinson, E. J. and Robinson, W. P. 1978. Development of understanding about communication: Message inadequacy and its role in causing communication failure. *Genetic Psychological Monographs*, **98**, 233–79.

Robinson, E. J. and Robinson, W. P. 1981. Ways of reacting to communication failure in relation to the development of the child's understanding about verbal communication. *European Journal of Social Psychology*, **11**, 189–208.

Wells, C. G. 1981. *Learning through interaction: The study of language development*. Cambridge University Press.

Whitehurst, G. J. and Sonnenschein, S. 1978. The development of communication: Attribute variation leads to contrast failure. *Journal of Experimental Child Psychology*, **25**, 454–60.

Whitehurst, G. J. and Sonnenschein, S. 1981. The development of informative messages in referential communication. In W. P. Dickson (ed.): *Children's oral communication skills*. New York: Academic Press.

Part IV
Social interaction in cognitive development

Cognitive development may be considered also as the appropriation by the individual of a cultural heritage. This appropriation is progressive and comes about through interactions with others. Various dynamics of social interaction that lead to cognitive development in the child are studied in the first contribution to this Part. The research carried out at Bologna and Geneva by Mugny, De Paolis and Carugati confirms the role that is played in the operational development of the child by the social confrontation of perspectives or focuses. Individual coordinations are appropriately considered as first of all the inter-individual coordinations of different perspectives. However, not all socio-cognitive conflict necessarily results in cognitive progress; though some regulations of a social nature can stimulate such progress, others can inhibit it. But it is precisely because inter-individual coordinations are constitutive of cognitive coordinations and because therefore they can assume the character of social necessity for the individual that they escape being arbitrary and that they are so widely distributed.

At first glance the conventions in our culture that govern the representation of distance do not enjoy the same status of necessity and generality. For all that, their links with perceptual phenomena, studied since the Renaissance and incorporated in the technique of photography, are not arbitrary. The research by Frésard shows how the mastery of these social and cognitive conventions is also achieved more effectively through social interaction.

8. Social regulations in cognitive development

GABRIEL MUGNY, PAOLA DE PAOLIS
and FELICE CARUGATI

1. A socio-psychological approach to cognitive development

1.1. A social mechanism: socio-cognitive conflict

Social interaction is not automatically a source of cognitive progress. For this a certain number of requirements have to be fulfilled. A central condition is that the interaction entails opposition of divergent cognitive responses. Such socio-cognitive conflict can arise for a variety of reasons and in a variety of situations. First, it can arise when the response systems of participants differ. This is the case in encounters between individuals whose different cognitive levels give rise to relatively divergent responses or actions with respect to the concept involved in the interaction (Doise, Mugny and Perret-Clermont, 1975; Mugny and Doise, 1978a). Socio-cognitive conflict can also emerge in the course of encounters between individuals who are at the same cognitive level and therefore possess the same operational schemas, but who make opposing centrations. This may occur, for example, in a task involving conservation of equal length. Two non-conserving subjects may both assume that one of the stimuli has become longer after a transformation of the perceptual configuration (reaching this conclusion by applying the same pre-operational topological schema, evaluating length as a function of only one of the differences without consideration of or compensation for the complementary difference). But they may disagree as to which stimulus is now the longer (Mugny, Doise and Perret-Clermont, 1975–6; Mugny, Giroud and Doise, 1978–9). Finally, socio-cognitive conflict can flow from an encounter between participants at the same cognitive level but occupying positions or points of view (particularly spatial) that generate divergent responses despite application of the same schema (Doise and Mugny, 1979).

Socio-cognitive conflict may be a source of cognitive progress for several reasons. First, the plasticity often found in immature thought allows the young child to make successive changes in response without experiencing any contradiction. Then only the simultaneous and more or less consistent opposition of another can bring the child to question his own system of responses and help him elaborate more advanced cognitive instruments allowing a more complete integration of contrasting points of view. (The term 'he', used for simplicity, refers to both sexes.) Thus the other by introducing a difference in response *may* render the child conscious of other points of view. To resolve this social disequilibrium, the child *may* be provided with points of anchorage for his construction. Thus the other's disagreement gives the child information which can be relevant to such an elaboration, though it should be stressed that this elaboration is often a collective one (and therefore more a matter of co-elaboration). It is not necessary, however, to provide the correct response (Carugati *et al.*, 1978; Mugny, Lévy and Doise, 1978; Carugati, De Paolis and Mugny, 1979, 1980–1), cognitive progress being the result not of the straightforward imitation or acquisition of a social heritage but of a collective construction. This derives from a social coordination of points of view, from their integration within a more general cognitive system which gives them a unity while accounting for the diversity of the viewpoints of different individuals (the elaboration of projective space is an obvious example here). Finally, socio-cognitive conflict *may* lead the child to be especially involved in the situation, essentially because the apparently cognitive problem the child faces in fact entails a social regulation of some kind or other. A search for inter-individual consensus constitutes such a regulation, as does the acknowledgement – transposed to the cognitive level – of an asymmetrical (or symmetrical) relationship between two or more participants. Cognitive development *may* result therefore from the social necessity of regulating a social situation characterized by an opposition of responses.

This conceptualization of cognitive development (expounded in more detail in Doise and Mugny, 1981), has received substantial experimental confirmation. But if it is true that social interaction is a source of cognitive development by virtue of the socio-cognitive conflict it engenders, it is nevertheless also true that there will exist other social events in the child's daily life which may keep such conflict from being a way to progress.

What types of difficulty might be encountered in social interactions that would prevent socio-cognitive conflict leading to cognitive development? Applying an articulated psychosociological perspective (Doise, 1978, 1982; Mugny and Doise, 1979a), factors may be distinguished in terms of different levels, namely at the level of the individual characteristics of the participants, at that of the characteristics of the encounters between participants, and finally at the level of the influence of more collective and general social representations. Let us first consider various general effects at these different levels which may modify the broad proposition that conflictual social interaction will be a source of cognitive progress.

1.2. Some apparent 'counter examples'

With respect to intra-individual characteristics affecting the course of social interaction, it should be noted that such interaction is not equally effective at all stages in the development of a concept. It has above all been the research by Perret-Clermont (1980) that has revealed the fact that there are essential prerequisites if a child is to participate in and benefit intellectually from social interaction. Just as cognitive progress is built upon social coordination of initially isolated schemas, so, if such coordination is to be possible, must these schemas have been elaborated in other social interactions on previous occasions. Furthermore, these prerequisites are not necessarily only cognitive in nature. It is equally likely that they will be social, though research has yet to come to grips with this crucial issue. We have found, and incorporated within our own conceptualization of the links between social interaction and cognitive development, that conflictual social interaction (whether between peers or children and adults) is most likely to induce cognitive progress at the point of initial elaboration of a concept (Mugny and Doise, 1979b). This is the point at which initially isolated schemas are ready to be combined into the first outline of a coordination. Finally, once the beginnings of this elaboration have been socially established, social interaction ceases to occupy a uniquely privileged position in development. The child is now able to perfect the equilibration of his coordinations also by working alone. From an initial social interdependence, and by virtue of it, autonomy of development emerges.

However, an individual's history cannot be written solely in terms of his 'individual' characteristics for their effects also vary according to the nature of the social interactions in which the individual is placed. Thus, for example, children who are less advanced with respect to some concept require stronger and more constraining collective situations than those who are intermediate, given the progressive automatization of development (Doise and Mugny, 1979). In the same way, one could envisage personality traits which may often have different effects depending on the nature of the social interaction with which the child is confronted.

The second type of factor determining the effectiveness of socio-cognitive conflict is located in the nature of the inter-individual encounters. Indeed, as our research has progressed it has become apparent that if cognitive progress occurs principally in situations of socio-cognitive conflict, experimental situations devised to stimulate such conflict none the less often fail to induce it in practice or do so without producing cognitive progress in all participants. Why? Because these situations are characterized by inter-individual dynamics which hinder the progress of socio-cognitive conflict. Let us consider a few examples. In these cases one often finds that the children involved have not attempted to coordinate their actions or their points of view. They have simply juxtaposed them, thereby avoiding conflict, or else one child takes a back seat to the other who becomes occupied with solving the problem alone. A strong compliance effect of this kind has also been observed when the interaction takes place with an adult. It is only through a style of interaction involving continual expressions of doubt that an adult can succeed in counteracting this dynamic of compliance. Thus even by (voluntarily) adopting incorrect responses will an adult be able to provoke cognitive progress in the child (Mugny, Doise and Perret-Clermont, 1975–6; Carugati, De Paolis and Mugny, 1980–1), though it is important that these responses are not made too explicit (Lévy, 1981). The more explicit the alternative the more likely is the adult, almost automatically, to exercise a constraint that inhibits any active construction of any other solution by the child.

As we have seen therefore, social interactions do not necessarily proceed in the same fashion irrespective of the nature of the partners (particularly peers versus adults). In fact, more general social determinants also intervene in these situations. Although not yet a fully-fledged member of society, the child is nevertheless already profoundly influenced by his social identities, both more immediately group-based and more generally category-based (as in peer groups), and also by a social position marked by dependence on adults (even though this asymmetry may vary according to social milieu). Elsewhere we have shown that cognitive décalages may be a function of children's sociological identity (Mugny and Doise, 1978b, 1979b; Perret-Clermont, 1980; Mugny, Perret-Clermont and Doise, 1981), and also that they can be attenuated through adequate experience of socio-cognitive conflict.

In the face of this accumulation of evidence indicating the existence of different processes in social interaction and socio-cognitive conflict, inducing different degrees of cognitive development, a conceptualization is now needed of the influence of these social dynamics and their effectiveness in the induction of cognitive progress. This we now propose to offer.

2. Social regulations of socio-cognitive conflict

Let us first consider Deconchy's (1971, 1980) work on 'an orthodox milieu in effervescence'. When orthodox subjects (who accept the regulation of their thought by the orthodox system) are led to recognize that certain of their beliefs are rationally false or unfounded, far from rejecting them they compensate this loss of rationality by psychosocial means. In particular they reinforce these beliefs by emphasizing their character in regulating membership of the orthodox community. In these experiments it seems clear that social regulation is supplanting regulation of a cognitive or rational order.

For the child confronted with a situation involving socio-cognitive conflict, the problem is much the same. If socio-cognitive conflict sometimes fails to produce the theoretically anticipated progress, could it not be that in an analogous manner the conflict was characterized by psychosocial regulation instead of a cognitive solution based on cognitive coordination of the various points of view?

Moreover, the difficulty could be of a double nature, arising both before and after the induced conflict.

2.1 Difficulties in the induction of socio-cognitive conflict

The difficulty 'before' is that a difference in response must be perceived and recognized if socio-cognitive conflict is to occur. In practice not all differences in response necessarily give rise to the kind of socio-cognitive conflict we have conceptualized as being a source of cognitive development. Why?

First, one might consider the lability of a young child's successive responses. What is large can become small, without contradiction. This is a feature of his style of thought. It can therefore sometimes seem perfectly legitimate to the child that there should be inter-individual differences in response. In such a case there is no conflict since the other's response is readily integrated within the child's own system of responses. What is involved here, however, is simply a matter of the initial cognitive and social competences of the child.

More significant are the inter-relational factors which may prevent the child from taking the response of his partner into consideration. We have already seen that these may reside in the partner's style of interaction. Hence, when one partner is assertive and denies the other much part in the interaction, the other fails to progress (Mugny and Doise, 1978a). It could be quite simply that the partner's response escapes the attention of the child who is dominated in this relationship. In the absence of any process of social comparison, socio-cognitive conflict cannot assume any reality for the child. This kind of effect reflects the unilaterality versus reciprocity dimension in relationships between peers (Carugati, De Paolis and Mugny, 1980–1), in which at one extreme there exists a kind of disregard of the response of the other. Similarly, the meaning of the instructions given by the experimenter plays an essential role; thus, what does 'Come to an agreement' mean in different situations? When it is a matter of sharing a drink (Perret-Clermont, 1980), consensus can assume significance because the relation of sharing is characterized by a norm of equality. Agreement on the equivalence of two villages cannot be socially marked in this way and subjects may more easily agree on a social resolution of the problem, such as one responding without the involvement of the other or each responding in turn (juxtaposition). Here also differences need not assume the significance of a socio-cognitive conflict.

Another, surely essential set of mechanisms comes into play at this level, namely the mechanisms of attribution whereby an individual accords meaning to the differences in response that he perceives.

First, there is a mode of attribution involving reference to the self (auto-attribution). Thus the child can simply attribute any difference to his own incompetence, this being somehow sufficient to deny the difference. The corollary to this is attribution of greater competence to the other. An attribution of this kind may depend on the identity of the partner, particularly on whether the partner is a peer or an adult if the environment is such that it is the adult above all who is considered the repository of knowledge and consequently the one responsible for development. In this case, the adult's responses necessarily constitute correct centrations (or at least correct in the sense of being adequate to a specific situation). Thus the child will more readily accept the adult's response as an appropriate centration or relevant point of comparison than he will consider the validity of a peer's response or even his own.

Furthermore, there are likely to be cross-cultural variations in this respect (Mackie, 1980).

In brief, there will exist dominant social regulations, rendered more or less salient according to the nature of inter-individual relations, which will determine the degree to which others' responses are accepted as valid centrations and hence used as bases for comparison with the child's own responses, a comparison which may then give rise to socio-cognitive conflict.

2.2. Modalities of socio-cognitive conflict resolution

Let us now suppose that a child recognizes a partner's contradicting response as a valid centration and 'accepts' a comparison with his own. At this point the conditions for socio-cognitive conflict will have been fulfilled. The central question now posed is what will the child do in the face of this conflict?

Here one could refer to theories of social influence. Are situations of socio-cognitive conflict not also situations of social influence? And in corollary fashion, are not social influence situations also socio-cognitive conflict situations? There is clearly a close connection between situations in which a child finds his judgments of the inequality in the length of rods, for example, contradicted and the situations created by Asch (1951, 1956), Sherif (1935), Moscovici (1976) and indeed Milgram (1974). Certainly one apparent difference is that the subjects in developmental studies have yet to elaborate instruments the validity of which will not be questioned further, whereas subjects in social influence experiments are often in the position of finding apparently obvious facts questioned. But all things considered, is it not the case that *before the social interaction* the former and the latter were certain of the correctness of their responses – or at least not preoccupied with this kind of question?

Recent work on social influence has also stressed the conflictual nature of social influence situations, visualizing the form of a socio-cognitive reorganization of responses in terms of this conflict (Moscovici, 1976; Mugny, 1981). Let us then try and conceptualize this issue of methods of socio-cognitive conflict resolution in the terms of this approach. What in effect will be the response to conflict once it occurs? Straight away one can anticipate that only certain methods or modalities are going to result in a new cognitive elaboration.

For the moment we will confine ourselves to defining the types of modality favouring cognitive development in terms of the negative case:

the conflict will be cognitively regulated (i.e. 'in operational terms' or tending to an operational solution of the problem) by a new cognitive elaboration when it is not regulated in terms of an exclusively 'relational' modality. Then we may witness an attempt to an elaboration (indeed a co-elaboration) of a cognitive instrument capable of integrating the various centrations within a coherent system that does not involve denying any of the centrations actually made by the various participants. Thus if two children believe that in one direction one of two rods is longer, but their respective centrations are opposed, they could without denying the respective points of view converge on a response of equality integrating these diverging centrations within a compensatory system. In the same way, Swiss and foreign children may integrate their respective positions without having to deny their own categorical identities by developing the reciprocity of the concept of foreigner thus: 'In your country, I am a foreigner, but not in my country where you are the foreigner.' And again in the same way, projective space allows integration of highly heterogeneous 'perceptual' points of view within a coherent system.

But not all modalities of socio-cognitive conflict negotiation involve the elaboration of such cognitive instruments. One can also identify processes of conflict resolution similar to conformity, to normalization and even to social differentiation. *In each of these instances one could claim that a relational regulation has supplanted a cognitive regulation.*

The relation of conformity may often occur within the context of a power relationship, and thus within the framework of an asymmetrical relation. In this case, conformity comes down to a form of negotiation aimed at the reabsorption of social conflict via an overt, socially explicit adoption of the other's response.

Various experiments have shown that this particular mode of social regulation appears in the relation of a child to an adult. On several occasions it has been possible to establish that a child has adopted an adult's response, whether correct or incorrect, without progressing subsequently. At the same time the impact of this asymmetry varies considerably with the adult's style of interaction which can facilitate either a more or a less relational resolution of the conflict (see Lévy, 1981; Carugati, De Paolis and Mugny, 1980–1). Other data have revealed the importance of the means by which the child leads the adult to believe that he has grasped the dimensions of a problem (Allen, in press). These responses are in some manner a reflection of normative influence (Deutsch and Gerard, 1955), wherein the problem for the child is to give a social response which will conform with what he perceives to be the expectations of his partner.

Other situations induce, instead of conformity, a kind of 'reciprocal negotiation' of the conflict, as in the situations devised by Sherif with respect to normalization. Elsewhere we have identified conditions at various levels affecting this type of inter-individual convergence (Mugny and Doise, 1979a). It is almost possible to take up the diverse variables influencing this phenomenon point by point. Specifically, one could note lack of 'involvement' on the child's part in a situation lacking any social necessity other than that of avoiding discord, be it simply as a result of the experimenter's explicit instruction that a consensus be reached. Such a convergence could also result from a perception of equality of status, as French (1956) has suggested. We have already seen that such reduction of conflict frequently takes the form of a juxtaposition of responses, a modality rendered more or less probable according to the type of situation. In fact certain paradigms allow a division of labour in which resolution of the conflict can consist in sharing the decisions, thus socially eliminating difference by avoiding social comparison. One can, of course, imagine other forms of compromise ('When *you* are looking it is bigger, when *I* am it is not' etc.). Generally there will be more chance that this modality will emerge among peers and when the social situation is sufficiently purified to abstract it from any other social regulation.

Another form of relational regulation could be envisaged which would involve affirmation of a difference (or differentiation, Lemaine, 1975), or indeed the creation of such differences. This would be the case in situations where the social positions of partners imply a social marking of a different kind (as in the example of the foreigner and the autochthon). Also, one might expect an affirmation of difference to be stronger when contrasts between groups or category memberships are salient and relevant to the task.

Certainly there has yet to be any systematic research on the various processes capable of interfering with the 'productive' development of socio-cognitive conflict. Nevertheless, in *a posteriori* analyses it has emerged with a certain regularity that various types of interactions can occur within the different paradigms we have used (cf. Doise and Mugny, 1981), and some experimental illustrations will be given later in the chapter. The reason for this gap in research is obvious; this set of mechanisms generally intervenes to counteract the emergence and 'productive' development of socio-cognitive conflict. Up to now research has, on the whole, tended to be concerned with socio-cognitive conflict, whether involving peers or adults, in terms of its effectiveness.

3. Social marking of cognitive responses

In many socio-cognitive conflict situations there exists a relationship, a correspondence of one form or another, between on the one hand responses of a cognitive order and on the other relevant social regulations or else regulations which are made salient in the situation. One could say of such situations that they are characterized by a social marking of cognitive responses.

3.1. Social marking of inter-individual encounters

Let us take as an example one of our own experiments (Doise, Dionnet and Mugny, 1978). Children who were non-conservers on a task involving conservation of unequal length were required in an experimental phase to judge the length of bracelets and then divide them either between a fat and a thin cylinder (the circumferences of which corresponded to the lengths of the bracelets), or between the self and an adult so that each could wear one on their wrist. Following the cognitive conflict thus created (identical in the two conditions), substantial progress occurred but only when the sharing was between the adult and child. Our interpretation of these results is simply that this superiority derives from the social marking of the task in this condition. It derives from the existence of a correspondence between preservation of the ordering of the two bracelets and the ordering derived from the necessity of social sharing. This social order accentuates the contradiction resulting from the child's initially non-conserving judgments.

Moreover, analogous effects can be expected regarding conservation of equality (of length, liquid, etc.) when this corresponds to an egalitarian social relationship. This is the case in the division of drink (cf. Perret-Clermont, 1980) particularly when the partners have previously socially earned such an egalitarian division (Finn, 1975; Doise, Rijsman, Van Meel *et al.*, 1981).

Thus certain forms of correspondence will favour cognitive progress, on the one hand because they induce a conflict between the child's spontaneous cognitive response and a response deriving from some social necessity, and on the other because the correct response (or one which is an advance on the cognitive level of the child with respect to the concept considered) is isomorphic with this social necessity. But for similar reasons other forms of correspondence can be opposed to such development.

If these latter forms of marking have not for the moment been studied, and again for obvious reasons, they can readily be imagined in terms of the earlier conservation example but this time with respect to equal lengths. Thus one might suppose that the social necessity of attributing a long bracelet to the adult and a shorter one to the child could favour a non-conserving child's spontaneous, incorrect response of inequality in a task of, on this occasion, conservation of equal lengths. For in this case there would be no conflict between the non-conserving response and the activity of social division also implicating inequality. In such a situation, isomorphism between the cognitive and the social responses would constitute a social obstacle to cognitive development.

3.2. Social marking of the task

Social regulation does not necessarily involve immediate modalities of interaction between social partners, as the preceding examples might suggest, wherein social asymmetry or symmetry between partners is entailed directly in their relationship.

Social marking is of a more general nature. *It connects relations of a cognitive order with those of a social order*, relations which can be activated in subjects *even in the absence of a direct relation with others*. In other words, social marking can be involved in a cognitive relation in a purely symbolic fashion, particularly when it directly characterizes elements or materials in the task. An example which might be given here is research carried out by Rilliet (cf. Doise and Mugny, 1981, pp. 166–9), the results of which have been replicated by De Paolis *et al.* (1981). Using a spatial transformation paradigm (Mugny and Doise, 1978a), materials without any salient social meaning were employed in a control condition. Subjects were asked to reproduce a village consisting of houses and a swimming pool on a base the orientation of which differed from that of the original village. This requires a complex transformation to preserve relations between elements in the spatial array. In the experimental condition the houses were replaced by desks 'occupied' by pupils and a larger desk 'occupied' by a teacher. This manipulation was based on the assumption that the teacher–pupil relationship involves spatial positions specific to participants in an educational relationship. In actual fact, in the classes where the study was carried out, the teacher occupied a distinct position in the corner of the room from which she could visually command the entire room. One might therefore expect that transformation of the various dimensions entailed in the task (in front/behind, left/right, near/far. . .) would have a greater probability of occurring in this situation because of the social necessity of conserving various relation- ships. Striking improvements did indeed emerge, both in the inter- individual interactions and on individual post-tests, for the situations socially marked in this way. Such improvements also occurred with subjects who worked individually during the experimental phase though these improvements were somewhat smaller than those achieved by children working in pairs. Hence, social marking also has certain effects for the child in apparently individual situations in which the social nature of responses is made salient by the use of socially meaningful material.

Recent research by De Paolis has confirmed these 'individual' effects for the social marking of materials. Among a sample of four to five year olds, substantial differences were obtained between those questioned individually with the materials lacking in social meaning (the village) and children tested with the socially marked material (the school room). In the social marking condition the majority of subjects offered intermediate types of solution while subjects in the socially unmarked condition gave responses stereotypic of an inferior level on this task.

In addition to show that the effects of this type of social marking cannot be reduced to simple explanations in terms, particularly, of familiarity, De Paolis compared situations involving the same doll figures in one case represented as watching television and in the other set in the previously described context of the school room. In spite of the use of these dolls in the television-watching condition, the superiority of the social marking condition remains. It seems that in this latter situation the dolls are somehow engaged in a social relationship implying specific spatial rules while in the former no such necessity exists.

Why is social marking so effective even in the absence of a direct inter-individual relation? Once again we believe the answer can be given in terms of socio-cognitive conflict. Responses (judgments, actions, placements of objects. . .) deriving from a social regulation (relative to sharing, to the respective positions of individuals in space, etc.) are in opposition to the responses the child would give spontaneously if he did not have to coordinate his cognitive schemas and his social representa- tions of these regulations. It is precisely from this socio-cognitive conflict that cognitive restructuring flows, though it should be stressed that there needs to exist a 'positive' correspondence which will not therefore counteract elaboration of a more advanced solution.

4. Some illustrations of an experimental paradigm

Our social conception of cognitive development may be illustrated with an experimental paradigm developed within the context of a collaboration between research teams in social psychology at Bologna and Geneva. This will enable us to clarify those dynamics of interaction which we believe determine modalities of socio-cognitive conflict resolution resulting in the presence or absence of cognitive progress among the subjects involved.

The task is based once again in conservation of spatial relations (Mugny and Doise, 1978a). It involves a model village constructed by the experimenter on a base depicting a reference mark; the child is required to reconstruct the same village on an identical but differently-oriented base. An individual pre-test (allowing retention within the experiment of non-conservers only) is followed by an interaction phase in which the experimental manipulations are introduced, and an individual post-test (permitting evaluation of each participant's progress).

Various modifications were introduced within the interaction phase of this paradigm (Carugati *et al.*, 1978). They were intended to isolate the social dimension of socio-cognitive conflict and thus differentiate the cognitive difficulty entailed in the task (due to the difference in orientation of the bases as perceived by the child) from the social opposition of a partner or partners. In order to separate these two possible and generally complementary sources of cognitive progress, it was decided to place experimental subjects in an 'easy' position from which the task would pose no cognitive problem given an identical orientation of the bases relative to the subject's view of them (Position X→E, Figure 1). They were confronted by partners occupying a 'difficult' position (Position Y→D, Figure 1) involving a cognitive problem by virtue of the fact that the orientation of the bases is reversed from this perspective, requiring transformations (inverting left/right and front/back relations) to preserve the relations between elements.

In an initial study this paradigm provided a demonstration of substantial progress on the part of subjects in the 'easy' position, progress which could be due only to the social conflict brought about by a comparison with the *incorrect* response of their partner or partners (Carugati *et al.*, 1978). Two conditions were compared in this experiment.

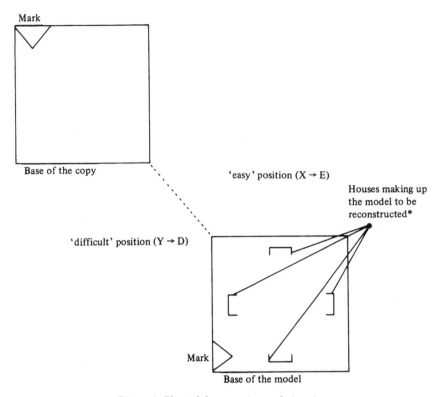

Figure 1. Plan of the experimental situation

In one (ExD), a subject in the 'easy' position was confronted by a single subject at the same pre-operational level in the 'difficult' position. In the other (ExDD), the subject in the 'easy' position was confronted by two subjects in the 'difficult' position. Post-tests show that subjects in the 'easy' position progressed more in this latter condition than those confronted by a single partner. This difference is not only apparent at the level of individual progress. Other results from this experiment illustrate the intervention of social regulations in the development of socio-cognitive conflict. An analysis of the interactions thus reveals a difference between the two conditions (Carugati, De Paolis and Mugny, 1979). In the ExDD condition, interactions involve more conflict and the subjects in the easy position more often take the final decision on the conflicting items than those in the ExD condition. This may indicate that the incorrect solution advanced by the two subjects in the difficult position has led their partner in the easy position to make a genuine comparison of the contradictory responses and has required a stronger defence of his own (subjectively obvious) correct solution. This implies a cognitive decentration consistent with trying to understand the points of view of others and refuting them as incorrect solutions. In the ExD condition, the subject in the easy position has less opposition to face, resulting in a more limited negotiation which is insufficient to allow reconstruction of the different dimensions involved in the task.

An interpretation of these data in terms of relational versus cognitive regulation of conflict is therefore plausible. In the ExD condition the subject possessing the correct solution predominates. Resolution of the divergence of points of view is therefore managed on a relational basis, thus preventing the subject from grasping the cognitive dimensions involved in the task. In contrast, in the ExDD condition the coalition of two partners obliges the subject in the easy position to take their point of view into consideration. This stronger social opposition cannot be resolved in an exclusively relational fashion. Hence, negotiation is located at the cognitive level (accounting for the defence by the subject in the easy condition of his correct solution to the conflicting items).

This is, however, only an interpretation. A double replication of this experiment was carried out with the specific aim of clarifying the operation of these social regulations directly (Carugati, De Paolis and Mugny, 1980–1). In one of these replications the child is confronted with a peer, in the other with an adult.

First, in the interactions between peers a crucial dimension emerges, that of the degree of unilaterality versus reciprocity in the decisions. Socio-cognitive conflict leads to development of new cognitive instruments essentially when decisions are shared among participants. This is not the case though when the division consists in a juxtaposition of responses and disregard of the responses made by the other, or when the decision-making is unilateral with one of the participants dominating the other (an effect already found by Mugny and Doise, 1978a). In fact, of the eighteen groups participating in the interaction phase, ten evidenced a unilateral regulation of the conflict and eight a reciprocal regulation. The index of unilaterality versus reciprocity was derived from the difference between the percentages of correct responses decided by each partner (the larger the difference the more frequently decisions are made by only one partner). On the individual post-tests eight out of the ten subjects in the easy position who had participated in unilateral interactions showed no progress while seven out of the eight from the groups involving reciprocal interaction progressed. If one considers the joint progress of the two partners, in only one out of the ten unilateral groups did both subjects progress and in six of these neither progressed. In contrast, in four out of the eight reciprocal groups both partners progressed with one of the partners progressing in the remaining groups.

In the second variation of this experiment the child interacted with an adult who, placed in the difficult position, gave systematically incorrect responses. From the (easy) perspective of the child the error was therefore obvious, the theoretical conditions for socio-cognitive conflict thus being assured. But what regulation will the child accord to this conflict and what will be the consequences for cognitive progress?

The results indicate that the children who oppose the adult most systematically progress on the post-tests. Those, on the other hand, who most readily accept the adult's incorrect solution without discussion (even though the adult engages in a process of questioning) and thus by their straightforward compliance accept a relational regulation of the conflict, do not progress. To demonstrate this we used as a criterion for differentiating the compliant and the 'resistant' subject the number of houses correctly placed during the entire interaction (a possible total of sixteen houses). This indicates whether the child has effectively resisted the adult's responses (since these latter always involve placing them incorrectly, in practice according to a 'translation' of the whole village). The thirteen subjects who showed progress on the post-test had on average correctly placed more than twelve houses during the interaction while those showing no progress correctly placed no more than six.

Accepting the adult as a source of the correct response despite the perceptual evidence, and adopting a strategy of compliance by respond-ing as a function of the adult's response, involves an essentially relational regulation of the conflict. This excludes progress, particularly to the degree that the specific response derived from this relationship is not isomorphic with the correct response. It is therefore to the problem of a difference in social status that these children respond rather than to the puzzling matter of the existence of several points of view which require a cognitive integration and coordination.

Using the same paradigm in a third experiment, De Paolis *et al.* (1981) were able to demonstrate the role that social marking may play not only as a condition favouring cognitive development but also as a (socio-cognitive) support for the child's resistance in the face of an incorrect solution advanced by an adult. It enables the child to confront the adult in a situation which would otherwise tend, as we have seen on various occasions, to favour a relational regulation in terms of compliance.

Two experimental conditions were compared in a situation opposing an adult and a child. One employed the usual material of the village, the other the socially marked material based on the school room. The latter, it will be recalled, allows the child to establish links between cognitive responses relevant to solution of the task and responses derived from social rules governing spatial relations between pupils and teachers.

In the 'village' condition children were less likely to set the evidence of their solution against the incorrect solution advanced by the adult, going so far as to reproduce the latter for on average more than six out of sixteen houses. Their post-test results were significantly lower than those in the 'school-room' condition. In this latter condition, the social marking of the material used in the interaction led to a superiority in the cognitive level displayed on the post-test with socially unmarked material (the village).

The reason for this progress clearly lies in the way that conflict with the adult is regulated during the interaction. In fact, children in this condition more frequently oppose the adult, responding to the social necessity of conserving various important spatial relations between pupils and teachers (after the manner of their actual relationships with their own classmates and teachers). The coincidence of cognitive evidence with the social rule symbolized in the task leads them to be particularly consistent and thus escape the 'social weight' of the adult partner. The proof is that on average they comply with the adult with respect to less than one placement out of the sixteen they have to defend. In this situation therefore a cognitive regulation of the socio-cognitive conflict is sustained by the correspondence between the 'good' and obvious response and the 'social rule' requiring conservation of certain spatial relations in a task symbolizing a socially hierarchic relationship. If social marking allows children to take the adult's perspective into consideration it is in order to reject its cognitive and social incongruence. Thus it allows the child to decentre from its own view point and recognize that there can exist various relevant dimensions in transformations and even to coordinate these within a more elaborated cognitive system (the proof of this being the cognitive level attained in the post-test).

5. Conclusions

The introduction of the notion of social regulation, like the more specific notion of social marking which has just been illustrated, seems to us to have facilitated an advance in the direction of a social conception of the development of intelligence in the child. The active construction by the subject of new cognitive instruments has been conceived as based on a social coordination of its own actions and judgments with the actions and judgments of others in situations characterized by socio-cognitive conflict. It is in this framework that we have tried to show the centrality of both the social regulations which manage the induction of these socio-cognitive conflicts and the modalities of their resolution. Moreover, these regulations may concern the more 'horizontal' relationships between peers and the more 'vertical' relationships between children and adults in a clearly differentiated manner. Finally, the notion of social marking enables us to encompass the dynamics involved in the isomorphism arising from a juxtaposition of responses relevant to application of a cognitive instrument with those reflecting a social rule or norm.

Acknowledgment

Most of the studies discussed in this chapter have been developed within the framework of the Convention between the Istituto di Scienze dell'Educazione (University of Bologna) and the Faculté de Psychologie et des Sciences de l'Education (University of Geneva), and supported by research grants 216.843 and 204.1427 (P. De Paolis) and CT 790107208 (F. Carugati) from the Consiglio Nazionale delle Richerche (Italy).

References

Allen, V. L. In press. The role of nonverbal behaviour in children's communication. In P. Dickson (ed.): *Children's referential communication*. London: Academic Press.

Asch, S. E. 1951. Effects of group pressure upon the modification and distortion of judgement. In H. Guetzkow (ed.): *Groups, leadership and men*. Pittsburgh, Pa.: Carnegie Press.

Asch, S. E. 1956. Studies on independence and conformity: A minority of one against an unanimous majority. *Psychological Monographs*, **70**, 416.

Carugati, F., De Paolis, P. and Mugny, G. 1979. A paradigm for the study of social interactions in cognitive development. *Italian Journal of Psychology*, **6**, 147–55.

Carugati, F., De Paolis, P. and Mugny, G. 1980–1. Conflit de centrations et progrès cognitif, III: Régulations cognitives et relationnelles du conflit sociocognitif. *Bulletin de Psychologie*, **34**, 843–52.

Carugati, F., Mugny, G., Barbieri, P. L., De Paolis, P., Gherardi V. and Ravenna, M. 1978. Psicologia sociale dello sviluppo cognitivo: Imitazione di modelli o conflitto socio-cognitivo? *Giornale Italiano di Psicologia*, **2**, 323–52.

Deconchy, J. P. 1971. *L'orthodoxie religieuse. Essai de logique psychosociale*. Paris: Editions Ouvrières.

Deconchy, J. P. 1980. *Orthodoxie religieuse et sciences humaines*. La Haye: Mouton.

De Paolis, P., Carugati, F., Erba, M. and Mugny, G. 1981. Connotazione sociale e sviluppo cognitivo. *Giornale Italiano di Psicologia*, **8**, 149–65.

Deutsch, M. and Gerard, H. B. 1955. A study of normative and informational social influence upon individual judgement. *Journal of Abnormal and Social Psychology*, **51**, 629–36.

Doise, W. 1978. *Groups and individuals*. Cambridge University Press.

Doise, W. 1982. *L'explication en psychologie sociale*. Paris: Presses Universitaires de France.

Doise, W., Dionnet, S. and Mugny, G. 1978. Conflict sociocognitif, marquage social et développement cognitif. *Cahiers de Psychologie*, **21**, 231–43.

Doise, W. and Mugny, G. 1979. Individual and collective conflicts of centrations in cognitive development. *European Journal of Social Psychology*, **9**, 105–8.

Doise, W. and Mugny, G. 1981. *La construction sociale de l'intelligence*. Paris: Interéditions.

Doise, W., Mugny, G. and Perret-Clermont, A. N. 1975. Social interactions and the development of cognitive operations. *European Journal of Social Psychology*, **5**, 367–83.

Doise, W., Rijsman, J., Van Meel, J. *et al.* 1981. Sociale markering en cognitieve ontwikkeling. *Pedagogische Studiën*, **58**, 241–8.

Finn, G. P. T. 1975. *The child's conservation of liquid quantity and its embedding in the social world*. Glasgow: Jordanhill College of Education.

French, J. R. 1956. A formal theory of social power. *Psychological Review*, **63**, 181–94.

Lemaine, G. 1975. Dissimilation and differential assimilation in social influence (situation of normalization). *European Journal of Social Psychology*, **5**, 1, 93–120.

Lévy, M. 1981. La nécessité sociale chez l'enfant de dépasser une situation conflictuelle. Unpublished doctoral thesis, University of Geneva.

Mackie, D. 1980. A cross-cultural study of intra-individual and interindividual conflicts of centrations. *European Journal of Social Psychology*, **10**, 313–18.

Milgram, S. 1974. *Obedience to authority*. New York: Harper and Row.

Moscovici, S. 1976. *Social influence and social change*. London: Academic Press.

Mugny, G. 1981. *El poder de las minorias*. Barcelona: Rol. (*The power of minorities*. London: Academic Press. 1982.)

Mugny, G. and Doise, W. 1978a. Socio-cognitive conflict and structuration of individual and collective performances. *European Journal of Social Psychology*, **8**, 181–92.

Mugny, G. and Doise, W. 1978b. Factores sociologicos y psicosociologicos en el desarollo cognitivo. *Anuario de Psicologia*, **18**, 21–40.

Mugny, G. and Doise, W. 1979a. Niveaux d'analyse dans l'étude expérimentale des processus d'influence sociale. *Social Science Information*, **18**, 819–976.

Mugny, G. and Doise, W. 1979b. Factores sociologicos y psicosociologicos en el desarollo cognitivo: Una nueva ilustraciòn experimental. *Anuario de Psicologia*, **21**, 5–25.

Mugny, G., Doise, W. and Perret-Clermont, A. N. 1975–6. Conflit de centrations et progrès cognitif. *Bulletin de Psychologie*, **29**, 199–204.

Mugny, G., Giroud, J. C. and Doise, W. 1978–9. Conflit de centrations et progrès cognitif, II. *Bulletin de Psychologie*, **32**, 979–85.

Mugny, G., Lévy, M. and Doise, W. 1978. Conflit sociocognitif et développement cognitif: L'effet de la présentation par un adulte de modèles 'progressifs' et de modèles 'régressifs' dans une épreuve de représentation spatiale. *Revue Suisse de Psychologie*, **37**, 22–43.

Mugny, G., Perret-Clermont, A. N. and Doise, W. 1981. Interpersonal coordinations and sociological differences in the construction of the intellect. In G. M. Stephenson and J. M. Davis (eds.): *Progress in applied social psychology*. New York: Wiley, vol. 1, pp. 315–43.

Perret-Clermont, A. N. 1980. *Social interaction and cognitive development in children*. London: Academic Press.

Sherif, M. 1935. A study of some social factors in perception. *Archives of Psychology*, 187.

9. The representation of distance in the individual and collective drawings of children

MARIE-DANIELLE FRÉSARD

1. Introduction

The characteristics of children's drawings, at least within the societies of Western culture, evolve in a systematic fashion with age. Numerous investigations, both classic (Piaget and Inhelder, 1948; Luquet, 1967) and more recent (Goodnow, 1977; Freeman, 1980) have made detailed investigations of the various characteristics of this development as they are linked to age. Our own long term intention is to reconsider these studies and determine whether a parallel can be established between the manner in which children discover techniques and strategies for graphically representing their environment and the manner in which these techniques have been invented, or reinvented, at various times in the course of the history of art.

The research reported here, however, has a more limited goal. Given that our current society has very precise rules, those of the classical drawing of perspective, for representing a three-dimensional space and more particularly for representing distance, we wanted to study the way in which children aged eight and a half to eleven and a half would manage to cope with an instruction to draw a road, a motorway and a railway going far into the distance.

According to the authors cited above and on the basis of our own pilot work, we could expect to find in the drawings of the younger children a significant effect of their 'realist' conception of distance representation. For these children, drawing a road which goes far is a matter of creating a drawing which takes a long time to complete and which involves a very long mark on the paper. We have previously established a lack of differentiation between the length of time taken to execute the task, the length of the image actually drawn, and the representation of distance.

An initial hypothesis was therefore that children of nine to ten years would still have difficulty in grasping that a drawing which is itself objectively short and requires little work may represent something spanning a considerable distance. Older children on the other hand (eleven to twelve years) would show greater mastery of the conventional rules of perspective and would be able to use them to represent distance with an image which is not itself very long.

This lack of differentiation between signifier and what is signified has been observed recently by researchers working in other areas. For example, Berthoud-Papandropoulou (1978) reports that when asked for a long word young children may offer the word 'train'; they do not differentiate between the length of the object evoked and the length of the word that evokes it. Similarly, some students of Mme Denis-Prinzhorn (unpublished research) have reported a lack of differentiation between temporal duration and distance among seven to eight year olds; when the same distance is covered either by car or on foot, they consider that it is shorter by car because the car goes faster whereas the pedestrian takes a longer time.

Furthermore, another set of ideas has guided us in the planning of this research. These ideas relate to the role of social interaction in cognitive development and have been developed by Doise and Mugny (1981; see also chapter 8 in this volume by Mugny, De Paolis and Carugati). The thesis of these authors is that socio-cognitive coordinations between individuals facilitate the individual acquisition of cognitive coordinations, particularly when individuals must coordinate their different and indeed opposing approaches in the course of a joint cognitive task. The construction of a graphical representation of distance, mastering traditional rules of perspective, is also a cognitive task. For this reason a phase involving joint work between two children was introduced within the experimental design for the research. In this way it should be possible to observe either, principally among the younger subjects, cooperation between children with broadly the same mode of representing distance, that is without any link with the rules of classical perspective, or among the older subjects cooperation between a child whose previous drawing reveals only a few elements of classical perspective and a child whose previous drawing has already shown more rudiments of the classical representation of distance. Opposing approaches should be much less frequent among younger than among older children.

Our groups would therefore reflect two different situations but with equal importance for understanding the stages in the construction of the concept of distance. For younger subjects interaction may have the effect of stabilizing schemas mastered individually by the partners. Thus, our younger subjects, making drawings of a road that are themselves long and involve numerous curves, are actually revealing a stage characteristic of their level of development, that of confounding the concept of distance with those of length and duration. As their centrations are identical, the interaction can only reinforce what each already believes and lead them directly to agree on a non-conventional representation of perspective. Such an outcome would follow from the fact that neither child would yet have integrated the rudiments of conventional norms in this area.

With the older children, interaction may be capable of facilitating the construction of new schemas, some elements of classical perspective being present in at least one member of the pair. In this case, interaction would lead to a collective construction or reconstruction of the classical methods currently conventional in our society. If the centrations of the two partners are opposed, the child already more familiar with the dominant norm will be more readily able to convey this convention, at the same time systematizing his or her own knowledge through confrontation with another mode of practice and the necessity of reaching a shared understanding.

2. Method

In order to test these hypotheses, 393 children drawn from urban and rural schools in and around Geneva were asked to draw on one occasion a road with trees along the sides, a week later to draw a motorway with traffic signs along the edges, and finally a week after that to draw a railway, again with trees. The children were told that the road, motorway and railway 'should go very far'. To examine the first hypothesis, children from three different age levels were selected, 8.5 to 9.5 years (fourth year), 9.5 to 10.5 years (fifth year), and 10.5 to 11.5 years (sixth year).

To examine the second hypothesis, a control group of 135 children completed the second task (drawing the motorway) alone, while the remaining 258 children, constituting the experimental group, completed this task in pairs or exceptionally in groups of three. Children worked on each of the tasks in their own classrooms in groups of 20 to 25 under the supervision of the author.

3. Results

The various analyses carried out on the drawings obtained have been described in detail elsewhere (Frésard, 1981). These were based primarily on the length of the images drawn (which varied between 0.1 cm and 300 cm on a sheet of A4 paper), the decreasing size of the road or railway toward the top of the drawing paper, and the type of sketch used. Within the scope of this brief chapter only the typological analysis will be discussed though the results it provided were convergent with those of the other analyses. The typological classifications were made by two independent judges who came to an agreement on the rare cases on which their judgements did not coincide.

While the children were very inventive in the forms they gave their drawings, some drawing roads in the form of an arc, others representing roads in a rectangular form, and yet others sketching road networks with numerous junctions, two types of drawing were nevertheless more frequent than others. Out of a total of 1,053 drawings obtained over the three phases of the experiment, 433 (41 per cent) were of a road or railway in a curved form, usually with several sharp bends (winding paths), and 402 (38 per cent) were clearly in the form of a complete or broken triangle (see Figure 1). In the case of each of these two types of drawing a strong developmental effect was obtained, but in each case in an opposite direction. Table 1 gives the frequencies of drawings in the form of winding paths, for each of the three tasks and at each age level.

The highly significant development effect ($p < 0.001$) evident here corresponds to an equally significant developmental effect with regard to the length of the image drawn. Our first hypothesis is thus strongly supported; the younger children more often draw longer images involving roads or railways with several curves or bends.

The analysis of frequencies of drawings in the form of triangles is in some sense complementary to the preceding analysis. The frequency of drawings in triangular forms increases significantly with age ($p < 0.001$). Table 2 gives a more detailed breakdown of these frequencies for triangular forms, giving the frequencies of different patterns of response within subjects across the three phases of the experiment. These results allow an examination of the scope of our second hypothesis, providing a comparison of development in children participating in social interaction with that in children working alone. For the fourth year there is apparent a clear dominance of negative stability; a pattern of performance over the three tasks which begins and ends with an absence of triangular forms

Table 1. *Frequencies of drawings in the form of winding paths for the three tasks and school levels*

	Task 1		Task 2		Task 3	
	Winding path	Other forms	Winding path	Other forms	Winding path	Other forms
School year						
Fourth	100	25	46	40	66	59
Fifth	81	48	25	62	39	90
Sixth	51	88	4	90	21	118

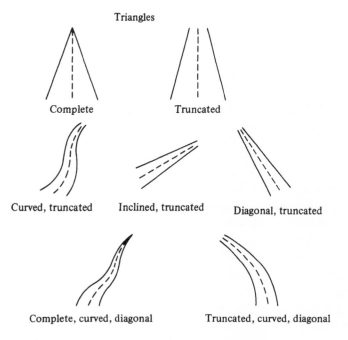

Figure 1. Examples of drawings with triangular forms.

constitutes 76 per cent of the total. That is to say, 95 out of 125 children do not draw a triangular form in their first and their last picture. There was no significant difference between the experimental conditions.

For the fifth year as a whole, patterns of performance ending with a triangular form are less frequent than those ending with a non-conventional form. Stability of a non-conventional type of response or change towards such a type is also as frequent as stability of a conventional type or change towards this type. In fact the directions of change are balanced; patterns change as often in a non-conventional as in

Table 2. *Frequencies of different patterns of performance across the three phases of the experiment*

Types of Pattern*	Fourth year Inter-action condition	Fourth year Control condition	Fifth year Inter-action condition	Fifth year Control condition	Sixth year Inter-action condition	Sixth year Control condition
+++	8	1	13	11	38	15
++0	0	2	5	0	1	2
+0+	1	1	5	0	1	7
+00	0	0	1	0	2	1
0++	11	2	8	4	22	3
0+0	9	1	6	2	16	2
00+	2	2	7	3	3	2
000	49	36	40	24	10	14
Total	80	45	85	44	93	46

Note: *+ signifies the presence of a triangular form, 0 signifies the absence of a triangular form. Thus, for example, ++0 indicates that in the first and second task a triangular form was used but such a form was not used in the third task. In the text we mean by 'patterns' the eight possible combinations of use and non-utilization of a triangular form across the three tasks.

a conventional direction. Otherwise the same type of drawing persists over the three tasks. Among children in the interaction condition, 39 per cent of patterns end with a triangle, or in 33 cases out of 85, while among those in the control condition, 41 per cent do so or in 18 out of 44 cases.

For the sixth year conclusions differ between the two conditions. In the condition without interaction patterns ending with and without a triangular form constitute 59 per cent and 41 per cent respectively, or 27 and 19 cases out of 46. These frequencies do not differ significantly from split half ($\chi^2 = 1.391$; n.s.).

For the interaction condition, on the other hand, positive stability and positive change were found to predominate. For the sixth year as a whole in this condition, patterns ending with a drawing containing a triangular form constitute 69 per cent or 64 cases out of 93. Patterns not ending with a triangle represent 31 per cent or 29 cases out of 93. These proportions differ significantly from split half ($\chi^2 = 13.172$, p<0.001).

Let us look a little more closely at the effects of social interaction for the oldest children (sixth year). For these we have drawn up a more detailed table, giving the frequencies of drawings in a triangular form in the second task as a function of the types of drawing made by members of the group in the first task.

Table 3. *Frequency of occurrence of triangular forms in the first and second tasks for sixth year subjects*

Control condition	Second task	
	Without triangle	With triangle
First task		
Without triangle	16	5
With triangle	8	17
Interaction condition	Second task	
	Without triangle	With triangle
First task		
No triangle*	6	10
Triangle by one group member†	1	16
Triangle by both group members‡	1	11

* On the first task neither member of the group had used a triangular form.
† Only one member of the group had used a triangular form in the first task.
‡ Both members of the group had used a triangular form in the first task.

First, an examination of the results given in Table 3 confirms the preceding conclusions. In the absence of social interaction (control condition) there is no clear stability of the conventional type of response; one third of the subjects (8 out of 25) having used a triangular form in their first drawing adopt another type of drawing in the second task. On the other hand, in the drawings resulting from joint performances, when the partners both used a triangular form in their first drawings, only a single regression was observed. What is more, in the groups in which only one partner had employed a triangular form for his first drawing, it was again with one exception this form that was retained in the collective performance. Finally, where no member of the group had individually adopted the triangular form, this type of drawing was invented by the partners in the course of interaction 10 times out of 16. Such collective inventions occurred more frequently than inventions of the same kind made by individuals working alone, the figures for the latter being 5 times out of 21 ($\chi^2 = 5.639$, p<0.025). It is worth noting that these effects remain relatively stable during the third phase of the experiment.

It would also seem to be appropriate to compare the collective products of the sixth year with those of the fifth. At the latter age level only one group out of 21 innovates by creating a triangle when no member of the group had adopted this form previously. On the other hand, when one member of the group had already adopted the triangular form during the first task, the other members go along with him in 10 groups out of 14 during the collective performance. This appears to show the predominance at this age of a modelling effect over a constructive effect.

4. Conclusions

The various results obtained clearly show that the manner in which the children examined represent distance is characterized by a strong developmental effect. Thus, as we have observed before, the lack of differentiation between such notions as distance, length and duration that is manifested by the younger subjects (fourth school year) is translated into 'realist' representations of distance. These children most often draw roads that are actually longer than the greatest dimension of the sheet of paper on which they are working; in effect, they give to the signifier (their drawing) the physical property of what is signified (length). The older subjects more often represent distance by more conventional means such that, for example, a drawing involving convergence is deemed to indicate distance more effectively than one based on length alone.

We should also note that, among the numerous strategies used by children to represent distance which we recorded, it was necessary to be selective and retain only those criteria for which a comparison between the different ages was possible. It is none the less the case that, in addition to drawings in the form of winding paths, children find other coherent means for representing distance or at least for suggesting distance. Indeed, a strategy we observed on several occasions consisted of portraying a road, motorway or railway either as ending in a tunnel or as concealed by the summit of a hill or the top of a mountain, or even as disappearing behind a hog's back. Even though no convergence is involved in such drawings, it is not impossible to imagine that, beyond the tunnel, summit or hog's back, the road, motorway or railway continues on as far as the eye can see, shrinking into the distance. This essentially suggestive procedure appeals to the imagination of the observer to envisage the entire scene, or even to recall images of things actually experienced, such as a road completely covered by an arch of thick leaves.

Among these 'disappearance' strategies we find several cases of roads or railways which wind across mountain or forest landscapes, becoming part of and blending so well with the scenery that they disappear into the background, giving an impression of depth and large spaces. In one drawing in particular this suggestive strategy seems to have been taken to the extreme; the child had depicted only a car at the entrance to a tunnel.

Another strategy designed to indicate distance consists of marking out the road, motorway or railway in milestones or signs carrying numbered indications as, for example, 100 Km and 1000 Km, but without a connection with the size of the space depicted between each of the signs. One is led to suppose, however, that in the minds of the authors of these drawings the road does actually go a great distance. Another procedure, similar to that of the milestone markers, consists of depicting signposts along the road, motorway or railway on which one can read, for example, 'New York', 'Grand Canyon', 'London', 'Paris', various indications signifying that there is effectively a great distance to be travelled.

Regarding the effects specifically of social interaction, it is worth recalling that the originality of collective was demonstrated most clearly for children in the sixth year. Study of the development of triangular forms across the different phases of the experiment clearly indicates that there are at least two processes via which social interaction can lead to greater progress. Now it appears that these processes are not equally evident at the same age levels. For children who could be considered as intermediates (fifth year), it is in particular interaction with a child who is more advanced that can result in progress. At this age level, pairs in which a child who has not yet used a triangular form interacts with a child who has will more often end up with a triangular form than pairs in which neither child used this form during the pre-test. At this age therefore the possibility cannot be excluded that some kind of modelling effect plays an important role in the interaction. It is surely no coincidence that children in precisely this age group, in one class of the control condition, reverted to using models drawn on 'educational cards' which were at their disposal.

Among the older children by contrast, even though such a modelling effect may occur, another process is at work in the groups where none of the children had used a triangular form during the pre-test, as the partners 'invent' a triangular form during the collective task. Of course, even though these groups were homogeneous in terms of the criterion of absence of a triangular form, they could have been heterogeneous from the point of view of other criteria (for example, length, decreasing height of trees in the scenery), and these differences could have led to new coordinations.

References

Berthoud-Papandropoulou, I. 1978. An experimental study of children's ideas about language. In A. Sinclair, R. J. Jarvella and W. J. M. Levelt (eds.): *The child's conception of language*. Berlin: Springer-Verlag, pp. 55–64.

Doise, W. and Mugny, G. 1981. *Le développement social de l'intelligence*. Paris: Interéditions.

Freeman, N. H. 1980. *Strategies of representation in young children*. London: Academic Press.

Frésard, M.-D. 1981. Etude génétique de certains aspects du graphisme enfantin. *Enfance*, **34**, 301–12.

Goodnow, J. 1977. *Children's drawing*. Glasgow: Fontana/Open Books.

Luquet, G.-H. 1967. *Le dessin enfantin*. First edn. 1927. Neuchâtel: Delachaux et Niestlé.

Piaget, J. and Inhelder, B. 1948. *La représentation de l'espace chez l'enfant*. Paris: Presses Universitaires de France.

Part V
Understanding the social environment

The social environment is constituted by a set of practices and institutions each of which has its own particular principles of regulation and functioning. If the individual actively intervenes in these regulations his own actions are none the less continually regulated and structured by pre-established functions. Cognitive mastery of social scenarios is at the same time a source of social competence and of individual organization. This kind of cognitive mastery is also acquired progressively, as is demonstrated in the contribution by Arcuri and his collaborators applying the notion of social scripts, or in that by Jahoda on comprehending the functioning of social institutions. Conditions of inter-individual interaction, studied in the preceding chapter, that stimulate and activate individual development are also involved in more institutionalized social regulations which are thus at the source of individual and inter-individual cognitive regulations.

However, not all individuals enjoy the same access, either objectively or subjectively, to use of different institutions; Jahoda shows how children manifest greater or lesser mastery in explaining the principles according to which these institutions operate as a function of their membership of different socio-economic groups. In other respects, though, similar elementary principles of organization seem capable of widespread diffusion in cultures and social milieux which appear at first glance very different.

10. Some trends in structuring social knowledge. A developmental study

LUCIANO ARCURI, ROSANNA DE NEGRI TRENTIN,
REMO JOB and PAOLA SALMASO

1. Script theory and the representation of social knowledge

As the child grows, his capacity to meet the demands of his social environment increases, and this becomes apparent from his overt behaviour – that is, from his ability to interact with things and people in a more and more flexible and effective way. These increasing abilities are connected with the acquisition of a series of concepts concerning the social aspects of reality. Each event of human interaction becomes in fact an occasion to develop 'theories', interpretations and explanations of the characteristics of people, their roles and functions, and the meanings and motivations of their actions. This knowledge, which constitutes the effective social competence of a child, is organized, we suggest, into structures varying in their degree of complexity and abstraction and which, in our opinion, may be assimilated to the construct of schema (cf. Nelson, 1981).

These same assumptions underlie the theory of scripts (Schank and Abelson, 1977). Scripts are defined as conceptual representations of stereotyped event sequences or, in other words, 'concrete' schemata, with a low degree of generality, applicable to frequent and/or conventional situations.

The original concept of schema, from which script theory derives, does not make any distinction between social and non-social knowledge, in that it aims to provide a unified explanatory framework for the processes of comprehension, memory and reasoning. The understanding and interpretation of an event are always the results of the activation of a schema-like structure. For instance, a causality schema could be basic either to associate two related physical events, according to a physical system of explanation, or in representing social causality, where the events are actions performed by people, so that the system of explanation has to include notions such as intention, goal, rule and so on. The possibilities offered by the schema concept are very stimulating from a theoretical point of view. However the term 'schema' is currently used to refer to a broad class of explicative notions (such as frames, definitions, plans, etc.) and so the overgeneral terms in which this 'higher-level' construct is formulated need to be specified in relation to the particular knowledge domains investigated. Scripts embody most of the conceptual issues raised by other types of schemata, yet are simple and well-structured enough to permit more focused analysis and experimentation (cf. Abelson, 1981).

The most important feature of the representation of social episodes by scripts is that of having a structure which preserves the temporal and causal connections among the events provided for in script. The theory assumes, moreover, that the set of the actions of a script could be represented by means of both general elements (high-level nodes) and more specific elements (low-level nodes).

As regards the development of script knowledge in childhood it seems that at least two problematic issues need to be clarified. The first concerns the ways event schemata originate and develop; the second concerns the role of cognitive processes and increasing social experience in under-standing and representing routine episodes by means of scripts.

Some informal observations on these topics are presented by Schank and Abelson (1977), who examined the verbal behaviour of a 2–3 year old child concerning eating at home, in restaurants and during a flight. The verbal reports supported the hypothesis that children are able to organize their cognitions into very simple script-like structures.

Only a few systematic studies have been conducted on the role of scripts in organizing children's knowledge. Nelson (1977, 1978, 1981, cf. also McCartney and Nelson) studied scripted knowledge in kindergarten children and showed that even at this age subjects possess a mental representation of this repeated familiar experience characterized by a 'skeletal sequential structure that is called up in context and is filled in as needed with appropriate optional slot fillers and details' (McCartney and Nelson, 1981). As age and experience increase, new elements are added to the skeletal sequence, and other elements, previously isolated, are linked into a longer structure (Nelson, 1977). Finally, from the analysis of children's dialogue (Nelson and Gruendel, 1979), it emerges that to the extent that children share common stock of social scripts (i.e. knowledge of pre-conditions and outcomes of actions, etc.) their dialogues become more and more communicative. In the authors' opinion this is due to the fact that the presence of an underlying script structure can help to overcome the child's egocentrism in language and thought.

The present work approaches the problem of children's knowledge in a different way. In fact we try to study if and how the children come to know the various components a script contains. That is to say, we aim to elucidate whether a performance of subjects shows a progressive transformation from a condition of a diffuse and undifferentiated knowledge to a condition of hierarchic integration for all the aspects of the script, and not only for its temporal sequence. We expect these possible lines of development to be characterized by qualitative as well as quantitative changes: they should correspond to some degree to an increase in the child's stock of concepts, but they should also reflect the development of semantic and conceptual competence in increasing independence from the episodic aspects of experience and increasingly based on categorical organization.

2. The research

2.1. Preparation of the experimental material

In order to obtain 'free association norms' for the components of some scripts, a free generation task similar to that used by Bower, Black and Turner (1979) was administered to a group of 58 children aged 12 to 13.

On being given the title of social event each subject had to:

(a) enumerate all the actions of the situation in question;

(b) underline the most important actions enumerated in (a);

(c) specify the principal goals and roles present in the script.

Four situations were studied:

(1) eating at a restaurant;

(2) hospitalization;

(3) a visit to a fun-fair;

(4) a trip to the mountain to ski.

The first two are 'strong' structure scripts (Abelson, 1981), that is to say, scripts characterized by a relatively fixed sequence of actions both as regards the temporal connections and the structure of the episodes.

The third and fourth have, in contrast, a 'weak' structure: in fact, if we exclude the initial and final phases, the internal order of the episodes may vary, and each episode can exist in relative independence from the others.

In Table 1 the actions and the roles quoted by at least 25 per cent of the

Table 1. *Actions and roles more frequently quoted by 12 to 13 year old children in the free recall task (basic actions in italics)*

Restaurant script	Hospital script

Actions

Restaurant script	Hospital script
Making an arrangement with your friends	Feeling unwell
Choosing a restaurant	Being examined at home
Meeting again outside the restaurant	Telephoning the hospital
Entering	*Going in*
Finding a table	Going into your room
Sitting down	*Undressing and going to bed*
Choosing the menu	*Being examined*
Ordering	Taking medicine
Waiting	Being operated on
Eating	Waiting for a visit
Speaking	Returning home
Joking	
Going for a walk	
Asking for the bill	
Paying	
Leaving	
Returning home	

Roles

Restaurant script	Hospital script
Waiter	Doctor
Cook	Nurse
Cashier	Ambulance driver
	Head doctor

Fun-fair script	Mountain script

Actions

Fun-fair script	Mountain script
Making an arrangement with your friends	Paying the organizer
Asking for some money	Waking up in the morning
Leaving home	Dressing for the skiing
Catching the bus	*Catching a bus or going by car*
Meeting your friends	Arriving at the meeting place
Going in	Getting on the coach
Watching the roundabout	Leaving
Choosing the roundabout	*Arriving in the mountains*
Buying the ticket	Arriving in the hotel
Getting on the roundabout	Going up to your room
Getting off	Renting equipment
Getting on again	Going to the ski-slope
Eating	Fixing the ski to your ski-boots
Walking	Queuing for the ski-lift
Speaking	Going up on the ski-lift
Returning home	*Skiing down*
Getting off the bus	Skiing with the instructor
Telling Mum	*Eating*
	Returning the equipment
	Getting on the coach again
	Returning home
	Returning to your hotel

Table 1. *contd.*

	Roles
Cashier	Ski instructor
Cake seller	Ski-lift operator
Roundabout man	Coach driver
	Hirer of equipment
	Chalet-owner

subjects are reported. From these normative data we selected the experimental material. In fact, using the criterion of average frequency of quotation and the judgement of importance the subjects supplied, we specified the episodes constituting the scripts and their basic actions. In addition, on the basis of the obtained frequency of quotation we distinguished central and peripheral roles for each script.

2.2. Experimental investigation

Phases of the research. The subjects took part in the following four tests: knowledge and evaluation of the roles; attribution of functions; a completion task, and a recognition task.

Subjects. Ninety-six subjects participated in the research. They were divided into three groups according to their age. The first group was composed of 32 Ss from 6 to 7; the second of 32 Ss from 9 to 10; the third of 32 Ss from 13 to 14. Each group was in its turn subdivided into four subgroups of the same number. The subjects of each group performed all the series of tests concerning a script up to the completion task; the recognition task, in contrast, concerned a different script.

1st test: knowledge and evaluation of the roles
Eight different roles regarding each script were presented to the subjects. They were printed on distinct cards. Two roles among the eight were central roles. They were the most mentioned roles in free recall task; the others, the peripheral, corresponded to the less frequently cited roles in the free-generation task; since in some cases these roles did not reach the number of six the authors added the necessary roles. The subject had to choose the 'four roles he thought most important within the given activity'; afterwards, he had to arrange the chosen roles in order of importance. (Examples of the roles used are given in the Appendix.)

Results. For each of the eight roles in the four scripts a score was calculated by multiplying the average of the evaluations of importance, varying from 1 to 4, by the frequency of quotation. Table 2 shows the weighted average scores for the central and peripheral roles, calculated for the three age levels and the two kinds of script. As the data show, in the case of strong-structure script as age increases, and particularly moving from the 2nd to the 3rd level, the difference between the two kinds of roles increases. In the weak-structure scripts, on the contrary, this difference, already small, remains on the whole the same as age increases. A more detailed inspection, moreover, reveals that in choosing the roles the script contains the range of choice narrows as age increases. That is to say, children at 1st age level tend to scatter their choice on all the roles, while at the 3rd level the same few roles are chosen by the majority of children. Finally, we observe an important difference between the 1st and 3rd age level in the evaluation of the importance of some roles. So, the peripheral roles 'owner' (restaurant script) and 'head physician' (hospital script) receive low evaluative scores by 6 and 7 year old children but very high scores by the older ones. This indicates that older children take into account some social rules connected with the dimension of power.

2nd test: attribution of functions
Two central roles and two peripheral roles were chosen to verify the knowledge of the functions associated with them. For each role two functions were prepared. The first one was general and synthesized the activity performed by the role (e.g. prepares the food); the other was a specific function concerning single actions the role was likely to perform (e.g. fries the chips).

The eight functions were displayed together to the subject and then the roles were presented one at a time with the request to choose, for each role, the two most appropriate functions. After each choice all functions were presented again and the subject was told that he could re-employ functions already chosen for a previously presented role.

Results. Table 3 shows the percentages of correct responses for age level and kind of role. The most notable finding is the progressive decrease in mistaken attributions as age increases, while important differences between central and peripheral roles or kind of script do not appear. A note of caution in deriving general conclusions is in order here, however. When collecting the data, in fact, we realized that the linguistic formulation of the functions prescribed for some roles tended, in some cases, to make the subjects' task easier, while in others it caused mistaken

Table 2. *Weighted average scores for central and peripheral roles in the* strong- *and* weak-*structure scripts at the three age levels.*

| | Strong structure | | Weak structure | |
	Central	Peripheral	Central	Peripheral
Level 1	16.01	8.01	12.50	8.92
Level 2	16.00	8.01	11.00	9.84
Level 3	20.00	6.67	10.76	9.75

Table 3. *Percentages of correct attribution of functions to the central and peripheral roles in the four scripts at the three age levels*

	Central	Peripheral
Level 1	64.06	58.59
Level 2	78.13	85.16
Level 3	96.09	97.66

attribution; thus, in the 'hospitalization' script there was the function 'to nurse the sick' which was attributed indifferently either to the doctor or the nurse, while it was prescribed as a function pertaining to the latter.

3rd test: passage completion task
In this phase the knowledge of the structure of the scripts was ascertained in a spontaneous production task. For each script a passage was prepared, composed of an introductory sentence, four intermediate episodes and a final sentence. Care was taken to express the four intermediate nodes using actions at the level of superordinate nodes. In one version of the passage nodes 1 and 3 were missing, while in the other version nodes 2 and 4 were missing. Each subject was presented with only one version and was asked to complete the missing parts upon reading it.

Results. The responses of the subjects were scored from 0 to 2 following this criterion: 0 was scored when a child did not answer or, instead of completing the missing episode, he paraphrased all or part of the text of an episode before or after the missing part (e.g. 'they all go to the restaurant': see Appendix, Completion task, Version 1).

Table 4. *Frequencies of 0, 1, 2 scores in the completion test for the four scripts at the three age levels*

	Scores		
	0	1	2
Level 1	42	17	4
Level 2	23	22	19
Level 3	8	17	39

One was scored when the child completed the script only in part, by mentioning a low-level action from the missing episode (e.g. 'They wait for the waiter': see Appendix, Completion task, Version 1).

Two was scored when the child completed the script correctly, mentioning the superordinate node appropriate to the missing episode (e.g. 'They order the "pasta" and the steaks': see Appendix, Completion task, Version 1).

The data inserted in a 3×3 contingency table (score and age level) were submitted to a χ^2 test and the differences were statistically significant ($p = <0.001$; 4 d.f.). Examining the trend of the scores (see Table 4) a remarkable increase can be observed from the 1st to the 3rd age level both for the strong-structure scripts and for the weak-structure scripts; moreover, the total number of maximum scores is considerably higher for the first kind of script than for the second (36 vs. 26). In conformity with this result a decrease in the 0 scores can be observed as age increases; 1 scores are constant for the three age levels, while they are more frequent in the weak-structure scripts (31 vs. 25). It is worth observing further that for the 1st age level there is a high number of mistakes or non-responses (42 vs. 21) that can be attributed to the non-reversible character of the child's thinking; we explain in this way the frequency with which children of the 1st age level complete the passage by summarizing the sentences following the missing part. Finally, we think that these data permit us to distinguish two phases of ability in the completion task. In the first children know the temporal sequence of the script, but produce only elementary actions; in the second, on the other hand, they succeed in integrating the meanings of the basic actions and in inferring from them the corresponding superordinate node.

Table 5. *Frequencies of congruent and incongruent recognitions at the three age levels*

	Congruent		Incongruent	
	General	Specific	General	Specific
Level 1	28	20	10	6
Level 2	44	15	3	2
Level 3	56	2	3	3

4th test: recognition task

This test aimed at verifying the congruence and the degree of generalization of the subjects in synthesizing the meaning of the presented episodes. In this test too four passages with the following structure were prepared: introductory sentence, four intermediate episodes, final sentence. Each episode was described by listing all the basic actions within it. Four kinds of sentences were prepared to sum up each episode: (1) general congruent; (2) specific congruent; (3) general incongruent; (4) specific incongruent. For the congruent–incongruent parameter the summarizing sentences contained actions suitable or unsuitable for the meaning of each episode, while the generality– specificity parameter referred to the degree of generality of the actions employed to summarize the episode. Thus sentences 1 and 2 contained actions of different degree of generality, but consistent with the meaning of the episode and they differed from sentences 3 and 4 because these, with a different degree of generality, contained actions which were most consistent with the meaning of the episode. Each subject read two episodes in a script and for each episode he chose among the four proposed sentences that summarized the episode in the best way.

Results. Table 5 shows the frequencies of kind of response for age level. As can be seen, older children preferably use high-level nodes, i.e. general congruent sentences, to meet the task requirements, while younger children do this to a lesser extent. Incongruent sentences, which are chosen very few times, tend to be chosen more frequently by younger children. The graph in Figure 1 shows the relationship between general congruents and specific congruents in the three age levels, while the graph in Figure 2 shows the relationship between congruents and incongruents. Regarding the latter, there is a clear difference between the 1st age level and the other two. The graph of the relationship between general congruents and specific congruents shows an increase as the age

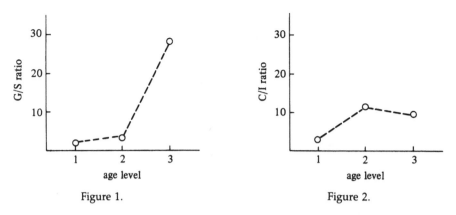

Figure 1.   Figure 2.

level increases; this increase is small between levels 1 and 2 while it is large between levels 2 and 3.

3. Conclusion

By and large, these findings show a developmental trend in the structuring of social knowledge, since only 13 year old children exhibit a performance adequate at the different levels of abstraction the script requires (cf. Graesser, 1978, 1981).

The incomplete reconstruction of the event chain given by 7 year old subjects seems to suggest a different picture of children's script knowledge from that proposed by Nelson (1977, 1978). She in fact found that even 3 year old children are able to verbally produce and to act out the basic elements of the script's structure. However, a direct comparison between the two studies seems inappropriate, not only because of the different experimental task required from the subjects, but mainly because Nelson's studies focused on the temporal sequence of scripted events, while we investigated the knowledge of the various components of the script and the interrelations among them. It is plausible to suppose that only this more 'articulated' knowledge shows a strong developmental trend.

Our results, instead, agree very well with those reported by De Negri and Salmaso (1981). In their study, children of different age levels were presented with a set of 12 drawings depicting which were high-level, low-level or atypical with respect to a given script, and were required to choose and order the 6 drawings that better described the entire script: younger children had some knowledge of the temporal structure of the script but used high-level nodes to describe it less frequently.

A last issue we would like to touch upon is the contribution of cognitive processes *sensu stricto* and the role of social experience in utilizing scripted knowledge. As emerges from the recognition task – where congruent sentences are compared with incongruent sentences, and general sentences with specific ones – even at the 2nd age level congruent sentences are chosen very frequently. In contrast, it is only at the 3rd age level that we obtain a large increase for the general sentences with respect to specific. In our opinion this difference between the congruent vs. incongruent on the one hand and the general vs. specific on the other can be explained on the assumption that this task demands both a cognitive component of a general character and specific social knowledge; the first is important in the comparison between general and specific, and therefore one obtains a relatively greater number of correct responses only when subjects have reached the logical-formal stage of thought. Social knowledge seems, on the other hand, mostly responsible for the choice between congruent and incongruent sentences, given that the judgements of incongruence, i.e. judgements about 'normality' or 'legitimacy' of behaviour are based above all on the proper acquisition of the rules of social interaction.

Appendix

Script: Eating at a restaurant

Roles	*Functions*
Cook	Prepares the food.
	Fries the chips.
Waiter	Serves at the table.
	Brings the menu.
Barman	Prepares the drinks.
	Gives the ice-creams.
Dish-washer	Keeps the kitchen clean.
	Polishes the saucepans.

Owner
Cashier
Door-keeper
Car-park attendant

Completion task

Version 1
John's family has decided to go and eat in a restaurant. They take their car and when they arrive in front of the place they have chosen they park it; they go in and sit down at a table.

. . . .

The waiter brings them the 'pasta' and everybody begins to eat. When they have finished, the waiter returns with meat and vegetables.

. . . .

John and his family go out of the restaurant and the waiter says goodbye to them.

Version 2
John's family has decided to go and eat in a restaurant.

. . . .

The waiter brings them the menu; mummy reads it and everybody chooses the food he wants to eat.

. . . .

After having drunk their coffee John's parents ask for the bill and then they pay. John and his family go out of the restaurant and the waiter says goodbye to them.

Recognition task

Version 1
John's family has decided to go and eat in a restaurant. Mom and Dad agree on the place where they want to go. Dad takes the car, they get in and they set off. When they have arrived they get out and Dad parks the car in the place the car-park attendant has shown him. When they go into the place the waiter meets them and shows them some free tables.

Summarizing sentences:
1. John's family goes to a restaurant (general congruent).
2. John's family leaves home (specific congruent).

3. John's family has a trip in the car (general incongruent).
4. John's family catches the bus (specific incongruent).

The parents choose a table and as soon as they are seated the waiter brings them the menu. Mom reads the menu and everybody chooses what he wants to eat. The waiter takes note of what they have chosen and goes away. The children go and wash their hands and then they come back to the table and they begin to eat 'grissini' and to look around.

Summarizing sentences:
1. John's family give their orders to the waiter (general congruent).
2. John opens the packet of 'grissini' (specific congruent).
3. John's family goes and buys some food (general incongruent).
4. Mom buys the lottery tickets from the waiter (specific incongruent).

Version 2
At last the waiter arrives with the 'pasta', they all put on their napkins, take their forks and begin to eat. When they have finished the waiter takes the dirty plates and carries them to the kitchen and returns with the meat and vegetables. After that they all take their knives and forks and cut the meat. The waiter returns, changes the plates and puts a cake on the table.

Summarizing sentences:
1. John eats his lunch (general congruent).
2. John cuts his meat with his knife (specific congruent).
3. John has a picnic (general incongruent).
4. John eats a sandwich (specific incongruent).

After drinking his coffee, Dad asks the waiter for the bill; the waiter goes to the cashier for the bill and Dad gives the waiter the money. The waiter returns with the change and Dad leaves a tip. John's family gets up, leaves the restaurant and goes home.

Summarizing sentences:
1. John's father pays the bill (general congruent).
2. John's father takes money from his wallet (specific congruent).
3. John's father lends some money to the waiter (general incongruent).
4. John loses the restaurant bill (specific incongruent).

References

Abelson, P. R. 1981. The psychological status of the script concept. *American Psychologist*, **36**, 715–29.

Bower, G. H., Black, I. and Turner, T. 1979. Scripts in test comprehension and memory. *Cognitive Psychology*, **11**, 177–220.

De Negri Trentin, R. and Salmaso, P. 1981. Social knowledge development: A script theory approach. Paper presented at the General Meeting of the European Association of Experimental Social Psychology, Sussex University (Brighton), April. Technical Report No. 53, University of Padua.

Graesser, A. C. 1978. How to catch a fish: The representation and memory of common procedures. *Discourse Processes*, **1**, 72–89.

Graesser, A. C. 1981. *Prose comprehension beyond the world*. New York: Springer-Verlag.

Graesser, A. C., Gordon, S. E. and Sawyer, J. D. 1979. Recognition memory for typical and atypical actions in scripted activities: Test of a script pointer plus tag hypothesis. *Journal of Verbal Learning and Verbal Behavior*, **18**, 319–32.

Graesser, A. C., Wall, S. B., Kowalski, D. J. and Smith, D. A. 1980. Memory for typical and atypical actions in scripted activities. *Journal of Experimental Psychology: Human Learning and Memory*, **6**, 503–15.

McCartney, K. A. and Nelson, K. 1981. Children's use of scripts story recall. *Discourse Processes*, **4**, 59–70.

Nelson, K. 1977. Cognitive development and the acquisition of concepts. In R. C. Anderson, R. J. Spiro and W. E. Montague (eds.): *Schooling and the acquisition of knowledge*. Hillsdale, NJ: Lawrence Erlbaum Associates.

Nelson, K. 1978. How children represent knowledge of their world in and out of language: A preliminary report. In R. S. Siegler (ed.): *Children's thinking: What develops?* Hillsdale, NJ: Lawrence Erlbaum Associates.

Nelson, K. 1981. Social cognition in a script framework. In G. H. Flavell and L. Ross (eds.): *Social cognitive development*. Cambridge University Press.

Nelson, K. and Gruendel, J. M. 1979. At morning it's lunchtime: A scriptal view of children's dialogues. *Discourse Processes*, **2**, 73–94.

Schank, R. C. and Abelson, R. P. 1977. *Scripts, plans, goals, and understanding*. Hillsdale, NJ: Lawrence Erlbaum Associates.

11. Levels of social and logico-mathematical thinking: their nature and inter-relations

GUSTAV JAHODA

1. Introduction

Studies of formal operational thinking have overwhelmingly followed the pattern originally set out by Inhelder and Piaget (1958) and confined themselves to logico-mathematical problems (Neimark, 1979). The only major exception is the work on moral reasoning, which has sometimes examined the links between the attainment of formal operations in logical reasoning and moral judgement (Lee, 1971; Kuhn *et al.*, 1977). There has been little concern with 'social thinking' in the sense of the development of ideas about the socio-economic structure of society. One notable exception has been the study by Jurd (1978) of children's understanding of historical processes. This author devised historical problems, administered in the form of a group test, that were structurally analogous to the logico-mathematical tasks usually employed in assessing formal operations. In order to be able to achieve this, pseudo-historical information had to be supplied and the task of the subjects was that of drawing appropriate inferences. On the basis of the findings Jurd claimed that they substantially conformed to the Piagetian stages.

The present author's interest focuses on the development of social thinking, especially within the economic sphere, outwith the conventional school subjects. The question posed is how children, utilizing the information available to them in their social environment, gradually construct increasingly realistic 'working models' of economic relationships. Unlike Jurd, therefore, no information is supplied in an attempt to elicit modes of reasoning characteristic of stages established within the logico-mathematical sphere; instead, children are expected to draw upon their own resources in solving problems. This means that it is not usually possible to label children's responses in terms of Piagetian 'stages'. There are reasons, discussed in some detail by Furth (1980), for believing that 'the distinction between concrete and formal operations [cannot] be easily transferred to other areas than the concrete physical world' (p. 86). This does of course not prevent the seeking of broad correspondences between the types of thinking displayed in relation to the physical and social worlds. Certainly the present study is intended to explore what might be loosely called 'formal thinking' in the socio-economic sphere. Within it, a distinction can be made between the understanding of clear-cut economic *systems* requiring the grasp of certain principles not unlike those necessary for understanding the physical world, and the unravelling of the complex aspects of socio-economic life which goes well beyond the relatively simple functioning of any particular sub-system.

The first, 'system', aspect was investigated in relation to the operations of shops and banks respectively. The second involved questions about the probable consequences of abolishing advertising and closing all schools permanently. These latter tasks require the consideration of 'theoretical or ideal possibility' regarded by Piaget as 'the most distinctive feature of formal thought' (Inhelder and Piaget, 1958, p. 245).

Another issue of concern was the relationship between each of these two types of social thinking and logico-mathematical reasoning. For this purpose two tasks were included, one dealing with correlation and the other with permutations.

2. Method

2.1. Samples

A total of 96 children was obtained from two different types of school. One was a fee-paying school for all ages, parents being uniformly in middle class (MC) occupations. The other two schools were located in a working class (WC) housing estate, one being a primary school serving as a feeder to the secondary school. Within each type of school 8 boys and 8 girls were drawn randomly from primary class 7 (P7), secondary 2 (S2) and secondary 4 (S4); mean ages were respectively 11 years 7 months; 13 years 10 months and 15 years 10 months. Since no significant sex differences were encountered, no further reference will be made to this variable.

2.2. Procedures

Each child was individually tested by one of two female research assistants, allocation being by odd and even code numbers so that each worked with a random half of subjects within each school. All responses, and prompts where applicable, were noted in full detail. The sessions, held in a quiet room, lasted on average 30–40 minutes. The sequence of administration was: shop, advertisements, bank, correlation, schools and permutations. Specific details of administration will be provided in the appropriate sections.

The treatment of the data relating to correlations and permutations was straightforward, merely following established methods. With regard to 'shop' and 'bank' the problems were, on the basis of preliminary work, structured so as to yield a set of pre-determined categories so that coding presented no difficulty. The remaining two themes were somewhat different, being entirely open-ended. In the case of the 'schools' theme an *a priori* conceptual analysis yielded a set of provisional categories, which required only slight modification in the light of the material obtained. On the other hand the 'advertising' theme proved more complicated: not only could no response categories be determined in advance, but even the pilot study provided only tentative cues about likely categories. An exhaustive content analysis of the responses obtained in the main study therefore had to be carried out, on the basis of which categories were created.

Issues of coding arose in connection with the verbal description of the strategy used in permutations, and both the 'schools' and 'advertisements' themes. All these were first independently coded by the research assistants, any discrepancies being resolved through discussion in which the writer took part.

In view of the categorical nature of most of the data and the departure from normality in some of the distributions, non-parametric measures were used in the treatment of the data, concentrating on age trends and social class differences. However, as will be explained later, a parametric analysis was subsequently done to check on the patterns of relationships obtained.

3. Results: I. Individual tasks

3.1. The functioning of economic systems: the shop and bank

The question at issue is the degree of understanding of certain principles underlying the working of economic institutions. In the case of the shop this is very elementary, but the bank requires a considerable level of conceptual sophistication that is only gradually achieved by some. For details of procedures and findings the reader must be referred to the full report of the study (Jahoda, 1981).

3.2. Hypothetical thinking: advertisements abolished and schools closed

Unlike the previous tasks concerned with existing institutions, these were designed to elicit open-ended thinking about hypothetical situations. Subjects were given the opportunity of bringing to bear whatever knowledge was at their disposal on anticipating probable effects of far-reaching changes in socio-economic institutions. The problem of the effects of eliminating advertising was selected because pilot work had shown that it reveals the level of thinking about aspects of economic processes, especially the determinants of prices, without triggering off learned (but not necessarily understood) formulae, which more conventional questions are liable to do. Similarly, the purpose of the 'schools closed' problem was to assess the extent to which subjects would be able to think through the consequences of the removal of one of the keystones of modern industrial society. In order to be able to do this, one has to have a grasp of the interconnections between various social and economic institutions, and the task was designed as a measure of such a grasp.

Beginning with 'advertisements', children were invited to suppose that a law were passed to stop all kinds, so that there would be no more advertisements in the newspapers, on the streets or on television. How did they think this would affect prices in the shops? Specifically, they were asked to consider whether they would become dearer, cheaper, or stay the same; unless a spontaneous justification was offered, subjects were requested to explain the reasons for their answer. A neutral prompt was occasionally used, mainly for clarification.

A coding scheme was devised distinguishing three levels of thinking about prices:
 (a) Naive ideas about prices;
 (b) arguments for chosen alternative showing some understanding of the factor(s) influencing prices;
 (c) awareness of complexity of issues involved;
 (d) irrelevant/don't know.

These categories will now be illustrated, together with some comments on the kinds of thinking involved.

(a) The most common conception was that every commodity somehow has a certain price attached to it, though how this comes about remained obscure. This notion took two distinct forms, one being that of an intrinsic value that cannot be changed; this is implicit in the extracts below;

'If they don't stay the same it would be cheating people.' ('What do you mean?')
'Just that it would be cheating to change prices.'

'Because people wouldn't know how much things cost and the shopkeeper would
cheat them into paying more.'

'People when they go into the shops there would have to be notices up telling the
prices, and that would make things dearer.' ('How would that be') 'Because the
shopkeeper would have to pay for the notices.'

The other idea held by only a few was that advertisements inform not
merely the customer, but also the shopkeeper, what the prices are.

'If the ads went off, shopkeepers wouldn't know how much the goods were, or
how much to put them up by – so they would stay the same.'

The remaining responses consisted of on-the-spot improvisations
indicating the absence of any coherent notions, of which one example
should suffice:

'Because if people didn't know the prices and went to the shops they might not
have enough money; shopkeepers would want them happy and put prices
down.'

(b) This was the largest response category and the ideas expressed lend
themselves readily to a brief summary. Almost a third of the children said
that prices would go down because firms would no longer have to bear
the cost of advertising. The remainder, apart from a handful of unusual
but sensible answers, were about evenly divided into two groups. One
argued that, without advertisements, prices would be lowered in an
effort to encourage buying. The other, holding an explicit or implicit
notion that profit levels have to be maintained, reasoned that in order to
do so with falling sales in the absence of advertisements, prices would
have to be raised. Most appeared to share the feeling that the issue was
really fairly straightforward, if not obvious.

(c) The small minority in this category reacted in precisely the opposite
manner, evidently being conscious that the issue was complex and that
they had to struggle with uncertainty. This will be illustrated with a
protocol wherein some of the arguments just described were understood
to be jointly applicable.

'A lot of products would probably disappear, but the ones that remain would
probably be a little cheaper – not very much. A lot of companies spend a lot of
money on advertising, so they could reduce prices; but a lot of firms rely so much
on advertising that their sales figures could go down and prices might go up.'

(d) These consisted of either irrelevant answers (e.g. 'They put prices
up nearly every day anyway!'), or simply 'don't knows'.

Table 1.

(a) 'Advertisements abolished' – distribution of response
    categories by age

Categories	Age groups			
	P7	S2	S4	All ages
a	15	11	3	29
b	8	16	22	46
c	1	–	4	5
d	8	5	3	16
	32	32	32	96

Note: Combining (a+d) and (b+c), χ^2 = 18.32; df = 2; p <0.001.

(b) 'Advertisements abolished' – distribution of response
    categories by social class

Categories	Middle	Working
a +d	15	30
b + c	33	18
	48	48

Note: χ^2 (corrected) = 8.20; df = 1; p <0.01.

The concordance rate among coders was 82 per cent, and detailed results are shown in Table 1. It is evident the age trend is from naive to oversimplified ideas, very few getting beyond that – though one of the youngest subjects did! There was also a significant social class difference in levels of thinking in this sphere.

For the 'schools' task children were told to imagine that after the end of the year all the schools would be closed and remain closed permanently, so that one would no longer get any education: what did they think would happen to the country if this were done? If objections were raised, e.g. parents protesting, it was explained that they were just to suppose it could be done, and think about what it would do to the country.

One difficult issue concerned the use of prompts, which might have a potentially great influence on responses. It was decided to confine these to two alternatives: first, where the effects on the country had been spontaneously mentioned and the child came to a stop, the interviewer would ask neutrally, 'Anything else?'; when there had been no such spontaneous reference, some appropriately phrased question about the effects on the country was asked.

A coding scheme was devised with the above purpose in mind, yielding five categories:

(a) no socio-economic consequences mentioned;
(b) some relatively isolated consequences;
(c) connected chain(s) of consequences, but short of envisaging general breakdown;
(d) connected chains of consequences leading to general breakdown;
(e) other.

It will be appreciated that the coding entailed a great deal of tricky subjective judgment, and in view of this the inter-rater agreement of 74 per cent seems quite acceptable; with two exceptions disagreements related to adjacent categories. Examples of typical answers will now be given, with prompts in brackets.

(a) 'People wouldn't be able to talk right or spell right. . .' ('Is there anything that might happen to the country?') 'If you went into a shop to buy rolls and that, and you got the change, you wouldn't know how much it would be. If you went to church and you were going to sing a hymn, you wouldn't be able to read the words.'

(b) 'If there were no education kids wouldn't have jobs in hospitals or anything like that where you need 0-levels and Highers; they wouldn't be able to get proper jobs where you need education.' ('What about the country, what would happen to it?') 'Youngsters would be just running around the streets getting into trouble.'

'Amount of people who were jobless would go up by millions. . . For every job nowadays you need a good education and if you don't have that education you're not going to get anywhere. . .' ('Anything else happen in the country?') 'There would be more vandalism . . . there would be pounds and pounds given out on the dole [i.e. unemployment benefit].'

(c) 'Unemployment would go up – employers would be looking for educated people and if there weren't any they wouldn't really want them. . .' ('Anything else?') 'The firms that needed educated people would probably have to close down and the country would come to a standstill; the standard of living would go down.'

'Parents would start teaching their children themselves they would grow up with possibly a rough idea of English and maths but not much knowledge of science – no science degrees, computers and all that. . .' ('How would it affect the country?') 'Industry would go down; technology would stop advancing; we would probably lose all the markets we had.'

(d) 'The whole economic system would collapse – a slow decline until about sixty years from now when there would be only very few skilled and trained people left alive. No more food, no more trade, industries closing down through lack of skilled labour. Farming would probably be the only thing that could continue, but on a very primitive basis – or fishing on a simple basis

Table 2.

(a) 'Schools closed' – distribution of response categories by age

Categories	Age groups			All ages
	P7	S2	S4	
a	10	8	4	22
b	12	12	11	35
c	6	7	8	21
d	–	5	8	13
e	4	–	1	5
	32	32	32	96

Note: Combining (a + e) and (c + d); $\chi^2 = 9.19$; df = 4; p = 0.056.

(b) 'Schools closed' – distribution of response categories by social class

Categories	Middle	Working
a + e	9	18
b	16	19
c + d	23	11
	48	48

Note: Rank-Sum Test Z = 2.57; p = 0.0051 (one-tailed).

using sailing boats and simple nets. There would be decrease in population – without modern agricultural techniques and fertilizers land wouldn't be able to produce enough food for everybody and people would starve.'

(e) 'Some people might leave it and go to other places to get schools.' ('What about people in this country, what would happen there?') 'They would have wee places where you could learn.'

The distribution of types of responses is shown in Table 2. Almost two-thirds of the subjects were unable to get beyond category (b), i.e. listing relatively isolated consequences; in fact the bunching within this category was evenly spread across all age groups, with the result that the age trend fell just short of significance in spite of the fact that a clear age progression is discernible among the other categories. The social class difference, on the other hand, was significant.

3.3. Piaget formal-operations tasks: correlation and permutations

Both types of tasks largely followed procedures described by Neimark (1970, 1975). The correlation task consisted of a deck of 12 cards showing a set of combinations of sick (S) and healthy (H) faces coupled with the presence (P) or absence (A) of germs in the following pattern: 4(H+A), 4(S + P), 2(H + P) and 2(S + A). Scoring was based on the subjects' manner of sorting through the deck (0–3), and their ability to select cards proving either that the germs do cause the sickness (0 or 1) or that the germs are unrelated to the sickness (0–2). Full details are available in Neimark (1970, p. 226); the meaning of some of Neimark's scores, i.e. 0+ and 0−, is obscure and such fine distinctions were omitted.

The correlation task is of course a very difficult one and on the basis of Neimark's findings one would not have expected even the older subjects to have fully mastered the concept of correlation. None the less it had been hoped that the various levels of approach to the task would be usefully discriminating. Results in Table 3 indicate that the outcome fell short of expectations. Subjects performed more poorly than Neimark's, about half scoring zero. A slight but significant age trend is visible, and there was no significant social class difference.

The permutations task (Neimark, 1975) was much more satisfactory, being readily understood by the children. They were asked how many different phone numbers they could think of, using the first four digits exactly once; they were encouraged to follow a plan, and then had to write down the numbers. When they had finished, they were asked to explain what their plan had been.

Three separate measures were obtained, the first one being a categorization of the children's account of their strategy: (a) no plan whatsoever ('none'); (b) description of some procedure, with no hint of understanding of systematic permutation ('some'); (c) a clear plan referring, at least by implication, to permutations. Examples are given below:

(a) 'I just mixed them up.'
(b) 'I just changed the numbers about and when I got to the end I made sure that I had the same numbers of 1s, 2s, 3s and 4s.'
(c) 'First of all 1, 2, 3, 4, then I used the numbers beginning with 12, 13, 14 and re-arranged the last two numbers; then began with 21, 23, 24 and re-arranged the last two numbers, and so on.'

Inter-rater agreement was 76 per cent, with the bulk of disagreement relating to the borderline between (a) and (b).

Table 3.

(a) 'Correlations' – distribution of responses by age

Scores	Age groups			
	P7	S2	S4	All ages
0	18	17	12	47
1	10	5	5	20
2	4	6	10	20
3	–	4	5	9
	32	32	32	96

Note: Combining scores 2 and 3, $\chi^2 = 10.10$; df = 4; p <0.05.

(b) 'Correlations' – distribution of responses by social class

Scores	Middle	Working
0	21	26
1–3	27	22
	48	48

Note: χ^2 (corrected) = 0.67; df = 1; n.s.

The second measure was simply the number of different permutations produced, and the third an index constructed by Leskow and Smock (1970) who called it 'initial marks held constant' (IMC). This is a convenient process score 'based on a frequency count of items held constant from one trial to the next in the first position, and in the second *only* when the first was also held constant' (p. 416). It may thus be regarded as a measure of the structural regularity of responses. Both number of permutations and IMC are of course entirely objective and would be suitable for parametric analysis. However, since the bulk of the data did not easily lend itself to that, the two measures were also cast into a categorical format.

Results are presented in Table 4 showing that all three measures exhibited highly significant age trends, and there were also significant social class differences.

4. Results: II. Inter-relations

The aim of this part of the work was to examine the relationship between traditional Piagetian formal operations tasks and those involving 'social

Table 4. *Permutations by age and social class*
(a) *Verbal plans*

	Age groups						Middle	Working
	P7	S2	S4	All ages				
None	14	5	3	22		None	3	19
Some	15	10	12	37		Some	22	15
Full	3	17	17	37		Full	23	14
	32	32	32	96			48	48

Note: $\chi^2 = 20.99$; df = 4; p < 0.001.   Rank-Sum Test Z = 3.16;
p = 0.0008 (one-tailed).

(b) *Number of permutations*

	Age groups						Middle	Working
	P7	S2	S4	All ages				
−13	15	5	6	26		−13	6	20
14–18	13	14	9	36		14–18	21	15
19+	4	13	17	34		19+	21	13
	32	32	32	96			48	48

Note: $\chi^2 = 15.99$; df = 4; p <0.01.   Rank-Sum Test Z = 2.65;
p = 0.004 (one-tailed).

(c) *Initial marks constant (IMC)*

	Age groups						Middle	Working
	P7	S2	S4	All ages				
0–2	17	5	10	32		0–2	12	20
3–11	12	16	7	35		3–11	17	18
12+	3	11	15	29		12+	19	10
	32	32	32	96			48	48

Note: $\chi^2 = 18.02$; df = 4; p <0.01   Rank-Sum Test Z = 2.04;
p = 0.021 (one-tailed).

thinking'. In view of the categorical nature of the 'social thinking' data it seemed appropriate to use Kendall's tau_b as the measure of association, and quantitative results of the other tasks were cast into the same format. It should be pointed out that tau_b is a rather conservative measure, which usually yields considerably more modest values than the corresponding product-moment coefficients of correlation normally employed. The overall matrices are presented in Table 5.

Table 5. *Matrices of tau$_b$* correlations (below the diagonal age is partialled out)

	2	3	4	5	6	7	8	9
1. Age	.59***	.36**	.46***	.27	.14	.39**	.35*	.28
2. Bank	X	.39**	.48***	.35*	.13	.42**	.31*	.29*
3. Shop	.23	X	.30*	.24	.19	.23	.22	.22
4. Adverts	.29	.16	X	.28	.12	.38**	.26	.24
5. Schools	.24	.16	.18	X	.11	.27	.27	.29*
6. Correlation	.06	.15	.07	.08	X	.33*	.20	.12
7. Perms. plan	.26	.11	.25	.18	.30	X	.56***	.59***
8. No of Perms.	.14	.11	.12	.20	.16	.50	X	.64***
9. IMC	.16	.13	.13	.23	.08	.54	.61	X

Note: * = p <0.05; ** = p <0.01; *** = p <0.001.
There is as yet no method for testing the significance of partial tau$_b$.

The top right half of the matrix, above the diagonal, gives values that are of course inflated by the effect of age. It is readily apparent that the most powerful associations link the three separate sub-tasks of permutations, which is of course not surprising. Some of the several measures of social thinking also show substantial associations; but the matrix at the bottom left below the diagonal, adjusted for age, indicates that the age factor seems to be relatively more important in mediating relationships among social thinking as compared with the permutation tasks.

In order to bring out the underlying structure more clearly, McQuitty's (1961) elementary linkage analysis was applied to the adjusted matrix. The outcome is shown in Figure 1(a), but before commenting on this an additional explanation is required. Some concern was felt that the structure emerging might, to an unknown extent, be a reflection of the characteristics of tau$_b$. Hence the entire set of computations was repeated, assigning arbitrary scores to the social thinking categories. There are of course technical objections to this, inasmuch as some of the distributions departed considerably from normality and thereby rendered the use of the product-moment correlation coefficient questionable. None the less, it was applied in order to provide a check on the tau$_b$ analysis. As may be seen from Figure 1(b), the result was reassuring. Both methods yielded a first cluster centred on permutations, to which 'correlation' is attached – in other words Cluster I consists of the traditional Piagetian formal operations tasks.

Cluster II comprises in both cases the social thinking tasks, but the internal structure is somewhat divergent. Although the 'bank' is central to both clusters, it is paired with 'advertisements' and 'shop' respectively;

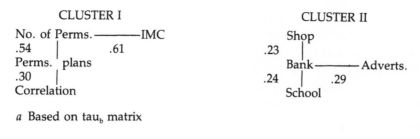

a Based on tau$_b$ matrix

b Based on product-moment matrix

Figure 1. Cluster analyses of matrices with age partialled out

and in the product-moment cluster the 'advertisement' task is in fact the most peripheral. Naturally there is no means of deciding on the basis of the available data which, if any, is the 'real' structure. The main point is that the two clusters are on the whole congruent and make good sense.

The emergence of two distinct clusters should, however, not be interpreted as a sharp disjunction between the two sets of tasks. If one scans the matrix in Table 5 it will be apparent that some of the social thinking tasks are almost as highly, and sometimes more highly, associated with the permutations tasks than they are with each other. It can therefore be at least tentatively concluded that the general processes of development involved in social thinking are not fundamentally distinct from those concerned with the logico-mathematical and scientific spheres that have been far more extensively studied.

5. Discussion

One intriguing issue is the social class differences encountered, which are not usually considered in research on formal operations. With the single exception of the rather elementary question of shop profit, middle class subjects reached a higher level than working class ones. As regards social thinking, one obvious interpretation that suggests itself is that the working class children grow up in a less rich information environment – a certain minimum amount of information is clearly a necessary prerequisite for being able to come to grips with the problems. However, there is the stubborn fact that a significant middle class superiority also emerged in the permutations tasks, for which all the necessary information was available to all subjects. Thus while information deficit may have been a contributory factor, it cannot be a sufficient explanation. The general problem of social class differences in cognitive functioning is of course beyond the limited scope of the present study. (For a recent review of the general issues, see Holling and Liepmann, 1980.)

One might return briefly to the generally modest level of social thinking revealed in this work that seems to characterize mid-adolescence. This finding is highly relevant to the area of political socialization, where research has tended to concentrate on information and attitudes rather than levels of thinking (Renshon, 1977). It remains an open, yet vital, question whether a spurt in the development of social thinking occurs in late adolescence, perhaps on entry into the world of work, or whether a majority of people grow up into citizens whose grasp of the functioning of the socio-economic institutions of society remains rudimentary.

Acknowledgements

The study was in part supported by the Nuffield Foundation and data analysis and writing were done while the author was a Fellow at The Netherlands Institute for Advanced Study at Wassenaar. I am also indebted to Hans Furth for many discussions which stimulated some of the ideas embodied in the study.

References

Furth, H. G. 1980. *The world of grown-ups*. New York: Elsevier.
Holling, H. and Liepmann, D. 1980. Zum Zusammenhang zwischen gesellschaftlicher Struktur und kognitiven Leistungen. *Kölner Zeitschrift für Soziologie und Sozialpsychologie*, **32,** 484–507.
Inhelder, B. and Piaget, J. 1958. *The growth of logical thinking from childhood to adolescence*. New York: Basic Books.
Jahoda, G. 1979. The construction of economic reality by some Glaswegian children. *European Journal of Social Psychology*, **9,** 115–27.
Jahoda, G. 1981. The development of thinking about economic institutions: The bank. *Cahiers de Psychologie Cognitive*, **1,** 55–73.
Jurd, M. F. 1978. An empirical study of operational thinking in history-type material. In J. A. Keats, F. K. Collis and G. S. Halford (eds.): *Cognitive development*. Chichester: John Wiley.
Kuhn, D., Langer, J., Kohlberg, L. and Haan, N. S. 1977. The development of formal operations in logical and moral judgement. *Genetic Psychology Monographs*, **95,** 97–188.

Lee, L. C. 1971. The concomitant development of cognitive and moral modes of thought: A test of selected deductions from Piaget's theory. *Genetic Psychology Monographs*, **83**, 93–146.

Leskow, S. and Smock, C. D. 1970. Development changes in problem-solving strategies: Permutation. *Development Psychology*, **2**, 412–22.

McQuitty, L. L. 1961. Elementary linkage analysis. *Psychological Reports*, **9**, 71–8.

Neimark, E. D. 1970. A preliminary search for formal operations structures. *Journal of Genetic Psychology*, **116**, 223–32.

Neimark, E. D. 1975. Longitudinal development of formal operations thought. *Genetic Psychology Monographs*, **91**, 171–225.

Neimark, E. D. 1979. Current status of formal operations research. *Human Development*, **22**, 60–7.

Renshon, S. A. (ed.) 1977. *Handbook of political socialization*. New York: The Free Press.

Part VI
Social construction of adolescent identity

Up to the present, studies of adolescence have developed in a variety of directions. Within psychology a developmental orientation has focussed on changes in behaviour and interests and in the self-concept that arise during and after puberty. A clinical orientation, using primarily a psychoanalytic frame of reference, involves studies of cases of adolescents with frequent psychological disturbances. A criminological orientation studies gangs of delinquent boys or else the deviant behaviour of adolescent males and females generally. Finally, a sociological orientation is concerned with the specific positions which the young occupy in society and with the factors that facilitate or inhibit their social integration.

The chapters in this Part try to indicate how problems in the study of adolescence can be approached from a more unitary perspective. The important contribution by Carolyn Wood Sherif draws together a series of systematic investigations carried out in collaboration with Muzafer Sherif on adolescence in industrialized society. If the differences between urban and rural, black and white, English and Spanish speaking, and male and female adolescents have an effect on the development of the adolescent crisis it is perhaps because they correspond to different social integrations. More specifically, the manner was studied in which such differences modify the self-system, the peer group structure, and the norms that develop in these groups.

The contribution by Zaleska and Malewska-Peyre illustrates the differentiation strategies among North African immigrant adolescents, both males and females, in the culture of origin and in French culture. Although the general mechanisms may be the same they may lead to different results in boys and girls, and also in well-adjusted individuals versus 'wards of court'.

Finally, the contribution by Carugati and his collaborators takes up the theme of the development of norms within adolescent groups. Individuals emerging from a long period of institutionalization were placed in small groups in a new environment with no imposed rules where they succeeded in constructing and defining novel life styles after negotiating a painful phase of disorganization. An understanding of processes implicating the whole group provides a more adequate account of the phenomena observed than does the study of individual dynamics alone.

12. Coordinating the sociological and psychological in adolescent interactions

CAROLYN WOOD SHERIF

Individual development during the adolescent period in modern societies proceeds within social processes differentiating adolescents from children and adults, different populations of adolescents from each other, and new small groups of adolescents. The collectively endorsed values or social norms (representations) that arise among particular adolescents are simultaneously reflections of the adult world, reactions to it, and creations of individuals participating collectively in activities with considerable motivational significance to them in everyday life.

Such social differentiations and the reciprocal (though not equal) give-and-take that each implies are the medium for an individual's development as a biologically growing human person, whose conduct and outlook is 'supposed' to change toward that of an adult. The collectively endorsed values or norms frame the directions of social processes and the intentions of individuals.

At a sociological level of analysis, the adolescent period is culturally defined and differentiated, between societies and within a society. But sociological imperialism that telescopes problems of human development and individual functioning into irrelevance is short-sighted. The social-psychological processes among adolescents and in individual development then come as surprises. How are we to understand young people whose sociological location points clearly to completing high school, but who drop out of school, one by one, consulting only each other? In a Mexican-American neighborhood spelling poverty, unstable families, low education and frequent crime, what could motivate a group of boys to walk daily across the city to a high school, becoming among the few graduates in the neighborhood despite derogation from their peers? Why would high school students in Soweto demonstrate in the summer of 1976 in the face of police brutality leaving hundreds dead, thousands injured and imprisoned? (The first two cases were reported by Sherif and Sherif, 1965; the last by Geber and Newman, 1980.)

At the other pole, psychological imperialisms have reduced problems of adolescent development to the biochemistry or physiology of growth, to a freakish stage of cognitive development characterized by 'adolescent egocentrism' or its sudden transformation into 'sociocentrism' (Piaget and Weil, 1951), or to search for an 'identity' of a kind available only to upper-middle class males in a prosperous country (Erikson, 1968).

Rejecting both sociological and psychological imperialisms, the position taken in this chapter is that the role of social interactions during adolescent development can be understood only by *coordinating* concepts and data at the sociological level of analysis with those on concrete social interactions among individuals and on their psychological functioning.

On one hand, the specific social situations encountered by individuals in daily living are composed from the larger social fabric and physical environment, with their historically accrued cultural meanings and values, from social activities, and other people located within larger social structures. They cannot be reduced to a particular individual's stream of consciousness or psychic struggles, but demand study as sociological, cultural and physical structures. If social interactions among individuals in these situations are patterned, their forms and contents are not reducible to discrete stimuli impinging on the person from moment to moment.

On the other hand, an individual during the adolescent period has lived at least a decade or so, and is experienced in social interactions. Barring severe early trauma, the child has established relationships with others as a boy or a girl within a particular milieu, relationships with his or her body and its capabilities, with social objects and values. Some of these established ties must change during adolescence, away from the dependencies of early childhood toward responsibilities, activities and modes of conduct more typical of adult men and women in the society. Simultaneously, the now familiar body grows at more rapid pace, accompanied by physiological and structural changes toward an adult male or female body. To collapse these two universals of development into 'incidents' of sociological analysis is to obscure individual contributions in social interactions and their role in development.

Coordinating the sociological and psychological implies a definite sequence of study. The sequence starts with independent assessment of the actual social situations encountered by adolescents, including their larger setting, proceeds to the study of social interactions among adolescents, then studies individual functioning in relationship to those social situations and interaction processes. In this chapter, research on naturally formed groups created by adolescents outside of adult supervision is summarized, following that sequence. It was conducted in large cities in the United States, which necessarily affected the specifics of adolescents' attitudes and actions (Sherif and Sherif, 1964, 1965, 1969a, 1969b; Sherif, Kelly, Rodgers, Sarup and Tittler, 1973).

1. Social-psychological bases for changed interactions during adolescence

The formation of 'natural' groups among adolescents and their considerable impact in the lives of individual members have social-psychological bases. The changing body, with its new experiences, changes in size and shape, and heightening sexuality cannot go unnoticed by the developing individual. Others react to the changes as well. Thus, even if the social transition to adulthood were to be arranged by the logic of the 'best of all possible worlds', the developing girl or boy has to alter psychological structures formed during the first decade of life. Such structures relate the body and its capabilities to the experiences of 'me', 'I' and 'mine', with the reactions of others and with cultural templates for what a growing and a grown female or male body should be. Thus, the individual's self system is propelled toward change.

What these changes are to be is not given, either by perception of one's own body or by clear guidelines and steps in the society. To the contrary, the latter are often uncertain, conflicting, and discontinuous with those already familiar in childhood. The distinctive properties of the adolescent period in contemporary societies may confront the individual with any or all of the following circumstances:

Discontinuities. Changes, more or less sharply defined, in adult expectations from now well-established patterns in childhood. The changes at times involve marked discontinuities, particularly in areas pertaining to dependence upon adults, responsibility and sexuality, especially if childhood segregates the genders and includes no preparation for sexuality. The areas of continuity or discontinuity from childhood may differ for girls and for boys.

Ambiguity. The steps and procedures for attaining adult status, beyond a legal 'adult age', are often by no means clear, though alternative pathways are indicated according to gender. Such lack of clarity is most striking when adolescents are effectively separated from the world of work, while told that the routines of daily existence are preparation for adult work and adult roles. It is also striking when there are few jobs available to adults in one's surroundings.

Divergent perspectives. When social changes in technological, economic, political and social modes of life are rapid, the perspectives of parents, teachers and other adults based on their own experiences of adolescence will differ from those of the current generation of adolescents. As a result, guidelines or constraints offered by adults may differ so sharply from the alternatives open to the current generation that adult precepts appear unacceptable to adolescents.

Contradictions. To the extent that the social institutions encountered by the adolescent are uncoordinated, even promote contradictory values, the developing adolescent faces considerable inconsistency in adult rules and expectations in moving from one to another or within the same institution from time to time. At times, the adolescent may literally be treated as a child, while at other times as an adult.

Marginality. To the degree that the adolescent period is also prolonged, owing to continuing economic and social dependence during school years or to lack of work opportunities, the transition period becomes neither childhood nor adulthood, leaving the adolescent betwixt and between. This state of suspension is recognized in some adolescent literature by including students or unemployed youth over twenty.

Inferiority. When, in addition to some of the above circumstances, the adolescent's gender, national or racial origin, or social class are marks for inferior status, for being ignored, scorned, or mistreated, some or all guidelines offered by the adult world may come to represent adult hypocrisy. The alternate pathways toward adulthood according to gender and to social class raise the possibility of marked discrepancies between images of adulthood portrayed in the mass media and the adolescent's base-rate observations of adults in his or her social surroundings. Personal prospects in adulthood dim from the contrast.

Listing such uncertainties, discontinuities and contradictions is not to suggest that adolescence is inevitably a period of 'storm and stress' or psychological trauma. Rather any one or some combination of such circumstances creates a dilemma sufficient, when coupled with a changing body, to disturb the psychological structures or schemata that have previously related the individual to his or her own body, with other individuals and groups, with activities, social objects, social institutions, and their values or norms. Further, though differing for the two genders, the greater independence allowed in physical movement, in use of leisure time, in choice of activities and friends, requires learning new behaviors, new activities and new modes of relating to others.

In short, the basic psychological problem during the adolescent period is the re-forming of those parts of the self system that are discontinuous with childhood experiences while forming new constructions in dealing with the changed circumstances and new experiences the adolescent is encountering.

The person's self system may be conceived as a system or 'constellation' of categorical structures or schemata, formed through interaction with the physical and social environment. They relate the experiences of 'me', 'I' and 'mine' with one's body and its parts, their capabilities and comparison with others; with significant persons, groups and categories (e.g. gender) and their relationships to others; with social objects, social institutions, and with the social values and status criteria each embodies – in short with significant features of the individual's effective social environment (Sherif and Cantril, 1947; Sherif and Sherif, 1969a; Sherif, 1976; Sherif, 1982).

The categorical structures in the self system are distinctive in that certain categories include the person and are, therefore, affect laden. The self-inclusive category is, in turn, related with others in the structure by rank (e.g. superior–inferior) and by affective direction (e.g. positively–negatively, acceptable–objectionable, friendly or hostile, etc.). The vaguely defined concept 'gender identity' refers to such a self-inclusive categorical structure, which incorporates specific myths, beliefs and attributions to self and others, including social stereotypes of the essential 'natures' of men and women (Sherif, 1982).

To the degree that such a self-inclusive category is high in the priorities of the self system, either because it is self-defining or because a situational context makes it focal, its involvement in psychological processes provides a categorical anchor for the individual's perception and appraisal of ongoing events related to it. We say that the person has become 'self-regulating'.

Such anchoring in the self promotes better recall of related events, heightened selectivity in attention and recall, shortened response time, and heightened ratings of self confidence or certainty in judgments (cf. Sherif and Cantril, 1947; Wegner and Vallacher, 1980; Sherif, 1982). Predictable assimilation and contrast effects occur in judgments of objects varying in discrepancy from categories acceptable to self (Sherif and Hovland, 1961; Sherif, Sherif and Nebergall, 1965; Sherif, 1980). Greater consistency is observed between the person's attitudes and purposive intentions, as well as between declared intentions to act and actions (Sherif et al., 1973; Sherif, 1980).

Any one of the distinctive properties of the adolescent period above, combined with the changing body and concerns over a future, can create dilemmas that shake established ties in the self system (for example, what it means to be male or female). What do individuals do when facing novel uncertainties and ambiguities, when few or contradictory guidelines are available for interpreting the circumstances and knowing what to do? Often they flounder about in confusion. But they also turn to other humans. If adults fail to provide satisfactory definitions and rules, often through no fault of their own, the adolescent searches elsewhere.

It is here that contemporary societies' age-related arrangements in school and community become decisive. In earlier times, such a search for human resources might have yielded no more counsel than a lonely adolescent's diary or daydreams. Today, adolescents can readily discover that other adolescents are in the same boat, experiencing similar dilemmas. The more frequent, more intense and more significant interactions with those of one's own generation, which are widely reported in the research literature, are the outcome.

The actual movement toward age-mates marks a general shift in emphasis within the self system, at least in those activities that are not adult dominated. Being acceptable to and accepted by age-mates become major concerns. Their eyes become those which *count* in several important respects, including whether *I* am 'normal', 'worthwhile', better or worse in various respects. Rosenberg's analysis of adolescents' self esteem (1967) revealed the extent of the shift. Adolescents whose school performance or behavior failed in measuring up to adult standards maintained self esteem through their collective agreement that adult standards were simply not important.

To be ignored, neglected or scorned at a time when one's self is changing is a painful experience, to be avoided if at all possible. When coupled with an earlier life history of insecure or unsatisfactory ties with family or age-mates, such experiences impel an almost frantic search to belong someplace, with someone, and at almost any price. For such reasons, inclusion by age-mates, even in a low status or marginal association with them, is preferable to isolation.

The fact that adolescents form their own standards for outlook, conduct and achieving status in the process of dealing with uncertainties of self is not a freakish event, unknown outside of that period. Nor is their preference for those standards over adults' a mystery when the circumstances are considered. Using the phenomenon of apparent movement of a tiny light in total darkness (autokinesis) as a metaphor for ambiguity, Sherif's laboratory experiments (1936) showed that adults also deal with uncertainties by forming their own rules for construing the situation.

When individuals with differing personal rules face such a situation together, over time they construct a new rule, a genuinely social norm, by which each regulates behavior, both when together and later when alone. Rooted in the human capacity to form rules, individually and collectively, such social norms spring from human relationships of trust. Even in the laboratory, interaction with a person who is distrusted leads to quite a different outcome. Sharply contrasting self and the other person, the individual moves away from the other, forming or maintaining a rule as different as possible (cf. Doise, 1978).

Unless parent–youth conflict is completely polarized, turning toward one's own generation during the period requires the capacity to form and to deal with loyalties to several reference persons and groups, simultaneously. A reference person or group is defined here as that person or social unit to which an individual belongs psychologically, or aspires to be part of (Sherif and Sherif, 1953, 1964). Now, there are at least two: family and peers. Certain significant social categories, such as gender or race, also become more salient psychologically during adolescence, as the young person observes the changing body.

The literature on adolescence presenting grand sweeping theories of the period sometimes fails to analyze such multiple anchors for the changing self and issues of the overlapping or conflicting loyalties they may imply. Like those parents who witness the psychological shift toward age-mates as a betrayal, much of the research on family and peer reference groups requires the adolescent to choose between parents and friends whose standards differ (e.g. Larson, 1972). Such a procedure assumes inevitable adult–youth conflict, which need not occur when adult and adolescent standards coincide, or when the priorities of adults and adolescents concern separate and distinct activities, which is often the case. The psychological shift toward age-mates can occur in the absence of parent–youth conflict.

Prado (1958) demonstrated the shift toward peer friends among boys with harmonious family relationships, and when with their favored parent. Compared with 8–11 year olds, 14–17 year old boys over-evaluated performance by peer friends, compared with their own fathers'. Conversely, the 8–11 year olds over-evaluated their fathers' compared with friends. Further, the process is reciprocal. Gecas (1972) reported that high school students' self esteem was highest in contexts with best friends of the same gender, followed by those of the other gender, with family contexts third. Their lowest self esteem was reported with 'adults in general', but particularly with teachers in the classroom.

In brief, the circumstances of the adolescent period which render parts of the self system shaky provide the impetus for adolescents to seek out peers. Interactions among them set the stage for the formation of 'natural' groups, that is, groups formed through their own initiatives, within, across and outside of adult supervised activities. Our research indicates common processes and properties among all such groups, but the social differentiations among them and the particular status criteria and norms they develop are not comprehensible apart from the effective sociocultural frameworks in which they form.

2. Effective sociocultural frameworks for studying adolescents

What happens as a consequence of the shift toward adolescent reference groups depends in large part upon the locations, facilities and arrangements where adolescents live, attend school and spend leisure time. One methodological contribution of the research project was to study the sociocultural framework that is effective, i.e. salient, to adolescents as conditions for their interactions.

This phase in the research consisted of three separate steps. First, census tract statistics were analyzed, guided by the Shevky-Bell Social Area Analysis (Shevky and Bell, 1955; Bell, 1958, 1965). The analysis permitted the location of each social area in a standardized matrix, which indicated the area's rank in socioeconomic status, conditions of family living (e.g. dwellings, fertility rates), and degree of segregation or mixture of racial or ethnic populations.

Social areas with residents of lower, middle and upper class were selected for comparative purposes. The areas differed widely in physical environments and their populations varied from all white, all black, all

Spanish-speaking to mixed populations. Second, each area was surveyed by observers in a geographic and descriptive analysis of dwellings, businesses, schools and recreational facilities. These surveys proved essential in understanding how and where group members spent their time, both inside and outside of the area. For example, problems of securing some privacy for their associations were different in lower, middle and upper class settings.

Third, opinion surveys were conducted on representative samples of students attending high schools that served the study areas. The purpose of the surveys was to detect the prevailing standards and aspirations deemed socially desirable among adolescents. The assumption was that the turning toward one's own generation would include concern with attitudes prevailing among other adolescents in the school where one had or was spending six to seven hours a day.

The extensive survey data, which are reported elsewhere (Sherif, 1961; Sherif and Sherif, 1964, 1965, 1969a) support several generalizations pertinent to understanding the social differentiations among adolescents and their interactions with one another.

2.1. Cross-class similarities

Despite great differences between schools, there were marked similarities and consensus across them that signified the impact of the larger framework of US society. Every sample bore the unmistakable impact of this larger culture, particularly its stress on individual comfort, material possessions and upward mobility or improving circumstances. Virtually all in every sample wanted automobiles, comfortable houses, televisions, radios and other possessions; their own 'spending money' for personal wants; and at least two hours a day to 'do what I want to do'. Such desires did not coincide with actual circumstances of adolescents in lower class areas, but did for those in upper class areas. For example, when asked where they would live 'if I had my way', the great majority of those in lower class areas responded with the upper class neighborhoods in their own cities. Only 5 per cent in upper class areas expressed any desire to move, and these to another city.

2.2. Upward mobility

Similarly, the ideology of upward mobility and individual achievement was represented in all social areas. For example, males in high social classes aimed at occupations on the level with their own fathers' occupations, but nearly half in middle and low class areas aimed at occupations higher in prestige and income than their own fathers'.

2.3. In-group preferences

Racial and ethnic preferences in choices of friends were obtained in response to a question that allowed one to make no choices based on race or ethnicity. Nevertheless, marked in-group preferences were found. The proportions explicitly responding that they did not choose friends on the basis of race or ethnicity varied from 10 to 16 percent, the variations not being significantly related to social class or area. In-group preference was strongest in the high and middle class white areas, where Spanish-speaking or black friends were infrequently chosen. In mixed and segregated middle or lower class areas with minority ethnic populations, members of ethnic or racial minorities chose their own groups first, but those from 'white, English-speaking' groups followed closely in frequency of mention. Only about half responded when asked who they would not want to make friends with, the most frequent responses by those being code words for lower class, racial or ethnic minorities (Sherif, 1961).

2.4. Gender differences

Across all areas, there were marked differences between the genders in occupational aspirations, and all items involving money. Greater upward mobility, higher aspirations and desires for more money by boys than girls were the rule. These differences reflected the actual low status of working women in the US, the lack of occupational prestige for the response of 'housewife' or 'mother', and the virtual separation of girls from the money economy except through 'allowances'.

2.5. Socioeconomic differences

Adolescents' conceptions of social structure and their own places within it differed markedly according to socioeconomic rank of their social areas and schools. These comparisons involved responses to questions that secured their estimates of what ranges of education, occupation, future income and current spending money were minimal for a person like themselves, were maximal for comfort or achievement, and their personal aspirations in these respects. It was not surprising to find personal aspirations varying by social class, or their realistic expectations for the future lower than aspirations. However, the very conceptions of acceptable categories, from minimum to maximum, also differed by social class. Thus, for example, the minimum amount of income conceived as 'barely enough to live on' differed significantly between low and high class areas. There was no overlap at all in confidence limits in the different areas for the median amount needed to 'be really well off'. Similar discontinuities were found between the areas in the range of acceptable occupations, a finding supported in a larger scale study by Haller *et al.* (1974). Finally, conceptions of the educational level needed to be 'educated' and 'for a person like me' differed significantly between social areas. This topic was one of the few, however, yielding no gender differences within areas. Educational aspirations differed within middle and lower class areas according to ethnicity, with black adolescents having higher aspirations than Spanish-speaking youth. Both for girls and black adolescents, the emphasis upon education in social movements is reflected in these results.

2.6. Social stratification within areas

Finally, in every respect mentioned, the homogeneity of responses was greater in schools serving areas of upper middle and high socioeconomic rank than the schools serving largely middle class or lower class areas. The heterogeneity of responses in the latter is important, since it did not reflect simply individual differences, but bimodalities related to social stratifications within the schools. The stratification reflected social status and ethnic or racial differences, but were by no means simple. Individual adolescents attending such schools are faced with issues of whether and how to be accepted by social circles stratified so clearly that adolescent lexicons include names for them, such as the 'Soches' (apparently from 'social'), 'Hoods', 'Greasers', 'Snobs', 'Yokels' or 'Townies' (cf. Schwartz and Merten, 1967). As Dunphy (1963) has suggested, the small informal group is a frequent medium for gaining entry to the desired social circle or 'crowd', which signifies the standing of members in the stratification system of the school.

These findings, then, represent social realities faced by adolescent boys and girls individually and collectively at their schools.

3. Formation of 'natural' groups among adolescents

Within each social area, one or more natural groups of adolescents was studied intensively and regularly by observers, for periods ranging from 6 to 14 months. The length of the study period depended upon the time required to complete a planned cycle of study (see below). The bulk of the data concerned groups of boys or young men (ages 13–19), although their relationships with girls and other groups in the area were of interest. Near the end of the project, 7 groups of young women (16–17 years old) were studied. The delay reflected the scarcity of women observers and important social structures restricting the movements and locations of adolescent girls (cf. Newson and Newson, 1976; Huston, forthcoming). Thus the under-representation of adolescent girls is an example of bias produced by social structures (cf. Sherif, 1976, 1979). In all, 47 groups were studied in the manner to be described.

Previous experiences in studying group formation among boys in summer camps in three field experiments (Sherif *et al.*, 1961; Sherif and Sherif, 1969b) suggested the study methods used and the general hypothesis about group formation.

The general hypothesis about the conditions conducive to group formation was as follows: individuals facing problem situations with strong motivational significance for them, which can be dealt with most effectively through coordinated interactions involving division of labor, will interact frequently, and over time will stabilize their relationships into a social unit, recognized by themselves and others and referred to as 'we'.

Relying on the sociological literature, the minimal properties necessary for such a social unit to be equated with a human group were defined as follows:

(a) Patterns of reciprocal behaviors during interactions that are mutually expected by the individuals (role relationships) and that can be ranked with respect to social power or status (defined as relative effectiveness in initiating, coordinating and controlling interactions, decisions and sanctions for conformity–nonconformity).

(b) A set of social norms, i.e. shared values, jargon, nicknames as well as rules for conduct, defining ranges or latitudes for individual differences evaluated as acceptable and as objectionable, at least in matters of mutual consequence to the members.

Reconstruction of the 'natural histories' of the natural groups of adolescent boys, on the basis of interviews with their members conducted at the very end of the study cycle, indicate that most of them had formed two to three years earlier. This period would have been when the adolescents left elementary school and entered junior high schools, or during junior high school. A few groups contained elementary school friends, and several and in the lower class neighborhoods, with little mobility except on foot, were composed of adolescents who were nearby neighbors. But the great majority of groups had members who lived in homes spread over wider areas. In fact, data on the spread of group members' dwellings support the hunch that the most cohesive or solidary groups were those whose dwellings were the most widely scattered.

Groups were not located by questioning either adults or adolescents. In fact, when questioned, both adolescents and adults tended to deny that there are groups, which they equated with 'gangs' who misbehave and cause trouble. Accordingly, the sole criterion for selecting a cluster of adolescents for intensive observation was that an observer reported frequent and recurrent associations among the same individuals over a period of time. When thus selected, the individuals in the observed cluster had not been in contact with an observer, though they had seen the observer in the area. The hypothesis was that such frequent and recurrent associations among adolescents were, in fact, small groups with the minimum properties for any group, and that they would be reference groups for individual members.

3.1. The observer being observed

Observers, who were in every case college or university students, were assigned to an area where their own backgrounds made them 'fit' in appearance, language and cultural knowledge. In no case was an observer in an area where he lived. Prior clearance with police and other authorities made it possible for the observers to circulate freely and to make observations, with the understanding that the reports would be available only to researchers, not to those authorities.

From the moment an observer entered an area, there had to be good reasons for being there, even to observe from a distance. The rationale for his presence, in turn, had to be that he was a harmless, neutral outsider with no authority in the area, especially over adolescents. The development of such an observer role was essential, owing to the psychological tendency to categorize a stranger in ways that suggest purpose.

Thus, for a period of time, the observer was being observed by the adolescents quite as much as he was observing them. It was only upon continued association, as they came to regard the observer as harmless, friendly and perhaps helpful, that the focus of attention returned to their own concerns. Observers were instructed not to take initiative in the adolescents' activities, nor to direct them in any way. The role was necessarily verifiable, since adolescents occasionally checked on the observer (for example to determine whether he was indeed assisting in a recreation center or whether he lived where he said he lived). Needless to say, the roles and activities of different observers varied considerably, depending upon the area studied as well as their own capabilities.

3.2. Study cycle

Once a cluster was identified and contact had been made, the observer proceeded through the research steps of the study cycle. First, observations focused on interpersonal interactions among the adolescents, to secure data on whether role and status relationships were stabilized. Observer ratings in these respects were supported by specific accounts of observed interaction, then later checked by the ratings of an independent observer on occasions when prolonged observation of the group members was possible. Finally, late in the study cycle, individual adolescents were interviewed informally to obtain their responses to sociometric questions concerning who was effective in initiating and in undertaking their activities of various kinds.

Next, the observer focused on evidence of normative regulation of behavior, on what were normative concerns in the group, on instances of praise for conformity or reproof for nonconformity. Such observations included reports on normative regulation of contacts with other adolescents outside the group and with adults. Observations were also made relevant to the degree to which group norms were binding for individual members, for example by noting decisions made when group norms conflicted with parental demands or relationships with girl friends. Finally, evidence was collected pertaining to the solidarity of the group, particularly as indicated by the degree and extent of secrecy maintained by members from other adolescents and from adults. A 'natural history' was the last step.

Clearly, the groups that were observed were among the more visible in their areas. The study cycle for some groups could not be completed, typically owing to an observer's difficulty in attaining access to the group's important activities. In every case, such groups were also highly secretive. Thus, there is reason to believe that the groups actually studied were not the most cohesive or solidary.

3.3. Differentiation of interpersonal relations

As fascinating as the variations among the groups were in terms of the status criteria employed and the different structures, this summary report will concentrate on generalizations common to all. From the viewpoint of the individual adolescent and from the social-psychological problems of individual–group relationships, these common findings are important in showing that interpersonal differentiations are consequential for the problems of the adolescent transition.

Briefly, these major generalizations are as follows:

Stability. In every group, the individual adolescents could be reliably ranked in terms of their effective initiative or power in social interactions over time across a variety of activities in which their individual skills clearly differed, using the combination of techniques already described.

Status hierarchy. The miniature social structures were invariably hierarchical with respect to social power, despite the fact that friendship choices by the members were typically reciprocated. Thus in the most solidary groups the structure according to liking or popularity of members was flat. Leadership roles were detected in all groups, even in those where members denied there were leaders or followers. What adults and outsiders saw as 'just friends' were organized groups, even though informally.

End-anchoring. Perceptions and judgments of interpersonal differentiations among members by both the observer and the members revealed a well-known principle in the psychology of serial judgments, viz. the principle of end-anchoring. Perceptions and judgments were anchored by the extreme positions, that is highest and lowest statuses. Such anchoring effects appeared in observers' judgments as lower variability in rating the status positions at the top and bottom of the status structure, *over time across different activities.* Further, the observers' ratings of their own confidence in their status ratings were higher at the upper and lower ranks than in the middle. Analysis of group members' choices of individuals who 'get things started' and 'get things done' in different activities showed similar end-anchoring. Their consensus across activities was highest at the upper and lower ranks. Observations of those groups whose status structure changed materially over the course of the study suggested that such end-anchoring in perceptions and judgments of the group may reflect important group processes. The observed changes, over time, in each case occurred when an important change occurred in the group's circumstances. For example, in one case, the opportunity arose for the group to compete in sports; in another, the acknowledged leader left town, while a third attracted a highly visible and skilled new member. In every case, the changes that occurred in the status structure involved movements upward or downward by members in intermediate ranks.

Relation to cognitive processes. The social structures of interpersonal relations in such natural groups of adolescents influence individual members' perceptions and judgments of one another in the performance of activities. By using tasks with ambiguous outcomes, the generalization of mutual expectations among individual members has been demonstrated. That is, judgments of individuals' performance vary systematically according to their status in the group, with considerable overestimation being typical for those with high status (Sherif, White and Harvey, 1954; Koslin, Haarlow, Karlins and Pargament, 1968).

Influence and stability. Confirming field observations, MacNeil (1967) studied the influence an individual member in an adolescent group could exert on another member of intermediate status in a laboratory situation. In groups with high solidarity, the influence of a high status member on another member's judgments was strikingly greater than that of a member with lower status. In the less stable group, on the other hand, both members with high and lower status exerted influence on the members with intermediate status, though not as much as a high status member in the stable groups.

In summary, despite their casual or informal appearance to outsiders, social differentiation within adolescent groups does occur with consequences for the perceptual and judgmental processes of individual members. Though products of their own interactions in their effective sociocultural surrounds, the status and role differentiations also reflect members' skills and achievements in social activities prized in the group. They reflect cultural values in their sociocultural framework, in particular those prized in the gender ideology, which differs in different social areas. Whatever they are, the criteria for status in the group define what is expected of self and of others as long as the association continues in stable fashion.

3.4. Social norms as products of interaction

The observational data reveal a plenitude of collective products, including group names, nicknames, special jargon, distinctive styles of dress, and rules for acceptable and objectionable conduct in treatments of one another and outsiders, and rules for the selection and conduct of collective activities. All such products acquire value for the members, hence may be referred to collectively as social norms.

The creation of social norms by adolescent groups clearly related to their experiences in interaction, as well as the larger sociocultural framework. It is tempting to document them in detail, for their novelty emphasizes their creativity. However, such documents are quickly dated. The norms of adolescent groups often change from one generation to the next. Therefore, this summary will concern (a) relationships between conformity to group norms and individuals' status levels in a group, and (b) an experiment demonstrating the autonomous regulation of cognitive processes by group members in line with group norms.

There is a tendency to see all or most behavior in groups as regulated by group norms, especially if that behavior is seen as undesirable or labeled 'delinquent'. The blanket label 'peer pressure' is then attributed as the 'cause' of anything that happened. We found that normative regulation of behavior was not evident in all spheres of group activity, as indicated by a wide range of individual differences among members which aroused no comment or overt response. Undesirable and even criminal behavior was normative in some groups; but instances of quite serious activities occurred in others with no evidence that they had been anticipated by the members, or that there were evaluative pressures for them to occur again. Convergence on customs and common evaluations by group members, with implied or actual sanctions for nonconformity, occurs in matters of some collective consequence to the group and its members.

By their very nature, the norms of a group permit, even recognize the play of individual differences. A norm defines a range or latitude for individual differences acceptable to group members, as well as a latitude for objectionable behavior to be met with disapproval or other sanctions, depending on the seriousness of the violation. Frequently, there are 'grey areas,' where neither acceptance nor rejection is encountered. In the study of group interactions, as well as in research on social categorization and attitudes (Sherif *et al.*, 1965), we have found it useful to designate such areas as a 'latitude of noncommitment', where reactions are neither accepting nor rejecting.

With these concepts in mind, certain generalizations are possible about the structure of social norms and about how binding a given norm was for adolescents with different status in the group.

Conformity and status. The latitude for acceptability defined by a group norm varied according to the importance of the activity or behavior for the group. It was sharply categorical and its range constricted for norms pertaining to the identity, maintenance or continuance of the group as a unit, such as loyalty in the face of intrusion or outside threat to major activities, especially from adults. Nonconformity or deviation in such matters called forth strong and consensual sanctions from others, even separation from the group. Nonconformity to less important customs aroused less opposition. A broad latitude of noncommitment, where individual variations aroused no evaluations one way or another, was found for minor norms.

Even in matters of central and common concern to members, the norms are not equally binding for all members. The latitude for acceptable action is narrower and more binding for members of higher status. Voluntary conformity to important norms represents one means of gaining and maintaining power in the group. The constraints on high status members were striking in actions with outsiders, especially with adults. A leader who risked exposing the group to adults was immediately chastised by other members. Few did.

On the other hand, in matters of less importance, particularly those strictly within group bounds, the high status members were far freer than those with lower status not to conform to its norms, or to innovate. On matters of custom strictly within the group, members with low status were more frequently corrected. A great deal of the exercise of power through sanctions in these natural groups occurred in relation to lower status members on such relatively minor concerns.

The great bulk of actions conforming to collective norms were self regulated by members without sanctions. A preponderance of autonomous regulation is not surprising when one considers that the adolescents associated and formed norms through their own initiatives and collective efforts.

Self regulation of cognitive-affective processes. Study of the social interactions in 7 groups of young women attending the same school provided the basis for making predictions about the psychological functioning of the individual members when apart from their groups. Group norms differing in their importance to these groups had been documented. Later, individual members participated individually in an experiment on social judgment. Certain predictions were made about how individuals in the different groups would make judgments.

The predictions were based on a theory of social judgment that considers self-defining values or norms as anchors in judgment (Sherif and Hovland, 1961; Sherif, Sherif and Nebergall, 1965; Sherif, 1980). The predictions were that individuals belonging to groups in which a norm is very important would use very few categories in judging pictures related to the norm, compared to a less important norm or to geometric forms (which are used for comparison only). Asked to label any pictures representing behavior acceptable or objectionable, those individuals would also show sharply defined acceptances and objections, with little noncommitment (i.e. failure to either accept or reject). More categories and more noncommitment were expected when the pictures concerned less important norms.

We found that, to a significant degree, the young women's individual categorizations reflected the observed norms and their relative importance within their respective groups. In brief, the experiences of participating in normative processes in their groups did affect their cognitive and affective functioning individually, outside of those groups (Sherif *et al.*, 1973).

4. Intercategory and intergroup differentiations

Adults, school and community authorities, and other groups of adolescents were important in the social ecology of the natural groups. Relationships with these outsiders were consequential for members and for the comparative stability and solidarity of their groups. Lines drawn by gender, social class and ethnicity were reflected in many of these relationships.

4.1. Gender and groups

Despite growing and often intense interest in the other gender, the young people observed in the research spent most of their leisure with persons of their own gender. The different groups varied considerably in the kind and frequency of contacts across gender lines by their members. When such contacts occurred, the social subordination of the girls was evident in several ways.

Differences between the groups in the relative frequency of contacts across gender lines were observed for both male and female groups. For example, both included groups whose members were actively pursuing the other gender, and spent a great deal of their time in their groups arranging to do so. Both included groups whose members seldom discussed or were observed to interact with the other gender. These groups were frequently absorbed in activities that were not highly prized in the adolescent norms of their social areas, such as serious intellectual activity, artistic endeavors, or (for girls only) team sports.

Within groups of boys or girls, the members were frequently observed in unifying activities directed toward common goals. But the only such activities including both boys and girls were organized music, drama and special interests groups attracting only a minority of the adolescent population in an area, and a small fraction of the members of groups observed. Thus, the chief mechanism for cross-gender contacts was 'dating', in which males took the initiative and in which the focus was sexual attractiveness. (The words used for that mechanism were not the same in different areas.)

Within all male groups, considerable time was devoted to discussing girls, whether members 'dated' or not. Those who did rated the attractiveness of various girls, and their sexual reputations. It used girls as objects to be exploited for status with one's own group.

When mixed gender interactions occurred, observers were asked to rate the 'effective initiative' (status) of girls in the situation as well as boys'. The girls' standings were invariably dependent upon those of the boys who attended them, and lower than theirs. A girl dating a boy with high status could at times veto suggestions made by lower status males. An exaggerated form of girls' status dependency was found in a lower class area (Spanish-speaking), where the status of every male in one group could be matched to that of a girl he dated in a distinct and separate group of girls.

The lack of activities in which boys and girls participated equally, the dependency of the dating process, and the emphasis by boys on female attractiveness and sexuality formed a social pattern supportive of the lower status of women in the larger society. Reflected in the informal associations of adolescents, such patterns clarify why a program of classroom instruction aimed at changing attitudes towards women's status failed among 14–15 year olds, specifically owing to the antagonism of the boys, to which girls were not immune (Guttentag and Bray, 1976). The program was highly successful in changing attitudes toward women's roles and status in the elementary grades.

4.2. Social class and ethnicity

The residential segregation in US cities and the marked in-group preferences by high school students surveyed in the research remove any element of surprise from the finding that members within each natural group were remarkably homogeneous as to social class, race and cultural background. The finding is significant, none the less, for in replicating the existing social order, these adolescents were also affirming the class and ethnic basis of their self systems. To the extent that their groups were stable with considerable solidarity, they provided standards for self evaluation of personal worth. The reported finding that black and white students in the US do not differ in rating their own self esteem would be expected, if each used their own reference groups as the basis for self comparisons (Rosenberg and Simmons, 1972).

The most cohesive groups, with highest solidarity, were formed in lower class areas by individuals who had experienced a gamut of influences giving the message that they were not wanted and were looked down upon. Living in crowded families, at times unstable, having difficulties in school, being barred from recreation centers, and observed by police whenever they ventured out of a segregated area, such youth turned to each other to find some basis for stable ties with *someone*. Competition for status with other groups did not bring them together, rather they were preoccupied with personal interactions, doing things together during their waking hours, and sharing secrets with others who paid attention to them. Such groups were the only ones observed who had adopted group names. Under such circumstances, self esteem relative to others in the group can be maintained, even when the group is an anathema to everyone else in the area.

In an interesting analysis of self–other comparisons, Tajfel and Turner (1979) proposed the 'basic hypothesis . . . that pressures to evaluate one's own group positively *through in-group/out-group comparisons* lead social groups to attempt to differentiate themselves from each other' (pp. 40–1, emphasis added). Our observations suggest that adolescent groups differentiate themselves for many other reasons than comparisons with other groups, and that members can evaluate their own groups positively while recognizing the reality of their social inferiority. Possibly the hypothesis is more appropriate when conflict between groups is already underway and focal in the group's concerns.

Relationships between adolescent groups are not always competitive or conflicting. In fact, observers recorded several episodes when members of one group went to great pains to avoid conflict with another, even at the risk of unfavorable in-group/out-group comparisons. Some Chicano groups maintained friendly relations or alliances with black groups in their neighborhoods, reserving their rivalries for other Chicano groups.

However, the ecology of certain neighborhoods and the prestige systems in several schools (the latter in middle and upper class areas) promoted intergroup conflict among adolescents. The very fact that a natural group formed in certain lower class neighborhoods meant conflict with others over the use of space and facilities. In many schools, the system for recognition, prestige and influence in the school was based on competitive struggle up the prestige ladder. Under such circumstances, any threat to a group's interests (for space, prestige or recognition) can provoke intergroup conflict. As the theory labeled 'realistic group conflict theory' by Campbell (1965) originally stated, such conflicts of group interest develop a 'life of their own' – a history that has to be understood in its own right over time (Sherif and Sherif, 1953; Sherif, 1966). As members of Los Apaches told the observer, they had 'always' fought with the Lakesiders, and 'always' would. As field and laboratory experiments also show (Sherif et al., 1961; Dion, 1979), during active intergroup conflict viewed by a group as 'successful', solidarity reached a peak seldom attained otherwise.

For adolescents, successful defiance of adult regulations gives a similar boost to group solidarity. The organization, conduct and aftermath of a post-dance party in a motel, in defiance of parents and several laws, marked the greatest solidarity of a group of upper class boys, who carried it off in greatest secrecy. In other cases, adult efforts to break apart members of a group were met with still greater secrecy on the adolescents' part, elaborate systems for liaison among members, or explicitly 'going underground'.

In general, therefore, relationships with the other gender, other adolescent groups, and with adults were significant contexts for the adolescent groups whose consequences in development depend heavily upon the sociocultural and ecological setting of interaction. When these contexts and the directions of groups in them were conducive to conflict, comparisons between groups assumed great importance for group members; but outside of conflict situations, members found many other bases for the formation and maintenance of their groups.

5. Impact of the changing times on adolescent groups

The research concluded as the waves of social movements of the 1960s and early 1970s involving many college-aged youth washed down into the nation's high schools. Contrary to reported circumstances in South Africa and Central American countries, adolescents in high schools in the US have not been prominent initiators of social protest. Such contrasts suggest that sociocultural conditions and social movements, not the developmental period *per se*, are the keys to understanding when adolescents are sensitized to the currents of larger social changes. Research on high school adolescents' attitudes toward the resurgent women's movement in the late 1960s showed high schools as hotbeds for reaction, not hotbeds for change. However, five years after the observations of girls' groups, a group of eight girls formed in the same school, whose members associated both informally and weekly as a study group on the status of women.

Similarly, the student movement, civil rights movement and antiwar movements of the 1960s were reflected in the nation's high schools. By 1968–9, 67 per cent of urban and suburban high schools reported incidents of student protest of serious enough proportions to be labeled 'disruptions' (Trump and Hunt, 1969). A striking instance of the impact of a social movement on an adolescent group occurred during the research. Within a few weeks, every black boy in the group had stopped getting a closely cropped haircut and appeared with the full hair style called 'Afro', which had been popularized by the 'Black Power' movement. After the project was completed, another observer returned to the neighborhoods observed in San Antonio, Texas to find that the Spanish-speaking boys (so derisively called 'Tex-Mex', or at best 'Latins', by the 'Anglos' in Texas) had adopted the dress styles and the self description of the 'Chicano' movement.

Such assertions of self and group identity within social movements are attempts to build new reference groups dedicated to social change. Their ideologies involve affirmation of group belongingness and self comparisons not only within one's own group, but deliberately of one's own group with groups more privileged than one's own. A social movement directed toward change is also, by definition, in conflict with groups opposed to change. Thus, social movements represent another circumstance where own group/other group comparisons become highly salient. When the aims of such movements are toward greater equality and more widespread social justice, the social inferiority of the new reference group is explicitly recognized, but the basis for the distinction is rejected in the movement ideology. Counter-movements re-asserting the basis for the distinction can then divide youth as well as adults, as they have since successfully done in the United States.

6. Conclusion

This chapter has viewed problems of social interaction among adolescents in development as a challenge. The coordination of what is sociological and of what is psychological, without dissolving one into the other, is necessary to meet this challenge. The research summarized here represented the effort to demonstrate what meeting the challenge involves. Since the sequence of coordinated steps requires tasks at the level of sociological analysis, of the interactions of individuals, and of their psychological functioning, learning and borrowing from both psychology and sociology become essential. Ultimately, a rounded picture of social interactions in adolescent development requires the coordinated efforts of researchers in these and other disciplines. If they accept the challenge, social psychologists can advance the study of their over-arching problem, that of intricate individual–group–society relationships.

References

Bell, W. 1958. The utility of the Shevky topology for the design of urban sub-area field studies. *Journal of Social Psychology*, **47**, 71–83.
Bell, W. 1965. Urban neighborhoods and individual behavior. Chapter 11 in M. Sherif and C. W. Sherif (eds.): *Problems of youth*. Chicago: Aldine.
Campbell, D. T. 1965. Ethnocentric and other altruistic motives. In D. Levine (ed.): *Nebraska symposium on motivation*, vol. 13. Lincoln: University of Nebraska Press.
Dion, K. L. 1979. Intergroup conflict and intragroup cohesiveness. In W. G. Austin and S. Worchel (eds.): *The social psychology of intergroup relations*. Monterey, Calif.: Brooks/Cole, ch. 13.
Doise, W. 1978. *Groups and individuals: Explanations in social psychology*. Cambridge University Press.

Dunphy, D. C. 1963. The social structure of urban adolescent peer groups. *Sociometry*, **26**, 230–46.

Erikson, E. H. 1968. *Identity: Youth and crisis*. New York: Norton.

Geber, B. A. and Newman, S. P. 1980. *Soweto's children: The development of attitudes*. London: Academic Press.

Gecas, V. 1972. Parental behavior and contextual variations in adolescent self esteem. *Sociometry*, **35**, 332–45.

Guttentag, M. and Bray, H. 1976. *Undoing sex stereotypes. Research and resources for educators*. New York: McGraw-Hill.

Haller, A. O., Otto, L. B., Meier, R. F. and Ohlendorf, G. W. 1974. Level of occupational aspiration: An empirical analysis. *American Sociological Review*, **39**, 113–21.

Huston, A. C. Forthcoming. Sex-typing. Pre-publication draft of chapter to appear in P. Mussen (ed.): *Carmichael's manual of child psychology*.

Koslin, B., Haarlow, R. N., Karlins, M. and Pargament, R. 1968. Predicting group status from members' cognitions. *Sociometry*, **31**, 64–75.

Larson, L. E. 1972. The influence of parents and peers during adolescence: The situation hypothesis revisited. *Journal of Marriage and the Family*, **34**, 67–74.

MacNeil, M. R. 1967. Power of status in norm formation under differing conditions of group solidarity. Ph.D. dissertation, University of Oklahoma.

Newson, J. and Newson, E. 1976. *Seven years in the home environment*. London: Allen and Unwin.

Piaget, J. and Weil, M. A. 1951. Development in children of the idea of homeland and relations with other countries. *International Social Science Bulletin*, **3**, 3, 561–78.

Prado, W. 1958. Appraisal of performance as a function of relative ego-involvement of children and adolescents. Ph.D. thesis, University of Oklahoma.

Rosenberg, M. 1967. Psychological selectivity in self-esteem formation. In C. W. Sherif and M. Sherif (eds.): *Attitudes, ego-involvement and change*. New York: Wiley, ch. 3.

Rosenberg, M. and Simmons, R. G. 1972. *Black and white and self-esteem. The urban school child*. A. and C. Rose Monograph Series in Sociology. Washington, DC: American Sociological Association.

Schwartz, G. and Merten, D. 1967. The language of adolescence: An anthropological approach to the youth culture. *American Journal of Sociology*, **72**, 453–68.

Sherif, C. W. 1961. Self radius and goals of youth in different urban areas. *Southwestern Social Science Quarterly* (December), 259–70.

Sherif, C. W. 1976. *Orientation in social psychology*. New York: Harper and Row.

Sherif, C. W. 1979. Bias in psychology. In J. Sherman and E. Beck (eds.): *The prism of sex. Essays on the sociology of knowledge*. Madison: University of Wisconsin Press.

Sherif, C. W. 1980. Social values, attitudes and involvement of the self. In H. Howe and M. Page (eds.): *Beliefs, attitudes and values*. Lincoln/London: University of Nebraska Press, pp. 1–64.

Sherif, C. W. 1982. Needed concepts in the study of gender identity. Presidential address, Division 35, American Psychological Association, 88th Annual

216 Carolyn Wood Sherif

Convention, Montreal, 3 September 1980. To appear, *Psychology of Women Quarterly*, Summer issue.

Sherif, C. W., Kelly, M., Rodgers, H. L., Sarup, G. and Tittler, B. I. 1973. Personal involvement, social judgment and action. *Journal of Personality and Social Psychology*, **27**, 311–28.

Sherif, C. W., Sherif, M. and Nebergall, R. E. 1965 *Attitude and attitude change: The social judgment–involvement approach*. Philadephia, Pa.: W. B. Saunders.

Sherif, M. 1936. *The psychology of social norms*. New York: Harper and Row.

Sherif, M. 1966. *In common predicament. Social psychology of intergroup conflict and cooperation*. Boston, Mass.: Houghton Mifflin.

Sherif, M. and Cantril, H. 1947. *The psychology of ego-involvements: Social attitudes and identifications*. New York: Wiley.

Sherif, M., Harvey, O. J., White, B. J., Hood, W. R. and Sherif, C. W. 1961. *Intergroup conflict and cooperation: The Robbers Cave experiment*. Norman: University of Oklahoma Press.

Sherif, M. and Hovland, C. I. 1961. *Social judgment: Assimilation and contrast effects in reactions to communications and attitude change*. New Haven, Conn.: Yale University Press.

Sherif, M. and Sherif, C. W. 1953. *Groups in harmony and tension*. New York: Harper and Row.

Sherif, M. and Sherif, C. W. 1964. *Reference groups: Exploration into conformity and deviation of adolescents*. New York: Harper and Row (reprinted H. Regnery, Chicago, 1972).

Sherif, M. and Sherif, C. W. (eds.) 1965. *Problems of youth: Transition to adulthood in a changing world*. Chicago: Aldine, chs. 1, 12, 13.

Sherif, M. and Sherif, C. W. 1969a. Adolescent attitudes and behavior in their reference groups within differing sociocultural settings. In J. P. Hill (ed.): *Minnesota symposia on child psychology*, vol. 3. Minneapolis: University of Minnesota Press, pp. 97–130.

Sherif, M. and Sherif, C. W. 1969b. *Social psychology*. New York: Harper and Row.

Sherif, M., White, B. J. and Harvey, O. J. 1954. Status relations in experimentally produced groups. *American Journal of Sociology*, **60**, 370–9.

Shevky, E. and Bell, W. 1955. *Social area analysis*. Stanford, Cal.: Stanford University Press.

Tajfel, H. and Turner, J. 1979. An integrative theory of intergroup conflict. In W. G. Austin and S. Worchel (eds.): *The social psychology of intergroup relations*. Monterey, Calif.: Brooks/Cole, ch. 3.

Trump, J. L. and Hunt, J. 1969. The nature and extent of student activism. *Bulletin of the National Association of Secondary School Principals*, **53**, 151–4.

Wegner, D. M. and Vallacher, R. R. (eds.) 1980. *The self in social psychology*. New York Oxford: Oxford University Press.

13. Social differentiation in adolescence: the case of North Africans in France

MARYLA ZALESKA and HANNA MALEWSKA-PEYRE*

The social differentiation process is the main component of the identity crisis in adolescence. The typical process consists in differentiating oneself from one's parents and from adults. To acquire a new identity often means changing, if not the membership group, at least the reference group (Newcomb, 1950).

The self image is strongly related to the awareness of group membership ('Us'), to the representation of Alter ('Them') and of the society (Zavalloni, 1973). A threat to the status or the image of the membership group is also a threat to the self image of the individual.

Since individuals in a society belong to several groups and are differentiated from others by a great number of social categories, there are numerous possibilities of making a separation between the ingroup and the outgroup. The actual awareness of any particular distinction between 'us' and 'them' may vary in the course of time since it depends largely on the social and situational context. A person may refer at one time to 'us', meaning the persons of the same sex, while at another time meaning the persons of the same religion – irrespective of sex – or those of the same nationality. There are virtually limitless possibilities of categorial differentiation, some transient and unstable, others permanent.

The problem we studied is that of the reactions and strategies adopted by adolescent boys and girls whose parents are North African immigrants in France. The empirical results reported and discussed here pertain, in particular, to the cultural differentiation of these adolescents with respect to their parents and the society of adoption.

1. Cultural differentiation

The culture of North Africans is different from that of the French. The dominant traits of this culture, once common to most Mediterranean

* The authors have decided to sign alternately in alphabetical and in the reverse order the papers on which they collaborated.

countries, are well known: for example, the inferior status of women, a strict division of roles between husband and wife, close family ties, a sense of honour and dignity based on the fulfilment of moral and social obligations, the importance of religious observance. The Moslem religion, which is central to the North African identity, accentuates the cultural difference between the French and the immigrants.

The problem examined here is that of cultural differentiation of the immigrants' children when they become adolescents. Whether they were born in North Africa or in France, they were exposed to the influence of French culture and to that of urban consumer society at school and in everyday life.

But at home, these boys and girls were exposed to the influence of their parents whose norms and values remain different from those of the society in which they live.

How do the North African adolescents react to the situation of conflict between the value systems of two cultures? How do they differentiate themselves from the culture of their parents and from the Western culture?

According to Camilleri (1979), the young generation confronted with this conflict would adopt the values and the norms of behaviour which appear more advantageous, profitable and convenient. We have suggested an additional criterion of choice: individuals may tend to preserve the values and norms of behaviour which are central and essential to their identity even if their retention may, in other ways, be to their disadvantage (Malewska-Peyre and Zaleska, 1980). Religious observance may thus be retained though it does not entail any advantage for the individual and may even expose him to danger or suffering.

The empirical data reported here are part of a larger study of the identity and deviance in adolescents of the second generation of immigrants. (This study was conducted by the Centre de Formation et de Recherche de l'Education Surveillée at Vaucresson under the direction of Hanna Malewska-Peyre.) The sample examined consists of about 500 young boys and girls in the juvenile justice system and of comparison groups composed of youngsters who had never appeared in court. The adolescents from North Africa and Portugal are compared to those from France of the same economic status. The families of all the youngsters in the sample are of low socio-economic level.

The data come from several sources: non-directive, biographical interviews, a version of the 'Who am I?' test, a sentence completion test and an alternative choice questionnaire.

The results reported and discussed here pertain, however, mainly to the North African boys and girls as compared to their French counterparts. These results were more interesting and unequivocal than those of the Portuguese, because the cultural distance between the North African and the French is thought to be greater than that between the French and the Portuguese.

The data relative to the cultural differentiation process are obtained by means of the alternative choice questionnaire. This questionnaire and the population sample are described below in greater detail.

2. Population studied

The results reported here were obtained from a sample of over 400 adolescents. The total number of North Africans – Moroccans, Algerians and Tunisians – was 217. Four subgroups can be defined according to the sex and the place of the adolescent in the justice system. There were 142 boys – 96 'mineurs de justice' and 46 boys of the reference group. (In the French justice system, the term 'mineurs de justice' refers to both delinquents and assisted youngsters.) Of the 75 girls, 37 were 'mineurs de justice' and 38 in the control group.

The answers of these North Africans were compared to those of the 185 French adolescents of the same age group. There were 107 boys (52 'mineurs de justice' and 55 control), and 78 girls (33 'mineurs de justice' and 45 control).

3. The alternative choice questionnaire

The instrument used for measuring the cultural differences between the adolescents of North African and those of French origin, as well as the perceived differences between themselves and their respective parents, was a questionnaire consisting of nine choice alternatives. The youngsters were requested to express their preference for one of each pair of propositions reflecting two different values or norms of behaviour, corresponding to the traditional form of culture and to that of industrial urban society.

Five of the choice alternatives concerned the rights and obligations of women and relations within the family: an example of one of these binary choices is given below.

– A woman's place is in the home. It is the man's duty to work and to support the family.

– Men and women should share the same domestic tasks and should have equal rights to work and to leisure.

The four remaining alternative choices reflect the relative importance attached to religious observances, the sense of honour, the attitude towards work obligations and towards relations with foreigners.

The youngsters answering this questionnaire were asked to give not only their opinion but also to indicate what they considered to be their father's and mother's opinion. Thus, by comparing the frequency and content of those statements on which the young people thought they disagreed with their parents, we were able to measure how they differentiated themselves from their mother and father.

This questionnaire was designed specifically for the purpose of the study by Isabel Leonetti and the authors.

4. Results

Before reporting the results, it is necessary to specify that very few North Africans in France occupy positions of high status. Most of them are manual workers and the first victims of unemployment. Because of their ethnic origin and low economic status they may be considered as an underprivileged minority group. Though the existence of any discrimination against them is officially denied, it is well known that they are not highly considered by a large proportion of French people.

In this situation of ethnic discrimination and of threat to the positive self image of the minority group members, the reactions of North African young boys and girls differ.

For the North African girls, our data show a considerable depreciation of girls from their own ethnic group and a much higher evaluation of French girls.

This depreciation of their own group and high evaluation of the French is reflected in the girls' answers to the following incomplete sentences from the sentence completion test:

– The girls from my country . . . .
– The French girls . . . .

As shown in Table 1, the percentage of answers reflecting a positive image is much lower for 'girls of my country' than for the French girls. The North African girls clearly hold girls of their own nationality in low esteem as compared to the French. From the interviews, we know that the French girls' independence and liberty are highly valued. As we shall

Table 1. *The positive image of the same sex in own ethnic group (per cent)*

	'Girls of my country'	'French girls'
North African 'mineurs de justice' girls	39	63
North African comparison girls	26	55
	'Boys of my country'	'French boys'
North African 'mineurs de justice' boys	48	58
North African comparison boys	48	42

see later, these answers confirm the attractiveness of modern values for the North African girls.

Unlike the girls, the North African boys tend to put their peers of the same ethnic origin and the French on an equal footing. This difference between the evaluation of their own group by the boys and the girls can be accounted for by the status difference between men and women in the Mediterranean traditional culture and particularly in Moslem societies. The North African girl is depreciated by the culture of her country of origin as compared to the boy. Moreover, she depreciates herself in comparison to French girls.

Since her identity, or to put it more precisely, the positive image of herself, is threatened by the cultural values of her country of origin, the North African girl's 'strategy' should be to change her values for those of the society of adoption, thus differentiating herself from her group of origin. As we shall see, the data obtained from our sample confirm this hypothesis.

5. Cultural differentiation of the North African boys and girls

It should be stressed at the outset, that the study on the identity crisis and deviance of adolescent immigrants of the second generation was not specifically designed for collecting data on the differentiation process. However, the answers to the alternative choice questionnaire yielded interesting quantitative results which can be examined from the point of view of the differentiation of the youngsters from their parents and from the society of adoption. The differences with respect to sex and status in the French justice system will be examined consecutively.

The variable used here is the mean proportion of choices reflecting a preference for norms of behaviour and values of the traditional culture. As expected, this proportion proved to be very different in the two ethnic groups – the North Africans and the French. It also proved adequate in demonstrating how adolescents differentiate themselves from their parents.

The average traditionalism, expressed by the mean percentage of traditional choices, of the young boys and girls, in the North African and the French groups, as well as the average traditionalism attributed by these boys and girls to their respective mothers and fathers, is presented in Table 2.

The most striking result is the consistent and extremely significant difference between the preferences of *all* the groups of young people and those attributed to their respective parents. This difference does not seem to depend on ethnic group, sex or status with respect to justice.

This result is, however, not very surprising. We expected to find that all adolescents would differentiate themselves strongly from their parents and that they would attribute to both their fathers and mothers a more frequent preference for traditional norms and values than their own choices.

The comparison between boys and girls of North African origin yielded more interesting results. *The delinquent North African boys are much more traditional than the girls* of the corresponding female group. (For the sake of convenience, we shall refer here to 'mineurs de justice' as 'delinquents' but the reader should keep in mind that the two terms are not synonymous.) The difference between these two groups is highly significant ($p<0.001$, t-test, two-tailed). (For all statistical tests, the probability reported is two-tailed.) Because of the overwhelming preference for the traditional values attributed to the parents, it follows that the girls' perceived disagreement with their mothers and particularly with their fathers is very strong. Thus, the average proportion of statements on which a different choice is attributed to the parents proved to be significantly higher in the female sample of North African 'mineurs de justice' than in the male sample ($p<0.01$ for the mother, and $p<0.001$ for the father).

The corresponding results for the comparison group of North African adolescents are even more striking. The girls in the control group also adhere much more often to the values and norms of industrial urban society – 'modern' values – than the North African control boys. The difference between the proportion of choices of traditional type made by

Table 2. *Percentages of traditional choices and perceived differentiation from the parents by French and North African adolescents*

Respondents	Mean % of traditional choices of the adolescent	Mean % of traditional choices attributed to the mother	Mean % of traditional choices attributed to the father
North African comparison boys	48	69***	69***
North African 'mineurs de justice' boys	39	69***	70***
North African comparison girls	29	71***	79***
North African 'mineurs de justice' girls	27	66***	84***
French comparison boys	20	35***	34***
French 'mineurs de justice' boys	31	44***	52***
French comparison girls	19	33***	39***
French 'mineurs de justice' girls	24	49**	54***

Note: The asterisks indicate the significance of the difference between the mother or father and the adolescent.
*** $p < 0.0001$
** $p < 0.001$

the female and the male comparison groups is extremely significant ($p<0.001$). Perceived disagreement with the mother ($p<0.001$) and with the father ($p<0.001$) is again significantly stronger in the group of girls than in that of the boys.

In contrast, there is *no difference between the boys and the girls of the comparison groups of French adolescents* and hardly any in the delinquent group. In only one respect do the girls in the latter group differ significantly from the boys: disagreement with the father is more frequent for the delinquent daughters than the delinquent sons ($p<0.05$).

The data obtained with the alternative choice questionnaire clearly show the difficulty of the North African girls' position. By choosing 'modern' norms and values, such as independence, liberty and equality between men and women, they differentiate themselves not only from their parents and thus probably from most adults of their ethnic group, but also from the young boys of the same origin. Their position appears, on the whole, closer to that of French adolescents than to the young males of their own ethnic group.

It is interesting to examine the propositions of the alternative choice questionnaire on which the North African girls differentiate themselves significantly from the boys.

As expected, there is a highly significant difference ($p<0.001$, χ^2) between the girls' and boys' answers when requested to make a choice of one of the following two statements.

– A woman's place is in the home. It is the man's duty to work and support the family.
– Men and women should share the same domestic tasks and should have equal rights to work and to leisure.

The difference between the preference of boys and girls is just as significant ($p<0.001$) in the case of the choice between the following statements referring to the girls' freedom in premarital sexual relations:

– A girl who is not a virgin when she marries brings dishonour to her family.
– It is not important that a girl should remain a virgin until she marries.

The third highly significant difference ($p<0.005$) concerns the religious observances: the choice given is between the following propositions:

– Religious observances such as prayer, fasting, celebration of religious holidays are very important.
– Religious observance is not really necessary.

Contrary to an often reported finding that women are more religious than men in Catholic and Protestant countries, the North African girls declare significantly less often than the North African boys that they attach importance to religious observance. The results obtained with the interviews confirm this finding. The number of girls who claimed that they were practising Moslems was significantly lower than that of the boys ($p<0.02$).

The prevailing tendency among the female North African adolescents is to differentiate themselves from their group of origin by adopting the norms and values of the country of adoption which are instrumental in attaining autonomy and equal rights with men. Since the dependence of the woman and her inferior status are an inherent part of the Moslem religion, the women from North Africa who want more independence and freedom of action are forced either to abandon the religion of their group of origin, or, at least, to become less involved in it. (According to some Moslem women their status is not inferior but different from that of men.)

6. Cultural differentiation of the North African boys in the 'mineurs de justice' and comparison groups

Further examination of Table 2 reveals that there are several other differences with respect to traditionalism between the various groups studied. It is worth noting that the North African male group of 'mineurs de justice' is more modern than the control group – the former having a lower proportion of traditional choices than the latter – while the reverse is true of the French boys.

Let us try first to explain the difference observed in the French sample.

The traditionalism of the French male adolescents is significantly related to the educational level of their fathers. The lower this level, the more frequent the attachment of the sons to traditional values and norms ($p<0.005$, χ^2). While the socio-economic status of all the parents is approximately the same, the fathers of the French delinquents are of a particularly low socio-economic and educational level. They are also perceived as more traditional by their sons – as well as by their daughters – than are the fathers of the control group ($p<0.001$, t-test). Thus, the significant overall difference ($p<0.02$) between the traditionalism of the French male delinquents as compared to the French control group is probably due to the difference of family background. The French delinquents seem particularly underprivileged from the socio-economic, educational and cultural point of view.

An explanation in terms of educational and cultural level cannot be applied to the North African boys. The traditionalism of their parents is different not only in degree but also in structure from that of the French (see Malewska-Peyre and Zaleska, 1980): the roots and the meaning of traditionalism are not the same for these two groups of adults.

As may be seen from the figures presented in Table 2, the difference between the North African delinquents and the control group of male adolescents is opposite to that between the corresponding groups of French boys. Contrary to the French sample, it is the comparison group which is significantly less modern ($p<0.02$, t-test) than the delinquents. Moreover, in the North African group, the traditionalism of the sons is not related to that of their fathers nor does it depend on the fathers' educational level.

An examination of their answers to the alternative choice questionnaire reveals that though there is a slight tendency among control boys to be more frequently in favour of traditional norms and values, the only significant difference between the North African male delinquents and controls pertains to the importance of religious observance (p<0.001, χ^2). These data are also confirmed by the interviews. The North African boys in the comparison group declare significantly more often than the 'mineurs de justice' (p<0.001) that they follow the rules and rites of their religion.

We can only speculate as to the reasons for this difference. As suggested elsewhere by the authors (1980), it may be hypothesized that the control group male adolescents have adopted a strategy of differentiating themselves from the French by holding to the religion of their fathers which seems to be an essential component of their culture of origin and of their sense of identity.

It may be conjectured that, on the contrary, the North African delinquents have made a different choice. It would seem that they had decided – perhaps neither deliberately nor consciously – to adopt a strategy of 'passing' from their group of origin to the French group.

There are other results suggesting that the North African delinquents are more attracted by French society than the controls. The reference group boys have a better knowledge of their country of origin, and choose more often to serve in the army of their native country during their military service period. Their answers thus indicate a greater attachment to their national identity. Conversely, the North African 'mineurs de justice' know little of their country of origin and often prefer to serve in the French Army. Finally, when responding to the 'Who am I?' test, they choose more often than the controls the attribute: 'I have the mentality of the French.' All these results form a consistent pattern suggesting that the North African delinquents are generally more attracted by the society of adoption than other boys of the same ethnic origin.

It appears then that various strategies of differentiation are manifest in the group of North African adolescents. These strategies represent different reactions to a situation of value conflict and racial discrimination. Before concluding, we shall briefly report some results concerning the discrimination experienced by these adolescents.

7. Experience of racial discrimination

Most adolescent immigrants from our sample report having experienced racism in all walks of life: at school, at work and in other relations with the French.

When all the positive answers to the question: 'Have you experienced racism?' are listed together, the following results are obtained:

North African 'mineurs de justice' boys   83%
North African 'mineurs de justice' girls   79%
North African comparison group boys   71%
North African comparison group girls   67%
Portuguese 'mineurs de justice' boys   68%
Portuguese comparison group boys   58%
Portuguese comparison group girls   55%

(The Portuguese community usually sends girls whose behaviour is undesirable to Portugal to avoid contact with French justice – for this reason it was impossible to form a large enough sample of Portuguese 'mineurs de justice' girls.)

A high proportion of adolescents declare having experienced racism: more than half of them in each group refer to it.

As would be expected, male and female adolescents from North Africa suffer more from racism than do the adolescents from Portugal ($p < 0.01$, χ^2).

Within each national sample, the 'mineurs de justice' felt racism more than did boys in the reference group ($p < 0.01$).

Finally, within each ethnic group, girls seem to be less exposed to racial discrimination than boys. This tendency is, however, not significant.

We have been able to establish several links between the declared experience of racism, and depreciation of self and own group. This is in no way surprising: during adolescence, which is the period of identity building, relationships with others are very important in constructing the self image.

The connection between the way adolescents complete the sentence: 'They think that I . . .' and perceived racial discrimination is significant ($p < 0.001$, χ^2). Other results confirm this correlation between the self image and perceived racism. The young immigrants who admit having experienced discrimination show a greater frequency of negative image of self and own group, and a lower frequency of positive and neutral image.

Behind these quantitative results, a painfully felt situation is often found. A Portuguese girl said: 'They think that I am Portuguese and nevertheless I am nice and easy-going'; 'I feel lonely.' (The respondents had to complete the sentences: 'They think that I . . .' and 'I feel . . .' among others.)

And Habib said: '. . . I wonder what they think of me. Nothing positive

. . . I spent my childhood in Tunisia, in total poverty, that's why I feel Tunisian. I don't want to be French. I wouldn't like to be Tunisian either. Later, . . . I intend to travel a lot. Until I find a country where I want to settle, Sweden or Canada. There is no racism there.'

And Farida: 'They think I am different. I feel that no one understands me.'

8. Some hypotheses in conclusion

As noted before, the research on the adolescent immigrants was not designed for the study of the differentiation process. This is why we do not have all the information necessary for a rigorous analysis of the factors which facilitate the choice of a particular strategy of differentiation.

We can, however, offer some suggestions here as to these strategies.

In the case of the North African girls, the results appear relatively clear-cut, unequivocal and coherent.

These girls are exposed to a double identity threat. Firstly, they are in general poorly considered by the society of adoption because of their low socio-economic status and their ethnic origin.

Secondly, in their own ethnic group, it is the man whose position is prominent and who is highly esteemed, while the woman is deprived of independence and freedom of choice. The self image of the North African girl is threatened because of the low status of women in the traditional culture of her own country.

The double devaluation by the society of adoption and by the society of origin is mirrored in the girls' answers to the sentence completion test. It should be recalled that their image of French girls is much more positive than that of North African girls.

On witnessing the apparent equality between French men and women, the North African immigrant girls have become aware of how their traditional culture threatens their own identity. This is probably why they seem to have preferred to differentiate themselves from their own group, often at the cost of an open conflict with their family over their right to freedom. It is worth mentioning that several girls from our sample have run away from their parents in order to avoid a forced marriage with an unknown man or to escape the tyranny of their father or brothers.

It should be stressed that by abandoning certain cultural values, particularly those of religion, the North African girls are loosening, if not cutting off, their ties with their family and their group of origin. They may be confronted with the problem of maintaining their identity as North Africans.

The North African comparison group boys have, on the contrary, apparently chosen a strategy of holding to their identity. These boys are forced by French society to remain in the low status group of manual workers and unemployed labour, and – for those who have not acquired French nationality – exposed to constant difficulties with the French administration. In this situation of threat to their self image and of intergroup conflict, they seem to have maintained an identification with certain aspects of their culture of origin and particularly with the religion of their fathers.

The attachment of North African boys from the comparison group to religious observances is nevertheless associated with a general tendency to adopt the cultural norms of behaviour and values of French society since they differentiate themselves significantly from their parents by a much more frequent preference for the 'modern' choices on the alternative choice questionnaire. As may be seen in Table 2, the proportion of traditional choices of this group is actually intermediate between that of their parents and the French youngsters.

Moreover, as shown elsewhere (Malewska-Peyre and Zaleska, 1980) the structure of their preferences seems to be different both from that of their parents and of the French, thus suggesting an emergence in this group of an original culture, integrating partly the norms and values of their own ethnic group and partly those of the society of adoption.

The response patterns of the North African male delinquents are the most difficult to interpret. Their abandonment of religious values and the low proportion of traditional choices, their apparent preference for French culture and society, their tendency to positively evaluate the French boys more often than they do the North African boys, all contribute to form a coherent picture of a strategy of 'passing' which in turn is based on a desire to assimilate into French society.

However, the choice of a strategy of 'passing' seems inconsistent with the frequency of experienced racial discrimination in this group. It may be conjectured that the failure of the strategy of 'passing' has increased the boys' frustration and resulted in a heightened probability of violence and other offences. But it is not clear why, despite the experience of racism and failure of their efforts to assimilate, these youngsters are apparently attracted by the society of adoption. We hope that future research will help to reach a better understanding of the cognitive inconsistency found within this group.

References

Camilleri, C. 1979. Crise socio-culturelle et crise d'identité dans les sociétés du Tiers-Monde. *Psychologie Française*, **24**, 3–4, 259–68.

Malewska-Peyre, H. and Zaleska, M. 1980. Identité et conflits de valeurs chez les jeunes immigrés maghrébins. *Psychologie Française*, **25**, 2, 125–38.

Newcomb, T. M. 1950. *Social psychology*. New York: Holt, Rinehart and Winston.

Zavalloni, M. 1973. L'identité sociale: un concept à la recherche d'une science. In S. Moscovici (ed.): *Introduction à la psychologie sociale*. Paris: Larousse, vol. 2, pp. 245–65.

14. Re-socialization processes in institutionalized adolescents

FELICE CARUGATI, FRANCESCA EMILIANI
and AUGUSTO PALMONARI

1. Institutional care

This chapter is concerned with the change in the behaviour and in the social relations of groups of adolescents which was brought about by means of their transfer from large residential institutions to small living units which were housed in normal city apartments. Psychology has, up to now, shown little interest in the developmental process of people who grow up in public, welfare institutions and not in families. An exception to this, in Europe, is the work of J. Tizard and his collaborators who, in a study of 1971 (King, Raynes and Tizard, 1971), emphasize that, among all residential institutions, those for children have particularly distinctive characteristics and that they can be placed along a continuum from child-oriented to institution-oriented management practices. In order to operationalize this conceptual dimension in children's institutions for the purpose of empirical study, these authors chose four areas of child management and staff interaction: rigidity of routine, 'block treatment' of children, depersonalization of children and the social distance maintained between children and staff (p. 106).

Our team has studied long-stay institutions for children in Italy at length and has focused, in particular, on those for normal children. In our country, in fact, residential care has been almost the only form of social assistance given to children in need. Many of these institutions are very large. They have often more than 150 inmates and are organized in a centralized fashion with one administrative and educational director to whom the entire staff is answerable. In many cases, these institutions are run by religious congregations (Sarpellon, 1979).

1.1. Social functions of institutions

The first fact that we discovered and that appeared to us important for an understanding of their social significance is that these institutions are not just a social care instrument intended to replace the family in cases of need, but that they also fulfil other important social functions. These are:

- as economic structures, the institutions are strongly connected with the economic life of the environment. The presence of a large long-stay institution for children may influence the economic and commercial structure of a territorial area as can the presence of an industrial or a military complex. There are, at least in Italy, some large areas whose livelihood is heavily dependent on the existence of a psychiatric hospital, or on a large total institution for children. In these cases, suggestions of closing the institutions raise far reaching social problems, causing definite and strong resistance on the part of local populations;
- the institutions are frequently run by groups that have acquired considerable social prestige precisely by means of the establishment and the running of charitable works for children. Many religious congregations and some lay, humanitarian societies are typical in this regard. These have their own tradition of charitable work which justifies, in their eyes, the pure and simple reproduction of the style of management by which they have always been characterized. The prospect of modifying the character of their own homes by putting them under the control of local authorities causes many congregations to react by closing their institutions. They also feel that they are being treated in a most ungrateful fashion;
- institutions are, furthermore, structures which perpetuate the existence of certain categories of under-privileged children. The terms 'Children's Home', 'Orphanage' and 'Institute for Poor and Abandoned Minors' indicate, in reality, long-stay institutions that care for children whose need for such care can be traced back to the precarious work-situations of their parents, to their lack of or the incompleteness of their families, to the inadequacy of school services and to the difficulties that exist with regard to adoption.

Institutional care confers a definite label on these children. This has many negative effects on their performance in school and on their self-esteem. These factors make the study of child-management in long-stay institutions even more important. If we compare, as we did in our previous studies (Carugati *et al.*, 1973) the life of a child living within his family, with that of one in a long-stay institution, we realize that the latter has a much more monotonous, homogeneous, heterodirected and fragmented daily routine.

1.2. Characteristics of institutional life

MONOTONY. In the institution, children have to follow a rigid timetable, which is essential for the functioning of the institution. Every day, without exception, the same activities are performed: getting up; washing; breakfast; school; lunch; studying; playing; supper; television and bed. None of these activities may be omitted; everything is compulsory, even playing. Each one of these activities must happen in turn at a given time, even playing, which is often confined to a specific game. All the activities take place in a fixed setting.

HETERODIRECTION. The daily behaviour of the children is prearranged by definite rules which are reinforced by the constant presence of an adult. The rigid organization of physical space and timetable fixity are the tools that reinforce the institution's power. Special authorization is required for every action that deviates from the established routine. The control is unlimited; if one of the staff members assumes a less rigid vigilance towards his charges, another member, hierarchically superior, may intervene to restore order. Permanent closeness between peers is a forced reality, a functional necessity for the control of the situation. The children are always together but do not communicate. The children's movements, even when they are outside the building of the institution, are always influenced by the authority of the staff. Their behaviour, therefore, is never autonomous and never creative of new personal relations, but involves merely movements from one place of activity to another.

HOMOGENEITY. This characteristic is particularly felt when the institution includes a school for children on the premises. In this case, the children do not have any chance of variation in daily life. The homogeneity becomes oppressive because of the close network of relations that binds the school world to the extra-school one. The children have no means of expressing themselves differently within various contexts, because neither adults nor peers allow it. This compels the children to maintain the same behavioural patterns.

FRAGMENTATION. This is a characteristic that can seem contradictory in such a homogeneous climate. Nevertheless, the burden that the timetable imposes on the daily routine makes it understandable. Everyone in the institution knows that all activities are compulsory but that, on the other hand, they cannot be prolonged beyond the given time. Therefore, the long day unfolds without any real interest in the assigned occupation and in the expectation of some key-moment when the discipline will slacken for a while. Knowing the impossibility of spending any more time than that allowed, the children do not care to make good use of it, even in cases where they are especially attracted to a particular activity.

The children, therefore, are living fragments of life, casually associated with one another, with a continuity that does not derive from their own experiences but from the rules of the institution.

Beyond these characteristics, the residential institutions often present some peculiarities, which Goffman (1961) defines as institutional ceremonies and underground life. These do not have to be described here. It will only be said that institutional ceremonies seem to be much more stereotyped than any family ceremony can be. Underground life depends on the size of the institution. Here various behavioural patterns appear: brawls between rival groups; nocturnal outings; incursions into forbidden areas (kitchens; staff offices; electric installations, etc.).

The literature on the long-term effects of prolonged periods of institutional care in childhood is partial and, in some aspects, controversial (Rutter, 1972, 1979; King, Raynes and Tizard, 1971). There is certainly a lack of studies on the way in which a transfer from one of these institutions to a family- or small-group-type situation influences the behaviour and the social relationships of the individual.

2. Experiments in re-socialization

In the past fifteen years in Italy, there has been a wave of criticism of total institutions, particularly of those for children, and there has been an attempt to overcome these criticisms by creating alternative forms of assistance. The effort to overcome the deficiencies of total institutions was given an important impetus by the assumption of direct responsibility for them by the local authorities. We have described this development and some direct consequences of it elsewhere (Palmonari and Zani, 1982). The programme which we will describe in this chapter started at the beginning of the 1970s in Bologna and in neighbouring cities. Their purpose was to provide a response to the needs of pre-adolescents and of adolescents. The programme involved the establishment of new structures of care called 'apartment groups' because ordinary apartments in different areas of the city were used to house groups of adolescents. Each one of these groups was supervised by three adults.

The first of these programmes, known as the Baraccano experiment, was implemented in Bologna during the year 1970/1. The programme was given impetus by the closure of a church-oriented institution which housed about 100 girls aged between 6 and 18 years. The girls came from small towns and from the countryside in the province of Bologna. They were of poor, generally farm families and they had been taken into care mostly because of the inadequacy of the school and study facilities available to them at home. This institution had to be closed after the religious staff had resigned due to a conflict with the institution's administrative council. The council, therefore, had to find another solution in the few months between June and September. It appealed to the Institute of Psychology in Bologna which proposed the following measures:

– a special financial aid programme, which would permit the girls who had originally been in the institution for economic reasons (about 75) to return to their families;
– the organization of four small autonomous groups for the girls who were not able to return to their families (about 25).

These groups were the first so-called 'apartment groups' and had the following characteristics:

– each group consisted of six to eight girls grouped according to age, as they had been in the institution, with three female adults; each group was then assigned a normal apartment in different areas of the city;
– the adults were either students of the Educational Sciences Faculty of the University, or graduates of the School of Social Work;
– the council of the institution paid a salary to one of the three adults, whilst the other two worked as volunteers with paid expenses;
– all adults lived and slept in the apartments;
– the council gave each group money to provide for the necessities of daily life; this was calculated according to the subsidies which had previously been granted to the institution. Moreover, the council directly paid the rent and the gas and electricity bills. Also at the expense of the council, a woman was engaged part-time to attend to the house-keeping;
– all the girls attended public schools, generally located near their apartments;
– each group was autonomous and organized its daily life according to the personal requirements of each member;
– the experiment provided for weekly meetings between all the adults and a psychologist from the Institute of Psychology, an expert in problems of the institutional care of children, to discuss the progress of the individual groups.

This programme lasted only a year because the administrators withdrew their support for it. They did not agree with the approach adopted by the adults and considered the way in which the latter dealt with the adolescents to be too *laissez-faire*. It proved possible to send most of the girls back to their families with some form of financial aid.

Despite the abrupt conclusion of the programme, the adults were able to draw up case histories of the groups using the contents of their weekly diaries. The Institute of Psychology requested that this information be given to them so that they could compare the results of the

experiment with those of an observation-study of ten mentally handicapped girls who had been transferred from a residential institution for
handicapped children that had 600 places to a boarding school in which
they lived in a small living unit with two nuns. On that occasion, it was
observed that, before finding their own style of constructive relationships, the girls went through a period (3–4 months) of intense
behavioural disturbance (Arfelli Galli and Palmonari, 1965). It was
therefore expected that the girls of the Baraccano experiment would go
through a similar period of disorganization and restlessness and that they
would achieve a life-style regulated by rules and norms that they
themselves had discovered, only after they had overcome this phase.

In fact, after a few weeks of well-being and enthusiasm for the new way
of life, the girls entered into a phase of over-excitement and confusion
which posed problems for the adults living with them. In only two of the
apartment groups did the adults succeed in confronting the behaviour of
the girls in such a way that, after months of continuous effort on the part
of the former, the latter were able to find acceptable rules and norms of
living together, to apply themselves to their studies and to take
responsibility for the everyday running of the apartment.

The development of the other two groups was, however, very
different. As soon as the person in charge of one of these was faced with
the first persistent signs of unruliness, she introduced a strict daily
timetable, assigned specific household tasks to each girl and imposed
definite study and meal schedules on her charges. In a short time,
therefore, the girls returned to an ordered life-style but this order was due
to rules and norms which were imposed from above and which were not
established by the girls themselves. Finally, in the fourth group, the
person in charge became involved in the behaviour of the girls; she did
not keep herself distinct from them. Because of this, the atmosphere of
confusion and incessant over-excitement continued until the end of the
experiment. However, the former two groups enabled us to confirm the
initial expectation that the girls would achieve a high degree of autonomy
only after a phase of confusion, already defined as one of 'regression'.

The programme outlined above and implemented in Bologna in 1970/1
was used as a point of reference for a later project which was started in
Ravenna at the end of the summer of 1971. This continuity was possible
because the same psychologist, who had carried out supervisory
functions in Bologna during the previous year, was asked by the local
authority of Ravenna to tackle, in the context of the Mental Health
Services, the problem of male adolescents of between 9 and 14 years of

age who had been refused admission by numerous welfare institutions either because of emotional disturbance or because of incidents of petty delinquency. This psychologist, together with two educators who had also worked in Bologna, was thus given the opportunity of implementing a programme based on the same principles as that in which they had previously been engaged. They did this by forming two apartment groups both of which began to function in the autumn of 1971. At the same time, the local authorities of Bologna and Imola started five and two apartment groups, respectively. These involved a total of about 40 boys between the ages of 10 and 13 years. The formation of the groups was the final step in a difficult and protracted process involving the closure of two large institutions for minors under the care of the local authorities. The most frequent reasons for the admission of the children to institutional care were neglect, desertion and emotional disturbance.

In the last two programmes, several differences from the initial one can be noted:

- the maximum number of boys in an apartment group was five;
- the educators were all paid by the local authorities and had specific social service qualifications;
- their presence in the apartment was determined by a regular schedule so that the work could be done in shifts. There were no housekeepers and all domestic work was done by the adults;
- the boys went to the public school from 8.30 a.m. to 5.30 p.m. with lunch at the school;
- the adults were directly responsible for the group and for the organization of a daily routine, but they did not have to account for expenses.

A similar programme was implemented in Ferrara where, in the winter of 1972/3, four groups, each one of five boys aged between 9 and 14 years, who suffered from severe psycho-physiological handicaps, were formed. During the period between the autumn of 1971 and the end of 1975, there were a total of 25 apartment groups operating in the cities mentioned.

These groups catered for a total of 130 minors, mostly male, between the ages of 9 and 15 years. Seventy-five adults, both male and female, were involved. In subsequent years, most of the groups were closed for a variety of reasons. In some cases, the closure coincided with the children's return to their families or with the boarding-out of young workers. This was particularly true for Bologna where the local authority, at the beginning of 1976, initiated a programme of domiciliary welfare for minors.

The adults involved in the apartment groups were employed in this programme. In the course of the programme, the minors were gradually returned to the care of their parents or to relatives and were followed in the first stages of their re-entry into family life by the same adults who had worked with them in the apartment groups. Other groups were closed down by the local authorities because of trade union problems with the adult staff (e.g. about hours of work), because of the local authorities' disapproval of the normative approaches adopted by the staff and implemented in the groups and because of tensions produced in the neighbourhoods by the sometimes unruly behaviour of the minors.

3. Life in apartment groups

The fundamental features that we have chosen to illustrate the extent to which this programme of apartment groups was innovative in the context of institutional care in general, are as follows:

- the integration of the programme with broader programmes of social security (adoption, fostering, vocational and educational programmes);
- the selection of apartments in residential areas of the city to facilitate the frequenting of public schools and entry into work;
- the direct responsibility of the adults for both the organization of everyday life and the overall development and welfare of their charges;
- the presence of supervisors who were external to the groups and who had the dual role of working with the adults to evaluate with them the progress of their groups and of acting as intermediaries between the groups and the local authorities from which position they could defend the autonomy of the adults involved;
- the elasticity of the roles of the adults, the absence of a rigid hierarchy among them and their refusal to model their behaviour in relation to the adolescents on parental roles;
- the availability of adults capable of maintaining relationships with both their charges and their colleagues and of sustaining group dynamics in a very difficult and demanding situation.

During the first year of the scheme, we followed, in a systematic way, the development of the five groups in Bologna and of the two in Ravenna. We made direct observations (two hours, every fifteen days) in each of the seven groups at different times of the day (lunch, dinner, evening hours before bedtime).

In addition, we conducted in-depth interviews with all of the adults, once in the initial stages of the group and once towards the end of the first year. In the course of 1975, we also conducted in-depth interviews about their lives in institutions prior to the establishment of the apartment groups, the initial stages of group life and the overall unfolding of the experiment with two-thirds of the adolescents involved. We were unable to carry out the same type of observation in the apartment groups of Ferrara and Imola. Thanks to periodic meetings with the people in charge of these two programmes, however, we were able to reconstruct the pattern of development of the groups in these two cities.

In five of the seven groups which were studied directly, a pattern of development consisting of three distinct stages was observed. It seems appropriate to describe the process in detail at this point. Although the length of each stage of development varied from case to case, the order in which they appeared was the same for all:

- an initial phase in which the way of life of the institution in which the adolescents had previously lived was reproduced and in which the different elements in the new way of life were discovered (duration 6–8 weeks);
- a phase of crisis (duration 3–4 months);
- a phase of reorganization (from the sixth month on).

3.1. Reproduction of the institutional way of life and discovery of new elements

When several adolescents came directly from the same institution, at first they manifested the behaviour acquired there and reproduced roles belonging to the previous context: for instance, leader, unruly rebel, clown, etc. At the same time, however, they found a great many aspects of the new environment which no longer corresponded to their preconceptions:

- a new physical environment, very different from that of the institution. The apartments were in the city, in normal houses organized like ordinary households, with a great deal of indoor light, whereas the institution had had none of these characteristics, a fact which the adolescents themselves noticed;
- they also interacted with the adults who were always ready to talk and listen to them, and to answer their questions. The latter were ready to change their opinions if these proved inappropriate; they did not simply impose upon the adolescents typical institutional punishments, such as beating them or putting them into dark rooms;
- they had the possibility of organizing their own schedules, of coming and going without having to account for these movements to anybody; they could meet the friends they liked outside the house.

The discovery of these changes greatly disorientated the adolescents but they expressed their confusion verbally only during the third phase which will be described more fully later. For the adolescents who did not come directly from institutions (for example those in Ravenna) this first phase was very brief, and was marked, above all, by their attempts to test the accessibility of the adults.

During the first phase the intention of the adults was to behave as follows:

– to be receptive to the requests of the adolescents;
– to be ready to provide explanations and justifications for their behaviour towards the adolescents;
– to be accessible and ready to take an active part in the various aspects of daily life, such as the housework, and the preparation of meals, without observing a strict timetable;
– to be discreet and lenient towards any disordered behaviour, manifested, for example, in unmade beds and uncleaned rooms.

This kind of informal and positive interpersonal relationship was the necessary condition for establishing an alternative way of life; the adults tried to provide the adolescents with the affection they had previously lacked, and thus offered them the possibility of constructing a critical framework in reference to the 'outside world'.

3.2. Crisis

This phase was very long (3–4 months) in all groups analysed. Generally speaking, it can be considered to be a group phenomenon, in the sense that it affected all the adolescents in the same apartment. Their behaviour was disorganized, apparently incomprehensible, and full of contradictions (e.g. they ate and slept when they felt like it regardless of the hour) but, at the same time, they wanted the adults to be present all the time.

The adolescents wanted the adults to be protective towards them. They sought physical contact with them: in some cases they shared their beds; they asked the adults if they could sit on their knees; and they wanted to know where the adults were and what they were doing all the time (e.g. they would telephone the adults when they were out of the house, question them about their activities, and continually enter their bedrooms). They tried to imitate the physical appearance of the adults. For example, they dressed in the adults' clothes, used their make-up, and also adopted their ways of thinking and acting, their personal tastes and opinions. They wanted to be reassured about the normality of their physical development. At times, the adolescents (above all the girls) displayed exhibitionist behaviour, in the presence of visitors. They refused any kind of involvement, whether in the running of the apartment or in school activities.

In our opinion this period represented an attempt by the adolescents to broaden their range of possibilities, activities and acquaintances. The adults, from their point of view, found this period one of continuous involvement, as the adolescents made constant demands on them. Meanwhile they also had to face numerous problems concerning school, the neighbours, the adolescents' parents, and even the police. The adults saw this phase as one of tension and frustration for themselves. It was during this phase in Bologna that four of the adults left the groups and replacements had to be found.

Although a direct causality between the behaviour of the adults and changes in that of the adolescents cannot be proved from the information gathered during the course of the programme, we are of the opinion that the adults in the two groups that did not develop according to the three-stage pattern outlined above, did not deal appropriately with the adolescents during the phase of confusion. In fact, when they were faced with the first symptoms of confusion, these adults adopted an authoritarian attitude and imposed strict rules on the adolescents.

3.3. Reorganization

In all the groups where the adults stayed on, a successive constructive phase emerged after this negative period: the third phase was characterized by more autonomous behaviour on the part of the adolescents. This change came about at different times in different individuals. The children regained their interest in the running of the house, keeping it in order and doing the chores.

During the first of these three phases the adults suggested – without insisting on the idea – holding discussions on their communal way of life, but these proposals met with no response. In the second phase, which we have just described, the adults chose not to renew the discussion of this issue. During this third phase, however, group discussions were set up dealing with the collective life in the apartments, and initiated by the adolescents themselves. The first of these discussions was set up ostensibly to solve everyday problems, such as household management and financial arrangements, but this led to more spontaneous discussions in which the issues were more personal and individual. For instance, personal experiences of the change from the institution to the apartment group were analysed. On such occasions new possibilities of linguistic expression were discovered, as these discussions allowed the adolescents to talk about themselves and their personal histories, to express the new image they had of the adults, and also to admit explicitly the senselessness of persisting in certain forms of behaviour which had characterized their life in the institution.

The adolescents said that they realized they were living through an original and personal experience which gave them an advantage in their encounters with normal adolescents, who – living with their families – did not enjoy as much freedom. This feeling was also accompanied, however, by a clearer awareness of their own difficulties arising from their family situations (separated parents, etc.). There was also a noticeable broadening of the adolescents' horizons, in terms of their perception of time perspective, and of their capacities for making plans for the future. It was also during this phase that their school interests began to reassert themselves, and their scholastic achievement markedly improved. During this period the adolescents also began to develop selective relationships with the outside world, to make new friendships.

4. Conclusions

The fact that at least in five groups studied the three phases were found in the same order, leads us to suppose that the phases do not succeed one another by chance, but rather seem to demonstrate a precise process of transformation, in which the crisis period plays a central role.

We here find ourselves face to face with one of the fundamental problems of the entire question: do the behaviour modifications manifested during the course of this programme represent merely temporary adaptations to a new, less structured and characterized situation, or do they truly represent a real process of change? Before answering any such questions, it is necessary to reflect on the factors which lie at the root of this problem, and which condition the process of personal change.

According to Gendlin (1964), any process of personal change is brought about within the context of a deep interpersonal relationship, and implies for the subject an intense surfacing of feelings. However, in the situations that have been considered, both of these phenomena occurred above all in one particular phase – the so-called 'crisis phase'. The adolescents experienced a considerable emotional upheaval, which had gradually developed during the first phase as they discovered the unexpected and unexploited range of possibilities which the new situation afforded, in terms of unstructured relationships with peers and with the environment, but above all with 'significant adults' (Berger and Luckmann, 1966), in this case, with the educators. This emotional upheaval reached peak moments of disorganization which sometimes lasted for several days. Relationships with the adults were characterized by explicit demands made on them: they had to be present when the adolescents wished them to be.

The adolescents came to feel the need for physical contact. Within the framework of exclusive relationships of this kind, episodes of very intense communication, especially on a non-verbal level, were quite frequent, as has already been described.

From the phenomena observed, it is evident that a real change did occur in interpersonal and intrapersonal relationships. From this point of view, we can now attempt a psycho-social interpretation of this change and of the consequent development of a set of autonomous and organized behavioural patterns. We can thus define the change as a process of de-socialization–re-socialization, as understood by Berger and Luckmann (1966).

According to these authors, any process which brings about profound changes during the so-called period of secondary socialization implies:

- a subjective feeling of total transformation: the individual has the impression of 'changing worlds';
- a radical reshuffling of the values of reality: certain elements of the social environment, previously predominant, lose their importance while other elements, previously subordinate in value, become predominant;
- the presence of intense bonds of affection with 'significant others': these bonds seem to be qualitatively comparable to those of the child with the mother during the early stages of social development.

That is, given the previous experiences of these adolescents, it is absolutely necessary for them to go through a phase in which the previous conventional structure of objective reality is demolished and disintegrates. This is called the de-socialization phase.

During this phase, behaviour seems confused, senseless and contradictory, as the subject negates the value of those parameters which he had used, until now, to give a certain degree of order to his actions. On the other hand, he is still unable to perceive clearly his new system of reference. It is precisely for this reason that the subject risks 'losing himself', since others will no longer tolerate his behaviour. They try to prevent this behaviour, and to push him back to positions he has already passed, or they leave him to himself which increases his confusion.

Such patterns of behaviour are similar to those manifested in the crisis phase, and also to those observed by Redl and Wineman (1951) during the well-known research they conducted in 'Pioneer House'. These are interpreted psychoanalytically as alterations of the functions of Ego control.

From a comparison of our observations and those of these two authors it can be seen that the behaviour of our apartment group adolescents fits the pattern of Redl and Wineman, and can be interpreted as symptoms of lack of Ego functions. However, it seems to us that the significance of the de-socialization which follows this phase in the sequence of change can be better understood if it is considered as an expression of real regression of behaviour (our concept of regression follows the operational definition given by Lewin, 1951, pp. 87–129). In fact, according to Lewin, regression essentially consists of a series of phenomena concerning not only the behaviour, but also the personal make-up of the individual. In practice, regression is indicated by less complex and more elementary organization of behaviour, by a lessening of the coherence of the individual, a restriction of his field of interests and activities, and a lessening of his capacity to distinguish between reality and unreality.

Judgements concerning the phenomena of regression must not be absolute, but rather they should make reference to the level of development of the individual's personal make-up and organization of behaviour at a given moment. Frustration is the principal cause of regression, yet there can also be phenomena of temporary regression (quite long-lasting at times) due to other intense emotional processes.

We believe that it is possible to classify those moments when the adolescents in the apartment groups lost the rhythm of their life as examples of temporary regression of behaviour: for example, those moments when they did not eat at regular hours; when they did not eat meals, but rather snacks, fruit, or cakes; when they slept during the day instead of at night; and when they abandoned themselves to creating 'incomprehensible' uproars which disturbed the neighbours.

We also cautiously put forward the hypothesis that various other forms of behaviour – such as thumb-sucking or sitting on an adult's knee – or, to put it more concisely, when the children communicate in a quasi-primitive and non-verbal manner, although rare in occurrence, can also be defined as phenomena of temporary regression of the individual. In this way the adolescents demonstrate that they can no longer do without physical contact with the adults.

Remaining within Lewin's frame of reference, these moments of regression are used by the child to break down the limitations on his 'free-movement space' which had been imposed by this previous institutional experience. New possibilities of working with the real world are thus opened up, possibilities which will consolidate themselves in the phase which we have called above the phase of re-socialization.

References

Arfelli Galli, A. and Palmonari, A. 1965. Fenomenologia del comportamento di bambine istituzionalizzate al passaggio da un istituto tradizionale ad un nucleo familiare. *Psichiatria generale e dell'età evolutiva*, **3**, 2, 3–22.

Berger, P. L. and Luckmann, T. 1966. *The social construction of reality.* New York: Doubleday.

Carugati, F., Casadio, G., Lenzi, M., Palmonari, A. and Ricci Bitti, P. E. 1973. *Gli orfani dell'assistenza.* Bologna: Il Mulino.

Gendlin, E. 1964. *A theory of personality change.* In P. Worchel and D. Byrne (eds.): *Personality change.* Chicago: J. Wiley.

Goffman, E. 1961. *Asylums. Essays on the social situation of mental patients and other inmates.* New York: Anchor Books, Doubleday.

King, R. D., Raynes, N. V. and Tizard, J. 1971. *Patterns of residential care.* London: Routledge and Kegan Paul.

Lewin, K. 1951. *Field theory in social science.* New York: Harper and Brothers.

Palmonari, A. and Zani, B. 1982. Towards a community psychology in Italy. In P. Stringer (ed.): *Confronting social issues.* London: Academic Press

Redl, F. and Wineman, D. 1951. *Children who hate.* Glencoe, Ill.: The Free Press.

Rutter, M. 1972. *Maternal deprivation reassessed.* Harmondsworth: Penguin.

Rutter, M. 1979. Maternal deprivation, 1972–1978: New findings, new concepts, new approaches. *Child Development*, **50**, 283–305.

Sarpellon, G. 1979. Censimento delle Istituzioni assistenziali collegate con la Chiesa. In Caritas Italiana (ed.): *Chiesa ed emarginazione in Italia.* Bologna: Edizioni Dehoniane.

Part VII
On becoming a worker

For a long time, entry into work has been a neglected phase in the study of individual development. It was considered evident that at this point the individual had acquired competencies which were now to be used within a framework defined by norms governing the organization of work.

Sociologists appealing to an interactionist perspective first attracted attention to this phase of individual history, showing how frequent are the discrepancies between individual expectations and experiences, and between the forecasts of the institution and the difficulties of adaptation for particular individuals. To these authors we owe the concept of moral career elaborated to account for modifications in the self-concept during different phases of the encounter with work.

Only in the last few years has social psychology begun to take an interest in these problems. The contribution by West and Newton here shows how entry into the world of work is accomplished in a different manner by males and females and also as a function of the schools attended beforehand. In his contribution Sarchielli uses different techniques to show the transformations that the first experiences with the world of work bring in the representations of occupations, in predictions concerning occupational future, and in the expectations expressed regarding fellow workers. It seems that modifications are produced which take account of the data of experience and which allow elaboration of effective strategies for coping with the difficulties of the work environment.

15. Social interaction in adolescent development: schools, sex roles and entry to work

MICHAEL A. WEST and PEGGY NEWTON

1. Introduction

The transition from school to work is a particularly important phase in adolescent development and it can be argued that the most significant milestone, the entry into work, has not been recognized either for the status changes it heralds in development or for the profound social-psychological influences exerted on the individual. But the transition from school to work is not a period during which the adolescent is merely worked upon and moulded by social institutions and forces. Heightened interaction between the adolescent and society occurs at a rapid pace and over a short period of time. Consequently, many adolescents (and adults) find this transition phase at once confusing, stressful, exciting and anxiety-provoking. Within this relatively short period, adolescents are expected to discard the role of dependent schoolchildren and assume the role of independent working adults.

The study we describe below emphasized the effects that school ethos and organization have upon individual development during adolescence and particularly during the entry to work phase. Our study focussed upon two schools which differed in their organizational structure. One school adopted a banding system in which roughly half of the students (considered academically more able) were assigned to the 'A' band, and the other half of the students (considered academically less able) were assigned to the 'B' band. The second school was run along 'mixed ability' lines, with a mixture of ability levels in classes being the general rule.

There is some evidence from a number of different sources, that streaming in schools has an effect upon the social organization of schools, and upon the attitudes and experiences of the pupils within them. However, there is almost no research which relates school organization to the transition from school to work. Swift (1973) has examined the differences in the experiences of grammar school and secondary school boys in the transition from school to work. Effects due to school organization in this study cannot therefore be distinguished from effects attributable to academic ability and social class background. Given that attitudes and experiences are influenced by school organization, it remains a possibility that attitudes and experiences during the transition phase might be similarly influenced. We therefore determined to assess whether such things as occupational aims, attitudes to work, attitudes to supervisors and hopes and expectations for the future, might be affected by school organization. Another area of possible investigation was differences in the transition from school to work between boys and girls.

2. The study

The study was designed to explore many different aspects of transition from school to work, including the issues described above, and was carried out in two traditional mining communities ('Woodbank' and 'Brookvale') in Nottinghamshire, England. Both towns also offered job opportunities in textiles, wood-machining and light engineering.

Defining the period over which the transition from school to work occurs is inevitably arbitrary. We have chosen to define the period as stretching from about six months prior to the date of leaving school to thirty months after the date of leaving. Accordingly, we interviewed 174 school-leavers (86 boys and 88 girls) within six months prior to their leaving school (Table 1). Ninety of the pupils were from the fifth form of Woodbank school, and the other 84 were from the fifth form of Brookvale school. Nine months into their working life, an effort was made to contact all of those who had co-operated in the first interview. We were able to contact 103 adolescents (48 males and 55 females; 52 ex-Woodbank and 51 ex-Brookvale pupils) and they were again interviewed at the schools. These interviews lasted approximately 45 minutes each and the adolescents were asked a wide variety of questions about their experiences since leaving school and starting work (Table 1). The final interview could not be conducted by teams of interviewers because of the logistical problems entailed in contacting all of the original sample and arranging for them to meet in one place. A questionnaire was therefore posted to all of those who had participated in the interviews conducted at the school shortly before they left (Table 1). Ninety-three returned the questionnaires completed, of whom 47 were males and 46 were females.

Table 1. *Interview schedules and goals*

Interview	Time	Areas of Enquiry
1	6 months prior to leaving school	Vocational preferences; knowledge about jobs and the means of getting jobs; opinions of careers interviews; parental wishes; attitudes towards teachers and school; expectations of the future; attitudes to sex roles; demographic data
2	9 months into working life	Examination passes; attitudes to careers service; length of time in finding first job; methods used to find jobs; help received from schools and careers service; job changes; attitudes to work, supervisors and co-workers; experiences on starting work; training required for jobs; pay and conditions; changes in home life; attitudes to society
3	2½ years into working life	Current jobs; how settled in jobs; opinions of help received from schools and careers service; number of job changes; reasons for job changes

Forty-nine former Woodbank and 44 former Brookvale pupils completed and returned the questionnaires.

At this time (two and a half years after the beginning of working life), we were also able to contact and gain information about the current jobs and job histories of a further 61 (in addition to the 93 already contacted) of the original respondents. This gave us up-to-date information on the job histories of 154 of the original 174 respondents.

3. The effects of school organization and ethos

Adolescents who attended the streamed school (Woodbank) were significantly less positive in their attitudes to both their teachers and their schools than were adolescents who attended Brookvale school. They were also more likely to choose jobs of higher status than pupils from Brookvale and, within Woodbank, the 'A' band pupils were much less likely to have jobs by the time they had left school, than were 'B' band pupils. Pupils from Woodbank also secured jobs, on average, of significantly lower status than those they had originally hoped for.

These differences between the attitudes and experiences of pupils from the two schools appeared to extend beyond the school walls. Differences in attitudes to training for jobs emerged, which appeared to be linked to the banding system in Woodbank. Former pupils of Woodbank, having left school, found their jobs less interesting than did workers who had attended Brookvale; they saw their jobs as offering them less in the way of promotion prospects, pay, useful learning or even social contacts; they were also less settled in their jobs and more likely to be considering a change of jobs.

This coherent picture of greater dissatisfaction among streamed school pupils is not easily explicable in terms of a single causal factor. The ethos of Woodbank certainly seemed to reflect the conflict which the banding system appeared to generate, with greater hostility expressed towards teachers, and greater rivalry between groups of pupils characteristic of Woodbank when compared with Brookvale. Another major difference between the two schools was the emphasis on academic values and the stress laid upon the rewards of hard work in Woodbank. The covert propaganda within the school may have given credence to the idea that by working hard at school, one's lot in working life would be better. The effects of this might then have been to raise expectations of working life throughout the school, with even 'B' band students being affected by the optimism of the 'A' band. Our finding that the Woodbank pupils had to take jobs of significantly lower status than they had originally aimed at, suggests that by some means, expectations of working life were raised more amongst Woodbank pupils than they were amongst pupils of Brookvale school.

Interestingly pupils from the unbanded school were more likely to describe co-workers as very easy to get on with than were those from Woodbank. They were also more likely to choose items describing favourable characteristics of supervisors. This latter finding is of considerable interest when taken in conjunction with the finding that they were also more favourable (on the same scales) in attitudes to teachers. It suggests that some socialization of attitudes to authority figures had taken place within the schools and that the attitudes had persisted and had been carried over to the world of work. Given that the kinds of jobs taken by the young people from the two schools did not differ in any significant way, it suggests that it was not differences between supervisors which produced the differences in attitudes. It appears more likely that attitudes to authority figures, engendered at school, persisted into working life.

An alternative explanation is that the less favourable attitudes to work held by former pupils of the streamed school, also affected their attitudes to supervisors. Thus, it might be argued, that their more critical view of working life (produced possibly by their disappointment at having to take jobs of lower status than originally aimed for) produced a more jaundiced view of almost all aspects of their work, supervisors being only one amongst many of these aspects. The finding that their attitudes to co-workers were less favourable would also be more consistent with this explanation and thus provides some support for it.

Whatever the explanation, it is apparent that some aspects of the organization and ethos of the schools affected subsequent attitudes to work and supervisors. The similarity of the catchment areas and jobs attained by pupils from the two schools makes explanations in terms of the schools themselves appear more likely. Rutter has argued that:

individual actions or measures (within the schools) may combine to create a particular ethos, or set of values, attitudes and behaviours which will become characteristic of the school as a whole . . . to an appreciable extent, children's behaviour and attitudes are shaped and influenced by their experiences at school as a social institution. (Rutter *et al.*, 1979)

So our findings provide support for Rutter's position that secondary schools do have important influences on their pupils' behaviour and attainments. What they also suggest however, is that these influences on behaviours and attitudes shaped and influenced by experiences at school, and by the group influence resulting from the ethos of school as a social institution, are likely to persist beyond school and into work life and may affect not only attitudes to work itself, but even social relationships within the world of work.

4. Sex differences in transition from school to work

How does the socialization of sex roles affect the processes of transition from school to work? Firstly, we found sex differences in attitudes to teachers, girls being significantly more unfavourable than boys in their evaluations of their teachers. How do such differences arise? Pre-adolescent girls' academic achievements are higher than those of boys, and girls perform better and are more likely than boys to work to their full ability in school (Emmett, 1954; Lavin, 1965). But early in adolescence, a proportion of girls begin to decline in achievement (Shaw and McCuen, 1960; Campbell, 1973). Ireson (1978) and Douvan (1979) have argued that during adolescence the female experiences a critical role conflict and this conflict may be partly responsible for the differences we discovered. Throughout childhood girls are socialized to be dependent and, at the same time, to be competitive, individualistic and achievement-orientated in school. Studies of adolescent self-concept have indicated that sex role identity is important to self definition during adolescence and that sex-linked interests and goals dominate adolescents' behaviour. Consequently, achievement-orientated, competitive, individualistic behaviour is less important for female sex role identity, since it is not sex-linked, nor is it central to sex role stereotypes of females (Coleman, 1961).

Such social-psychological processes may therefore be the underlying cause of the sex differences in adolescence in attitudes to teachers which we discovered. The girls' changing attitudes to academic achievement may have been reflected in their attitudes to teachers.

Attitudes to work of the females in our sample tended generally to be less positive than those of boys. The simplest and most obvious explanation for this is our finding that the conditions of employment for the females in our survey were objectively worse than those enjoyed by the boys. For example, there were real sex differences in training received for work. Girls were far less likely to receive training than boys – a highly significant finding. Of the boys, 60 per cent were given apprenticeships or formal training, compared with only 14.5 per cent of the girls (Table 2). Girls were more likely to receive only informal training with no set length or course of instruction.

It might be that the discrepancies between training provided for boys and girls are merely due to the skills demanded by the jobs chosen by women. Over the nation as a whole, women tend to be employed largely in jobs such as catering, cleaning and hairdressing, clerical jobs and jobs in textile, clothing and footwear industries (HMSO, 1978). In our survey, this general pattern was obtained, most of the girls being employed as machinists, shopworkers or office workers. It might be argued that such jobs require little formal training and that it is this fact that is responsible for the discrepancy between training for boys and training for girls.

A more likely explanation, however, may be that proposed by Mednick *et al*. (1975). They point out that labour force participation of women tends to be intermittent because of attitudes and policies of employers *themselves* (e.g. no paternity leave) and that jobs requiring training entail a perceived risk for the employer. Employers would therefore see jobs requiring little training as better alternatives for women (though such a policy ignores the fact that there is no single employment pattern for women).

After nine months of work, females were significantly less likely than males in the sample to express strong positive attitudes towards work and significantly more likely to express strong negative attitudes. Thus, at nine months, nearly half the males said they loved their work, compared with about one in four of the females. Moreover, whereas none of the boys reported hating their jobs at this time, 13.5 per cent of the girls did so.

Table 2. *Type of training received by young people entering work*

Type of training	Number of respondents	%	Males	%	Females	%
Apprenticeship	21	24.4	19	50.0	2	4.1
Formal (set length and course of instruction)	9	10.5	4	10.5	5	10.4
Informal	41	47.7	8	21.1	33	68.8
No training	15	17.4	7	18.4	8	16.7
N =	86	100.0	38	100.0	48	100.0

These results suggest that, for girls, the early experience of work was far less favourable than the early experience of work for boys. We would see as the most likely explanation of these sex differences, the greater discrepancy between the expectations of the world of work and the reality, experienced by the females in comparison with the males in our survey.

When the attitudes to work of males and females were measured at thirty months into working life, it was discovered that the sex differences evident at nine months had disappeared. At thirty months into working life, 50 per cent of the women reported loving their work (compared with 26.9 per cent at nine months). This highly significant change in the females' attitudes to work appeared to be accounted for largely by respondents who had previously reported only liking their jobs. The number who were indifferent to, or disliked their jobs remained nearly the same.

This change in female attitudes is explicable in terms of the adjustment of attitudes which occurs during socialization to work. Thus, we would see the young female worker as holding conflicting attitudes – expecting more of working life than she perceives herself receiving, yet at the same time expecting to be moderately satisfied in working life. The possible resolution of such a conflict would then lie either in changing jobs, or in altering attitudes. Some job changing does occur and, as a result, more realistic expectations of working life may be fostered, since available alternative jobs might be no more satisfying. It is also likely that the tension created by the conflict is reduced by the individual altering her attitudes and expectations. Attitudes and expectations would then be expected to change in the direction either of greater liking, e.g. 'Now I know the job better, I really love the work' or in the direction of indifference – e.g. 'I used to hate the job at first, but now I just while away the time by chatting.'

At nine months into working life, all the subjects were asked about how interesting they found their jobs. The vast majority (85 per cent) found their jobs at least 'somewhat interesting', 41.5 per cent finding them 'very interesting'. However, in the replies to this question, there were highly significant sex differences. Females were less likely to describe job interest in strong positive terms. This conforms with the previous finding of less favourable attitudes to work amongst women, and suggests that they may have expected more interesting jobs, or that work would provide a more interesting environment than they found to be the case. It is unlikely that initial expectations differ between boys and girls (there is no evidence that this is so), but more likely that it is the kind of work they do which differs. Alternatively females may be less happy in working life than males generally because of a variety of reasons (e.g. lower job status, rates of pay, conditions, etc.) and may therefore be less likely to express strong positive attitudes towards any aspect of work.

Female workers were less likely than males to see their jobs as offering promotion prospects. Generally, however, the females in our survey were unlikely to have jobs offering good promotion prospects. Maizels (1970) also found that females were significantly less likely than males to have good promotion chances, as rated by both employers and school-leavers themselves. The female workers in the present study did not see their jobs as teaching them something useful. The relative scarcity of formal training for female school-leavers may have led the women to the conclusion that their work was not teaching them anything useful, since it did not require training.

Whereas 40 per cent of males reported working overtime most weeks, only 27 per cent of females did so. Females were also less likely to work weekends and less likely than males to have any additional benefits from their work, such as extra money, or benefits like travel expenses and luncheon vouchers. Whereas 47 per cent of the males had such benefits, only 27 per cent of the females reported receiving them. Such forms of discrimination must contribute in no small way to the greater dissatisfaction and unhappiness of women in working life. Perhaps more importantly, the way wages were worked out also differed significantly between the sexes. Nearly one-third of the females in the sample were paid on a piecework system. Very often, females working in the textile industry were paid according to the amount of work they produced. However, if there was no work immediately available, their pay was considerably reduced. None of the males was paid in this way.

5. Life changes

Almost all of the young workers reported that beginning work had changed their lives considerably. Amongst the males, there appeared to be a strong feeling that changes in their lives were due partly to their meeting new people and learning to get on with them, but having money, independence and freedom were also frequently mentioned as important factors. Amongst the females, the most important factor in life changes resulting from their starting work was reportedly having money (21 per cent of all female responses). A large number also mentioned that they had grown up and become more mature and confident, and many mentioned that going out to work had made them more responsible. Other factors mentioned included a changed perspective of the world (e.g. 'I see things from a different point of view now, and I have a broader outlook'), going out more in the evenings, and having to get up earlier!

In answer to questions relating to expectations and hopes for the future, girls appeared to see their future identity more in terms of marriage and children, whereas boys tended to emphasize work and jobs more. This result is not confined to the present survey – the salience of marriage and motherhood for women, in future expectations, has been found to be paramount in previous studies. Veness (1962) found that marriage was mentioned by 94 per cent of the girls and 67 per cent of the boys in their life histories. Wilkins (1955) found that references to marriage dominated the replies of the girls to questions relating to what they hoped to be doing by the age of 25. In Maizels' (1970) study, though references were also made to continuing in work until the arrival of children or, in some cases, to the return to work when the children were older, two in three of the girls in her sample referred exclusively to their hopes for a family life.

It was possible, from the measures we used, to get some hint of the way in which the individuals in our survey saw themselves in relation to society generally. We were particularly interested in whether the differences between males and females would be reflected in the responses to these measures. One set of questions we used dealt with the degree of alienation from society felt by people within it. Srole (1956a, b) has conceptualized this alienation or 'anomie' as a psychological state which refers to 'the individual's generalised, pervasive sense of "self-to-others belongingness" at one extreme, compared with "self-to-others distance" and "self-to-others alienation" at the other end of the continuum'. In other words, alienation describes the extent to which the individual feels separated from, and unsupported by, others in society. To measure alienation or anomie, Srole devised a scale consisting of five statements. Subjects were asked to rate how strongly they agreed or disagreed with each of these statements, and an overall alienation score was derived by adding together the number of statements with which the individual agreed. Investigators who have administered the Srole scale to various samples in the United States have uniformly reported that alienation is highest among minority and disadvantaged groups, e.g. old people, the widowed, divorced and separated people, the less educated, those with low incomes and low prestige occupations, people experiencing downward social mobility, black people and immigrants.

Females in the present survey were more alienated than the males and this was a highly significant finding. On every statement, a greater proportion of females expressed agreement than did males. The average number of statements agreed with was 2.9 for females and 2.1 for males.

Even prior to leaving school, there is evidence that males are prepared better for the world of work than females. Boys' vocational aspirations are usually well-developed by middle adolescence, while girls hold less articulated occupational aims and are less well-informed about the educational requirements for the jobs they choose (Douvan, 1979). Ireson (1978) has referred also to the pattern of limitation evident in girls' occupational development. Girls indicate much less varied occupational aims and both sexes consider fewer occupations open to women. During the adolescent years, when girls' academic interests decline, the range of occupations chosen by girls also narrows. The social pressures on adolescent girls to aspire to sex-appropriate occupations and to relinquish ambitious, achievement-orientated career plans are undoubtedly strong. Within the present survey, there was evidence that girls making inappropriate sex role choices were pressured into changing their choices by both institutional agents, such as careers officers, as well as by family and friends. Behaviour such as striving to achieve, which is not seen as compatible with the role of wife and mother, is thus discouraged. Television further contributes to this socialization process (Sternglanz and Serbin, 1974). Children's television programmes and advertisements portray sex roles in rigid stereotyped ways (Locksley and Douvan, 1978).

Overall, the period of transition brought more changes in the lives of males than females in the present study. The males felt that they had acquired freedom and independence and saw themselves as treated with more respect and as more responsible and mature. The females felt that they were more mature and confident since leaving school, but fewer females than males reported that their home lives had changed. For males, adulthood appears to be marked by the entry to work, whereas for females marriage and motherhood appear to represent adult status. It appears that the major tasks society expects a woman to carry out are to get married and to have children. This is the norm which is communicated to women, and full adult status appears to be contingent upon its fulfilment. The male's task appears to be mainly to secure and keep full-time employment.

The most disturbing aspect of this research has been the discovery of the consistently unfavourable experiences of females leaving school and starting work. Whilst this aspect is obviously a reflection of more general sex discrimination in our society, we were surprised by its extent, particularly in training provided by firms for employees. The enormity of this problem is best judged by the degree of alienation reported by the girls in this survey (relative to the boys), and the very real effects their social experiences in leaving school and starting work must have upon individual development. The influence that schools can have upon development at the end of school life may have been underestimated in the past and the importance of both school organizations and work organizations as social institutions influencing individual development may become apparent as research in this area develops.

References

Campbell, P. 1973. Feminine intellectual decline during adolescence. Unpublished Ph.D. thesis, Syracuse University, New York.
Coleman, J. S. 1961. *The adolescent society*. New York: The Free Press.
Douvan, E. 1979. Sex role learning. In J. C. Coleman (ed.): *The school years: Current issues in the socialization of young people*. London: Methuen.
Emmett, E. 1954. Secondary modern and grammar school performance predicted by tests given in primary schools. *British Journal of Educational Psychology*, **24**, 91–8.
HMSO 1978. *Equal opportunities commission second annual report 1977*. London: HMSO.
Ireson, C. 1978. In A. H. Stromberg and S. Harkness (eds.): *Women working: Theories and facts in perspective*. Palo Alto, California: Mayfield.
Lavin, D. 1965. *Prediction of academic performance*. New York: John Wiley.
Locksley, A. and Douvan, E. 1978. Problem behavior in adolescents. In E. Gomberg and V. Frank (eds.): *Sex differences in disturbed behavior*. New York: Bruner Mazel.

Maizels, J. 1970. *Adolescent needs and the transition from school to work*. London: Athlone.

Mednick, M. T. S., Tangri, S. S. and Hoffman, L. W. 1975. *Women and achievement: Social and motivational analyses*. London: John Wiley.

Rutter, M., Maugham, B., Mortimore, P. and Ouston, J. 1979. *Fifteen thousand hours: Secondary schools and their effects on children*. London: Open Books.

Shaw, M. and McCuen, J. 1960. The onset of academic underachievement in bright children. *Journal of Educational Psychology*, **51**, 103–8.

Srole, L. 1956a. Social integration and certain corollaries: An exploratory study. *American Sociological Review*, December, 709–16.

Srole, L. 1956b. Anomie, authoritarianism and prejudice. *American Journal of Sociology*, **62**, 63–7.

Sternglanz, S. and Serbin, L. 1974. Sex role stereotyping in children's television programs. *Developmental Psychology*, **10**, 710–15.

Swift, B. 1973. Job orientations and the transition from school to work: A longitudinal study. *British Journal of Guidance and Counselling*, **1**, 62–78.

Veness, T. 1962. *School leavers – Their aspirations and expectations*. London: Methuen.

Wilkins, L. T. 1955. *The adolescent in Britain: the social survey*. London: HMSO.

16. Work entry: a critical moment in the occupational socialization process

GUIDO SARCHIELLI

1. Introduction

Many of the problems that characterize the relationship between the individual and the world of work (difficulties in adaptation, dissatisfaction, lack of job involvement, ambiguity in attitudes towards trade unions, etc.) which are prevalent, above all, among the juvenile population, are now being reconsidered by focusing greater attention on the processes by which subjects achieve their complete socialization into the work process.

The term 'work socialization' would ideally indicate a field made up of various phenomena, including: the procedure adopted by different socializing agencies for introducing the 'newcomer' into the work setting; the modalities required from subjects for acquiring values and outlooks typical of working reality; strategies adopted for understanding specific organizational and social context and elaborating appropriate behaviour.

This complex phenomenon has been studied in terms of a linear process for the transmission of information, values and behavioural models that the subject should assume in so far as they are universally held to be suitable for pursuing a satisfying occupational career (Moore, 1969). Possible misunderstandings and uncertainties or different points of view may come to be considered as dangerous deviations from the legitimate professional path mapped out by socializing agents and for this reason they are opposed by means of meticulous programming of the subject's career, enforcing a system of rewards, punishments and modelling (Weiss, 1978) – the very features on which the entire socialization process is inherently based.

Reality seems to be much more complicated and heterogeneous; the phenomena of 'dissonance' from the behavioural models dictated by individual work settings cannot be considered as marginal deviant phenomena which can be dealt with by a more rigorous 'work training' regime.

There exist doubts as to the legitimacy of occupational roles as well as common values and goals. There are uncertainties concerning the rules, the norms and the very skills necessary for work performance; divergences exist regarding the social significance of the work experience (Havighurst and Gottlieb, 1975). These viewpoints on work seem to be most clearly expounded by young people who are faced with the possibility of a number of occupations after a long period of education (Rousselet, 1974).

Therefore, it seems to us somewhat inappropriate to conceive of work socialization as a process designed to uniformly mould people, according to abstract models, even if these have been consolidated by tradition. Currently this approach seems to be even more inadequate in as much as the inevitable exposure of the individual to a large number of heterogeneous messages and differing socializing agents does not guarantee a final outcome which is both coherent and 'secure' (Shuval and Adler, 1980).

In our opinion the work socialization process has a relatively clear final objective; that is, the assumption, on the part of the subject, of the adult roles of consumer and producer.

The above premise must not, however, be considered as uniformly applicable nor should it be taken for granted. In fact, it is possible to imagine the adoption of different styles in handling these roles and, most importantly, in the various ways in which the subject may interact with the 'world of work'. Such interaction can, in fact, reveal itself as a moment of strong pressure to discipline one's behaviour or, on the other hand, as a favourable opportunity for pursuing one's personal development, realizing one's expectations, feeling oneself autonomous and satisfactorily located in a social environment (Kleinman 1981; McKeon et al., 1981; Sarchielli, 1978).

The studies which have been carried out to date emphasize the necessity of identifying a sequence of crucial moments in the process of occupational socialization that, in fact, correspond to the objective stages of the occupational career (Feldman, 1976) and that seem to convey significant variations in the way in which the individual relates to his working life. In this sense the pre-work phase comes to be understood as the most favourable opportunity for the subject to develop his attitudes towards work and prepare himself to decide on which job to choose. The moment of *actual entry* into work represents a point at which the discrepancy between the subject's expectations and his working reality must be confronted: this will have real effects on his assumption of the adult consumer–producer role. Subsequent work experiences (job changes, promotion, etc.) provide the opportunity for further verifying the correspondence between work behaviour and the expectations of organizational settings (Waterman and Waterman, 1976).

Given the limited knowledge of this phenomenon it could be considered legitimate to assume this periodization for its value in descriptive terms. However, it subsequently becomes necessary to take note of the actual conditions in which the work socialization process occurs and identify *if* and *how* the subject has the possibility of maintaining a questioning and critically active stance to the organizational setting and of adopting appropriate 'personal counter-measures' to the influencing pressures exerted within the working environment.

In other words, if one conceives of work socialization as a specific process of interaction between two social factors (the individual and the organizational setting) then one should be able to analyse how such interaction develops in each of the phases mentioned above; above all, one should try to understand the modifications entered into by each of the two factors in order to establish a satisfying relationship for both parties.

It seems clear that if work experience does not represent a simple fulfilment of those expectations, goals and behavioural models which were elaborated by the subject at school, then the interaction between the individual and his organizational setting can appear to be fairly complex.

If for example the subject arrives at work with a 'set of expectations' different from that of the organization it is very probable that he will start to express negative judgements and as a result, considerable pressure will be exerted to bring the subject back into line with pre-established rules. In this case, the possibilities of posing resistance and of negotiating a working career in line with one's expectations are reduced. The subject depends on the quantity and quality of personal resources, but, more importantly, on the way in which he relates to various social groupings in the work environment (Shein, 1968; Van Maanen, 1976). In fact these groupings can often represent a concrete opportunity for 'alternative socialization', developed as it is from viewpoints which differ from those proposed by the formal organizational setting and from ways of acting that are both convincing and incisive. All this confirms for the subject the possibility of increasing his discretionary powers and thus he may choose to assume or correct approved behavioural models; that is, he can carry out his job without sacrificing goals, values and expectations he regards as important for preserving self-identity.

2. Research on the first contact with the world of work

The phase of entry into full-time employment, whether preceded or not by partial work experience, represents a crucial moment in the work socialization process. One is dealing with a fairly complex phenomenon that tends to be conceptualized in relation to: differing psychological and socio-psychological processes which are sparked off by the interaction between the individual and his work setting; the widening and increasing articulation of the subject's cognitive structure (Hall, 1971); explicit or informal negotiation of goals and the psychological orientation of one's actions entered into with one's most important interlocutors (colleagues and superiors) (Mortimer and Simmons, 1978); the comparison between the subject's expectations and the resources at his disposal (Wanous, 1977); the reinforcement or transformation of personal identity in relation to the requests and judgements of various actors interested in the subject's working career (Van Maanen, 1976).

In the present state of affairs there does not seem to exist a perfect correspondence between conceptual intuition and empirical verification: the phenomenon of work entry has not yet been fully studied, although interest has grown (not only on the part of psychologists) in the dramatic problems regarding the transition from school to work (OECD, 1977; Neave, 1978).

From the *empirical research* that has been carried out on this theme we can consider, following the categorization of Mortimer and Lorence (1979), those who have adopted the *occupational selection* model and those who, specifically studying work entry refer to the *occupational socialization hypothesis*.

The *first type* of research is founded on the basic assumption that the subject who has settled in a job has selected it on the basis of psychological characteristics which have already been formed at school and which have shaped his professional identity and laid the foundations for his future working career.

Vocational psychology, above all, has worked in this direction, gathering useful and interesting results in the vocational guidance sector. However doubts have arisen as to its relevance for understanding individual working experience even amongst its advocates (Holland, 1976) and marked differences have been discovered between those who occupy the same job positions.

Holland (1976) gives particular attention to the relative instability of plans and aspirations pertaining to a professional career. After analysing the longitudinal study of Benjamin (1968) on 229 engineers he concludes that important changes in work preferences and aspirations are not only attributable to biographical characteristics (type of choice made, sex, type of school experience, etc.), but also to actual experience in the work role and to relations with colleagues and other important people in the work environment.

On the other hand the limitations of studies on occupational choice in developing understanding of work socialization have been highlighted by Roberts (1968). He underlines how often one tends to underevaluate the moment of the beginning of the working career and not to consider the possibility that the preferences which the subject expresses when he is already at work, derive from new and more precise processes of evaluation and social confrontation brought about by this newly experienced situation. In this sense the large surveys into the attitudes and expectations of young people towards work, for example Rousselet *et al.* (1975) or ISFOL (1977), seem to be more pertinent for understanding the most relevant interests of a particular social group (ways of relating to adults, influence of familial values, etc.) rather than for focusing on specific strategies for studying the relationship between these subjects and the world of work.

These initial observations allow us to re-evaluate the classic study of Carter (1962) on 200 school-leavers, interviewed once at the end of their school career and twice after they had begun work. The majority of these subjects affirmed that they had not found the work they had expected or envisaged on leaving school, but that they weren't particularly dis-satisfied with this. In fact, they were more directly affected by the characteristics of the work setting (work tasks, limitations, precepts, interpersonal relationships, etc.), so removed as they were from those they had already experienced, that numerous attempts at adaptation were required above all from those who had not been able to take advantage of formal induction schemes or who could not count on the informal support of older colleagues.

Carter (1962; 1966) explains these results by calling attention to the subjects' characterization and conception of work ('a job is a job'), to their awareness of the absence of concrete occupational alternatives, to the actual pursuit of one goal – the status of worker – perceived to be central with respect to his self-identity.

In other words, in the entry phase it isn't so much the discrepancy between expectations and working reality that seems to dominate (although it is present and occasionally assumes the features of a 'reality shock' (Form and Miller, 1949; Ondrack, 1975)), but rather the effort required to identify minimally realizable goals in a concrete situation, the limits of which are discernible.

One of the studies that we carried out on a group of 24 apprentices, in the framework of a wider study on adolescence (Palmonari *et al.*, 1979) produced similar results.

For these subjects, the salience of attaining certain personal goals (breaking with school and family past and acquiring a newly defined status) makes the idea of 'becoming a worker' assume a wider and more positive significance, namely that of guaranteeing a minimal personal identity. Thus they under-estimate the difficult conditions in which they actually work. The subjects don't feel inspired to negotiate improvements in working conditions and, indeed, feel the necessity to commit themselves to carefully carrying out all of the tasks requested of them; they seek to take maximum advantage of their present situation in order to have themselves recognized as adults who are different from their student contemporaries.

They don't, however, develop positive feelings for their position as apprentices, but remain fixed on the hyper-realistic objective of individual mobility in a work setting.

The second research prototype, based on the occupational socialization hypothesis, presupposes a more direct influence of working experience on subjects until the beginning of *their relationship with the work process*.

Feldman (1976) studied 118 workers (40 per cent of whom had been employed for less than a year) in a New England hospital, taking into consideration the successive stages of work socialization. Some variables can be identified for each stage, which determine the final outcome in the socialization process; these can be measured according to the level of job satisfaction, type of personal involvement, possibility of influencing working decisions and of regulating one's own behaviour on the basis of intrinsic motivations. It emerges that the more a subject finds a correspondence between organizational resources, specific needs and personal ability (congruence) and the more he achieves a realistic and accurate description of working reality (realism) then the more the learning of tasks, adaptation to team work, definition of new roles and self-evaluation of activities prove to be less problematic. Indeed the success in this first phase will have positive effects on subsequent socialization phases.

Lurie's research (1981) also underlines the need for an accurate re-elaboration of the way in which one conceives of work. He studied 46 professional nurses, first during the formation phase and then 6 months after entering work. He utilized interviews, questionnaires and conducted prolonged observations of their working situation. Even though the study confirmed the importance of the pre-work period in inducing values, knowledge and professional attitudes, the research demonstrates how the personal autonomy of the subject and the possibilities of negotiating one's work role come to be limited by the influences of a rigid organizational structure. This structure, in fact, turns out to be centred around the hierarchical figure of the doctor and contrasts with images previously held of the job which were based on the possibility of participating in decisions and dealing with the patients autonomously.

According to Lurie (1981), the newcomer tends to realize that working in an organizational structure can only be dealt with through a more balanced relationship between personal interaction, negotiation of activities, and the concrete limits imposed by the work setting: awareness of this factor must represent one of the objectives of a coherent socialization process.

Wanous (1976) documents the occurrence of changes in the ways of conceiving work during the work socialization process. He finds, after considering questionnaires completed by 753 business school graduates (employed for less than a year), that the expectations based on intrinsic factors (personal development, autonomy, etc.) tend to be lowered, while those connected with extrinsic factors (money, working time, working conditions, etc.) either remain stable or assume greater importance. Using these findings one can say that, after a brief period, work entry produces a greater degree of realism (concreteness) regarding expectations and that (as a trend), the attractiveness of an organization decreases after first contact.

Similar results have been obtained by Hazer and Alvares (1981) in a study carried out on two groups of town policemen first interviewed at the end of professional school and then after 4 and 6 months of working experience. A certain stability in the general significance attached to work becomes clear in the time period taken into consideration, even if the intensity of expectations relating to extrinsic factors had risen. The work entry process above all – whether temporary or full time – produces consistent effects: those who find themselves in a temporary working situation suffer greatly from the initial stress, demonstrating a clear diminution in their job involvement and so they define their work in terms of its extrinsic value.

Again Wanous, in a subsequent survey of research on work

socialization (1977), underlined the double need to gather information on this subject and to collect the most detailed empirical evidence possible. In this survey he defined the above mentioned phenomena with the term 'organizational entry effect': he added, by way of conclusion, that the more the importance attached to work and professional expectations turns out to be naïve, non-specific or illusory then the more the impact of the organization will have negative repercussions on the subject's career: thus we see dissatisfaction, working instability and turnover. In this sense, the use of realistic job previews can present a useful and practical support for facilitating the evaluation processes that occur in the first phase of work socialization and thus positively direct successive phases of socialization.

3. Two studies in Bologna

The research analysed so far, above all that dealing with work impact, seems to agree on the possibility of the work entry phase representing a particularly intense moment of work socialization: one can hypothesize that the levels of receptiveness and availability to adapting to, and accepting, new rules and appropriate behavioural models (even to the detriment of previous personal expectations) can be understood as a practical strategy designed to overcome the discomforts and difficulties caused by the first impact of the world of work.

In other words, work entry can have the effect of desocialization (unfreezing phase, Shein, 1968) and thus provides a difficult test of the newcomer's ability to exercise an 'active presence' in his working environment, to realize both the plans and expectations that he has elaborated in the pre-work phase and to negotiate his eventual social and professional standing.

However, systematically gathered information on eventual long term effects does not yet exist. It seems to us that it is still necessary to develop further specifications of the more immediate effects that surface during work entry.

This study seeks to evaluate whether work entry (defined in a fairly arbitrary way as a period of less than six months' working experience) can produce specific effects on the way the subject perceives work and his future professional career. In other words, it is asked whether the images of work and the significance attached to it show traces of the way in which the subject settled into his first full-time employment.

We tackled this subject in two ways: firstly, an exploratory survey designed to illustrate some typical elements of the work entry situation was carried out on a group of young apprentices; secondly, a more accurately refined research design was drawn up for two groups of young people awaiting first full-time employment and who had been working as apprentices for less than six months.

3.1. Exploratory interview study

Twenty-three subjects were considered in the exploratory study, all of whom came from the same geographical area and were all from working class families. They had been working as apprentices for less than six months. All the subjects were interviewed individually on the following themes.

First weeks at work. Problems relating to the good performance of work tasks were emphasized (16 subjects mentioned these compared to 8 who emphasized interpersonal relations and 3 who raised the questions of loss of free time and working conditions). The strategies adopted to overcome these difficulties were either to ask the help of older colleagues (15) or increase personal effort (7) rather than resort to seeking external help (parents, trade unions, etc.).

Present and future work. In the majority of cases the strategies adopted seemed to have produced good results, that is, from the moment in which there was a positive evaluation of present work (the ratio of advantages to disadvantages of work equals 1.53; the ratio of interesting to non-interesting aspects of the job equals 1.16). The planning of their future professional career seems to be linked to their present situation: the majority of subjects (14) intended to remain in the same type of work for the following 5 years and only 7 subjects considered the possibility of changing their situation by taking up further studies. Among those who intended to change their jobs there prevailed the expectation of going into business on their own.

Significance attached to work in general. The apprentices freely reported on the significance attached to work by those adults whom they considered important (parents or older people) and by themselves in their role as apprentices.

The 157 statements that were given were classified into 9 content categories. The categories used most frequently (i.e. aspects relating to money, working conditions, the burden of the work involved, possibilities of self-realization) accounted for 68.1 per cent of the content provided. Those that were used more rarely (i.e. social relations and professional development) accounted for 5.8 per cent and the intermediate categories (i.e. work performance, link between work and other activities, claims on work) accounted for 26.1 per cent. It should be noted that among the categories most frequently used, those that were held to be typical for adults concerned the heaviness of the workload and self-realization, while those aspects which related to working conditions and pay were attributed to themselves in their role as apprentices.

In short, the data which emerged provide an example of how young apprentices integrated themselves within the work setting. They seem to have adopted an integration strategy based on the realization of their capacity to respond to contingent problems posed by work, even to the partial detriment of a more definite concern with projects of self-realization that lie outside it, and thus, they establish an equilibrium for their present work experience.

Considering these qualitative indications, it seems to us that one can hypothesize that the work entry situation induces the subject to reformulate his cognitive structures in order to achieve a more accurate evaluation of the work setting and to develop a more precise definition of available resources. This enables him to act with greater effectiveness and possibilities of success. In other words, we hypothesize:

(a) that the description of work in general and the criteria the subject establishes for his ideal job will be modified in the work entry phase in such a way as to privilege those concrete elements that relate to work performance;

(b) that in the planning of the future professional career there exists a greater concern for working conditions than for social relations and personal development.

3.2. Comparative study

Method. Sixty young people between the ages of 18 and 24 were studied, all of whom came from the same geographical area and cultural background and who had all obtained secondary school diplomas. They were listed on a large public service register whose function was to offer them relatively stable jobs.

On the basis of a preliminary investigation 60 subjects were identified who had given positive judgements of their school career and who had

had a normal school experience. Among these some had found a job less than six months before (30) while others found themselves still awaiting their first employment (30).

Therefore, one is dealing with a particular group which is reasonably homogeneous in its distinctive features (level of scholastic attainment, judgements on past school career, geographical area and cultural background) and orientated towards relatively similar work activity (in fact, the law almost exclusively offers work in the public service sector).

One found oneself, therefore, in the most unfavourable situation for identifying differences that were a result of recent work entry.

The subjects were submitted to an interview of 30 minutes' duration during which they were asked to choose from a list of affirmations that defined work in general, those that were regarded as most suitable for defining the importance attached by the subject to *work as human activity* (the statements provided were partly derived from a study by Williams, Morea and Ives (1975) and had been tested in a previous exploratory research); the subjects were subsequently asked to focus attention on statements that expressed their preferences for *their own work*, choosing the most suitable statements from a list of 12. After exploring the features which were representative of a future professional career, a version of the techniques already used by Wallace (1960) for the study of time perspectives was adopted and personally re-elaborated. In short, the subjects were asked to express facts, events and happenings that they believed could turn up in their future working career, arranging them, within a pre-determined temporal scale, and evaluating them according to their level of importance.

Results. Table 1 indicates those subjects who utilized each item posed in order to define work in terms of its general significance. As one can note, the majority of subjects concentrated their attention on those positive aspects about which there exists a strong social consensus, while avoiding those which have a more explicit negative connotation. Between the two groups there emerged a perceptible difference in attributing to work the significances of social utility, economic opportunity and social recognition.

Table 2, constructed in the same way, demonstrates how the subjects of the two groups utilize different statements for identifying expected and preferred work; while everyone chose those items that expressed interest in work as an end in itself, in a good salary and in a good quality of life, there were still noticeable differences regarding relationships with work

Table 1. *Distribution of respondents* to various definitions of work in general*

Work is	Employed N = 30	Non-employed N = 30
(1) A means to produce something	26	23
(2) An obligation	1	1
(3) A way to provide resources (i.e. money)	11	18
(4) Socially useful	20	11
(5) Tiring and a pain	0	5
(6) What one likes to do	3	6
(7) A way to be socially accepted	7	11
(8) A way to be proud of oneself	10	10
(9) A way to be self-accomplished	18	20

* Each interviewee was allowed to choose up to 4 definitions.

Table 2. *Distribution of respondents* to various definitions of preferred work*

Work is preferred if it	Employed N = 30	Non-employed N = 30
(1) Is interesting in itself	21	23
(2) Allows a good quality of working life	15	15
(3) Facilitates relationships with colleagues	5	12
(4) Is free, without hierarchical controls	11	7
(5) Secures a good salary or wages	20	18
(6) Allows a career	11	9
(7) Allows security and stability of the workplace	16	11
(8) Allows social status and prestige	6	5
(9) Is in a well-managed organization	9	10
(10) Is not too tiring	9	6
(11) Is in a small work organization unit	9	12
(12) Does not take up too much of my time	2	1

* Each interviewee was allowed to choose up to 5 definitions.

colleagues, security and stability of position, hierarchical controls of work activity.

Having taken account of these trends we proceeded to check whether overall evaluation of work in general and of the work preferred could present an adequate criterion for controlling intragroup homogeneity and the heterogeneity between the groups of subjects. In other words, the question was whether the global profile obtained from the responses of these subjects who were established in employment was significantly different from that identified by those who were still awaiting employment. We availed ourselves of discriminant analysis, which would allow for the verification of the distinction between the two groups of subjects studied, using to this end one or more of the discriminatory functions given by a fixed set of variables *a priori*. In our case this function was constructed by combining those items considered relevant for the definition of work in general and of the work preferred by the subject. The core of discriminant analysis is that of reclassification of the subjects into groups in relation to discriminant function: that is, a first evaluation was carried out on the similarity between individual profiles and subsequently each individual was placed in the group to which he had the greater probability of belonging. The results of the analysis appear in percentage form for the correctly completed classification.

On the basis of discriminant analysis only 2 subjects belonging to the employed group and 4 from the unemployed group do not possess predicted group membership. Essentially the two groups turn out to be clearly distinguishable (the percentage of 'grouped' cases correctly classified is 90 per cent) on the basis of the two representations of work. (Analysis was carried out separately on the definitions of work in general and that preferred. The results for the discriminant analysis, as far as they were less explicit, express the distinction between the two groups with an accuracy of 68.3 per cent and 63.3 per cent respectively.) The strongest relative contribution to the discriminant function, calculated through the standardized canonical discriminant function coefficients, was given by items concerning: the provisions of resources (0.84); a job which is free, without control (0.69); security and stability of the positions (0.37); tiring work (0.61); the interest in the work itself (0.49); the possibility of relating to colleagues (0.67); what one likes to do (0.44). The first three items were chosen mainly by stably employed subjects while the others were chosen by the non employed subjects.

The events and circumstances considered by the subjects as relevant for their future were first provided spontaneously and then classified by two independent judges into four large categories: (a) security and stability of workplace; (b) personal features; (c) social dimensions; (d) well-defined job performance and work activities. Subsequently, the density index was calculated (Trommsdorff, Lamm and Schmidt, 1979) considering the number of events in each category divided by total events produced by the subject. Such an index expresses a partial aspect of the cognitive structure for the future reflecting the interest or the preoccupation of the subject with the area considered. By adopting this index, comparisons are possible between the various thematic areas provided by the members of each group.

The employed group demonstrated a more reduced production of contents ($x = 2.7$ contents per subject as to $x = 3.9$); they concentrated on well-defined job performance (frequency 38.3 per cent; density 0.37) and on security (frequency 33 per cent; density 0.41); while contents of personal type (frequency 14.8; density 0.11) and social (frequency 13.6; density 0.11) were all of secondary importance.

The other group placed relatively less emphasis on the categories expressing qualities inherent in work defined as it was in a limited sense: well-defined job (frequency 28.4; density 0.27); security (frequency 31.9; density 0.35). There is instead a persistent presence of references of a personal type (frequency 28.4; density 0.28), while those relating to contents of social type turn out to be modest (frequency 11 per cent; density 0.11).

The difference between the density relating to contents of a personal type turns out to be statistically very significant for non employed subjects (t = 3.36; df = 58; p<0.001).

As far as the extension of the future time perspective is concerned (evaluated on the basis of events, experienced in brief, medium and long periods) we limited ourselves to underlining the marked utilization of briefer times for both groups which, therefore, do not present significant difference in this regard. Our subjects, confirming the results of previous research (Teahan, 1958), demonstrate a strong reality orientation in identifying events located in narrow temporal perspective.

4. Conclusions

Our subjects turned out to be a fairly homogeneous group from the point of view of educational background; they opted for the type of work proposed by the public service and were part of the same social and cultural community. What is more, having a reasonably high level of education, one can suppose that they would aspire to those jobs offered which corresponded to their level of scholastic achievement. In this framework, their positive orientation towards work in general seems to be understandable, reinforced as it is by the lack of references to those negative aspects (obligations, hard efforts, etc.) that are part of the common sense definitions of work in general. However, even in such favourable conditions as these for the passage from 'outsider' to 'insider' status in the organizational framework, notable transformations can be discerned in the subject.

The brief period of work experience appears to be capable of shifting the attention of the subject from personal demands to characteristics that define the work setting, particularly in terms of job position and professional performance. In this way the future professional career is structured with a greater degree of detail by the young employed, who give greater weight to the experience of the new environment in which they are experimenting with their work roles. The criteria by which preferred work is judged come to be better defined, more simply, more realistically than the global expectations which were usually referred to in the pre-work period. While those young people awaiting first employment seek to find in work the possibility of spontaneously expressing themselves, of developing interesting relations with colleagues, even of working very hard provided that the activity is interesting in itself; those who already work give greater weight to the security and stability of the job and emphasize the kind of authority that regulates their working relationships.

One can therefore affirm that becoming an effective member of a work organization constitutes a specific outcome in the phase of first entry into full-time work. The subject finds himself immersed in an involving situation in which he must establish what the meaningful features of his work are and come to terms with not only his own expectations, but also the concrete requests of his colleagues and superiors which he must deal with immediately.

The pressure of dealing with such a situation is translated in a sort of compromise: the subjects we studied appear to be prepared 'to come to some sort of understanding' with working reality, a reality which is perceived on the whole as positive, and concentrates on particular elements that can guarantee a rapid adaptation to the new situation.

References

Benjamin, D. R. 1968. A thirty-one year longitudinal study of engineering students' interest profiles and career patterns. *Dissertation Abstracts*, **28**, 4421.

Carter, M. 1962. *Home, school and work*. Oxford: Pergamon Press.

Carter, M. 1966. *Into work*. Harmondsworth: Penguin.

Feldman, D. C. 1976. A contingency theory of socialization. *Administrative Science Quarterly*, **21**, 433–52.

Form, W. H. and Miller, D. C. 1949. Occupational career pattern as sociological instrument. *American Journal of Sociology*, **54**, 317–29.

Hall, D. T. 1971. A theoretical model of career subidentity development in organizational setting. *Organizational Behavior and Human Performance*, **6**, 50–76.

Havighurst, R. J. and Gottlieb, D. 1975. Youth and the meaning of work. In R. J. Havighurst and P. H. Dreyer (eds.): *Youth*. University of Chicago Press.

Hazer, J. T. and Alvares, M. K. 1981. Police work values during organizational entry and assimilation. *Journal of Applied Psychology*, **1**, 12–18.

Holland, J. L. 1976. Vocational preferences. In M. D. Dunnette (ed.): *Handbook of industrial and organizational psychology*. Chicago: Rand McNally.

ISFOL (Istituto per lo Sviluppo della Formazione professionale dei lavoratori) 1977. Atteggiamento dei giovani nei confronti del lavoro. *Quaderni di Formazione*, **28**, 1–248.

Kleinman, S. 1981. Making professionals into 'persons'. *Sociology of Work and Occupations*, **1**, 61–87.

Lurie, E. E. 1981. Nurse practitioners: Issue in professional socialization. *Journal of Health and Social Behavior*, **22**, 31–48.

McKeon, J., Gillham, J. and Bersani, K. 1981. Professional identity and interaction: A case of a juvenile court. *Sociology of Work and Occupations*, **3**, 353–80.

Moore, W. 1969. Occupational socialization. In D. A. Goslin (ed.): *Handbook of socialization theory and research*. Chicago: Rand McNally.

Mortimer, J. T. and Lorence, J. 1979. Work experience and occupational value socialization: A longitudinal study. *American Journal of Sociology*, **84**, 1361–85.

Mortimer, J. T. and Simmons, R. G. 1978. Adult socialization, *Annual Review of Sociology*, **4**, 421–54.

Neave, G. (ed.) 1978. *Research perspectives on the transition from school to work*. Strasburg: Council of Europe.

OECD 1977. *Education and working life*. Paris.

Ondrack, D. A. 1975. Socialization in professional schools: A comparative study. *Administrative Science Quarterly*, **20**, 97–103.

Palmonari, A., Carugati, F., Ricci Bitti, P. E. and Sarchielli, G. 1979. *Identità imperfette*. Bologna: Il Mulino.

Roberts, K. 1968. The entry into employment: An approach toward a general theory. *The Sociological Review*, **2**, 165–84.

Rousselet, J. 1974. *L'allergie au travail*. Paris: Seuil.

Rousselet, J., Balazs, G. and Mathey, C. 1975. L'idée du travail, de réussite et d'échec chez des jeunes de milieux scolaires et sociaux différents. *Cahiers du centre d'études de l'emploi*. Paris: Presses Universitaires de France.

Sarchielli, G. 1978. *La socializzazione al lavoro*. Bologna: Il Mulino.

Shein, E. H. 1968. Organizational socialization and the profession of management. *Industrial Management Review*, **9**, 1–16.

Shuval, J. T. and Adler, I. 1980. The role of models in professional socialization. *Social Science Medicine*, **14**, 5–14.

Teahan, J. E. 1958. Future time perspective, optimism and academic achievement. *Journal of Abnormal Social Psychology*, **57**, 379–80.

Trommsdorff, G., Lamm, H. and Schmidt, R. W. 1979. A longitudinal study of adolescents' future orientation (time perspective). *Journal of Youth and Adolescence*, **2**, 131–47.

Van Maanen, J. 1976. Breaking in: Socialization to work. In P. Dubin (ed.): *Handbook of work, organization and society*. Chicago: Rand McNally.

Wallace, M. 1956. Future time perspective in schizophrenia. *Journal of Abnormal Social Psychology*, **52**, 240–5.

Wallace, M. and Rabin, A. I. 1960. Temporal experience. *Psychological Bulletin*, **3**, 213–36.

Wanous, J. P. 1976. Organizational entry: From naïve expectations to realistic beliefs. *Journal of Applied Psychology*, **1**, 22–9.

Wanous, J. P. 1977. Organizational entry: Newcomers moving from outside to inside. *Psychological Bulletin*, **4**, 619–33.

Waterman, A. S. and Waterman, C. K. 1976. Factors related to vocational identity after extensive work experience. *Journal of Applied Psychology*, **3**, 336–40.

Weiss, H. 1978. Social learning of work values in organizations. *Journal of Applied Psychology*, **6**, 711–18.

Williams, R. S., Morea, P. C. and Ives, J. M. 1975. The significance of work: An empirical study. *Journal of Occupational Psychology*, **48**, 45–51.

Concluding remarks

17. Characteristics of contemporary socialization studies

WILLEM DOISE and AUGUSTO PALMONARI

1. An assessment by H. R. Schaffer

The editors felt that the best way to end this book was to recall at some
length the remarks made by H. R. Schaffer concerning the current state of
research on 'Early Development and Socialization' at the International
Congress of Psychology in Leipzig (July 1980):

Some of the major changes that have taken place in the last 20–30 years in our
thinking about the nature of early social development:

1. A change has occurred from a primarily negative attitude (emphasizing what
children *cannot* do) to a positive attitude (concerning what children *can* do).

2. At one time the first social relationship formed by the infant was thought to
represent the prototype for all subsequent social relationships. This is no longer
accepted uncritically; consequently the motivation for investigating early social
development lies in this phenomenon in its own right; the ability to relate to
another person is an extraordinarily complex set of skills, and the aim of the
investigators now is to attempt to isolate, describe and understand these.

3. A change has taken place from an interest in products to an interest in
processes. We are, for instance, not so much concerned now with the description
of the attachment bond as such but increasingly with the way in which the
relationship develops and the underlying mechanisms that are responsible for
this development.

4. Instead of seeing socialization as a unilateral process in which all-powerful
adults shape passive infants, a view that stresses the reciprocal nature of the
relationship has gained ground. This applies even to the youngest infant, who is
already capable of controlling to some extent the kind, amount and timing of other
people's stimulation.

5. Questions are increasingly being asked about how children's social behaviour
goes from one development point to another, what continuities there are between
these points, and what the continuities (or discontinuities) are due to. Thus
instead of focussing on isolated age points as previously, attention is now paid to
the nature of developmental change.

6. Whereas previously only the child's relationship to the mother was of interest,
other relationships are now also being investigated. This refers in particular to the
father but also to peers.

7. The previous point refers to a widening of focus, i.e. from the study of just a single relationship to the child's totality of relationships. This widening of focus is now being taken still further, in that these relationships themselves are being viewed in their social context – as defined by the family, social class, nation, culture, etc.

We would adopt these views as our own and thank the author for allowing us to reproduce them here. In addition we believe that many of them are applicable not only to the first phases of development but equally to all studies on the social development of the individual and we hope that the present book demonstrates this.

2. Further comments

Let us, however, emphasize certain points. The research reported in this book is, to be sure, concerned with the elucidation of specific processes occurring at different points in development. As such they illustrate the need to elaborate a number of models, such as that of socio-cognitive conflict or that of social identity, to provide an account of individual development. These models are by nature very varied and, at least at first glance, do not necessarily have much in common with one another.

In general terms it is none the less necessary to acknowledge the interpenetration of several dynamics intervening in the development of the individual, even if any articulation between the different models intended to describe these dynamics has rarely been achieved. We would look for such articulation in the direction of a reciprocal interdependence between individual and social dynamics. As individual autonomy necessarily develops out of the dynamics of social interdependence, so also these dynamics of interdependence can only evolve on the basis of a continual development of individual potentiality. This general conception is not only at the root of the theoretical approaches developed in this book, it has also successfully guided the action research reported by Carugati and his colleagues.

Ideas of a very general bearing can thus be effectively employed to direct intervention and research activities. But progress in understanding will only take place through a detailed analysis of specific processes. Fortunately, this is a characteristic of current work on social interaction in individual development, in contrast to earlier anthropologically and culturally inspired approaches which often used psychoanalytically derived notions to account in global terms for both the development of the individual and the specificity of cultures. If there is a basic personality structure, its functioning and development can still only be grasped bit by bit.

The multiplicity and indeed variety of processes which link individual development and social dynamics show how the social development of a personality is in every case a complex story which it is difficult to provide an account of scientifically. One could also easily conceive how this development could be hindered in various ways, but even if there are difficulties it is perhaps the very multiplicity of processes that renders them to some degree substitutable for one another with the effect that very few forms of psychosocial dysfunctioning appear irreversible. If clinicians are above all concerned with the study of these pathologies of development, the contributors to this book often seem to practise a more optimistic approach, researching and studying those widely distributed conditions that allow an individual to construct himself in and through his relationships with others.

Author Index

Abelson, P. R., 159, 160, 161
Adler, I., 262
Ainsworth, M. D. S., 69, 93
Allen, V. L., 134
Allport, F. H., 13
Alvares, M. K., 267
Antinucci, F., 102
Arcuri, L., 158
Arfelli Galli, A., 236
Asch, S. E., 133
Asher, S. R., 114
Atkinson, M., 98
August, D. L., 116
Austin, J. L., 72

Baldwin, A. L., 42
Bandura, A., 2, 4
Bates, E., 97
Bell, R. Q., 42, 67, 93
Bell, W., 198
Benjamin, D. R., 265
Berger, P. L., 242, 243
Bernstein, B., 17, 42, 52
Berthoud-Papandropoulou, I., 148
Bestuzhev-Lada, I. V., 44
Billig, M., 16
Black, I., 161
Blurton Jones, N. G., 25, 32
Boden, M., 120
Bourdieu, P., 10, 11, 14
Bower, G. H., 161
Bowlby, J., 2
Bray, H., 211
Bronfenbrenner, U., 43
Brown, R., 97
Bruner, J. S., 2, 95, 98
Bullowa, M., 107
Butterworth, G., 6

Camaioni, L., 92, 98, 100, 104
Camilleri, C., 218
Campbell, D. T., 19, 212

Campbell, P., 253
Cantril, H., 195, 196
Carter, A. L., 107
Carter, M., 265
Carugati, F., 1, 7, 78, 126, 128, 130, 132, 134, 139, 140, 141, 148, 190, 231, 282
Castelfranchi, C., 78
Changeux, J. P., 15
Charney, R., 94
Child, I. L., 69
Chomsky, N., 15
Clark, R., 99, 104
Cole, M., 17
Coleman, J. S., 8, 254
Collis, G. M., 98
Cranstoun, Y., 81
Crook, C. K., 71, 72, 78, 80

Damon, W., 5, 6
Davis, A., 42
de Castro Campos, M. F. P., 100
Deconchy, J. P., 131
De Gelder, B., 97, 98
de Leeuw, J. A., 16
de Lemos, C. T. G., 96, 100
De Negri Trentin, R., 168
Denis-Prinzhorn, M., 148
De Paolis, P., 1, 7, 126, 128, 130, 132, 134, 137, 138, 140, 141, 142, 148
Deutsch, M., 134
Didillon, H., 32
Dion, K. L., 212
Dionnet, S., 136
Doise, W., 1, 2, 6, 13, 16, 120, 127, 128, 129, 130, 132, 135, 136, 137, 139, 141, 148, 197
Doob, L. W., 4
Douvan, E., 253, 258
Dumaret, A., 17
Dunn, J. F., 3, 93
Dunphy, D. C., 201
Duvernoy, J., 33
Duyme, M., 17

Eckensberger, L. H., 6
Eibl-Eibesfeldt, I., 25, 32
Eisenstadt, S. H., 8
Elder, G. H., 8
Emiliani, F., 64, 78
Emmett, E., 253
Erikson, E. H., 8, 9, 192
Ervin-Tripp, S., 72
Eysenck, H. J., 17

Feffer, M., 16
Feingold, T., 17
Feldman, D. C., 262, 266
Finn, G. P. T., 136
Flavell, J. H., 2, 6, 71, 116, 117
Fodor, J. A., 97
Fogel, A., 94
Form, W. H., 266
Francesconi, C., 99
Freeman, N. H., 147
French, J. R., 135
Frésard, M. D., 126, 150
Freud, S., 68
Friedenberg, E. Z., 8
Furth, H. G., 173

Geber, B. A., 192
Gecas, V., 198
Gendlin, E., 242
Gerard, H. B., 134
Giroud, J. C., 120, 127
Glezerman, G. E., 44
Godard, D., 29
Goffman, E., 234
Goodnow, J., 147
Gordon, L. A., 44
Gottlieb, D., 262
Graesser, A. C., 168
Grant, E. C., 25
Green, F. L., 116
Green, M., 25
Gremillet, H., 32
Gruendel, J. M., 160
Grusec, J. E., 66
Guest, A., 25
Guillaume, P., 99
Guttentag, M., 211

Haarlow, R. N., 206
Habermas, J., 43
Hall, D. T., 264
Haller, A. O., 201
Halliday, M. A. K., 104, 107
Harper, L. V., 67
Harré, R., 78
Harvey, O. J., 206
Havighurst, R. J., 42, 262
Hazer, J. T., 267

Heiskanen, M., 59
Hess, R. D., 42, 43, 52
Hildyard, A., 110
Hinde, R. A., 2
Hoffman, M. L., 69, 74, 75
Hogan, R., 69
Holland, J. L., 264
Holling, H., 186
Hollingshead, A., 8
Holter, H., 43
Hovland, C. I., 196, 209
Hunt, J., 213
Huston, A. C., 202

Inhelder, B., 147, 173, 174
Ireson, C., 253, 258
Ives, J. M., 271

Jahoda, G., 158, 175
Jaspars, J. M. F., 16
Jurd, M. F., 173

Kamin, L., 17
Kanter, R. M., 44
Karabenick, J. D., 114
Karlins, M., 206
Katz, I., 17
Kaye, K., 93, 94
Kelly, M., 193
King, R. D., 231, 234
Kister, M. C., 117, 119
Kleinman, S., 262
Klopov, E. V., 44
Kohlberg, L., 4, 6
Kohn, M., 43, 44
Koskenniemi, M., 48
Koskinen, P. L., 59
Koslin, B., 206
Kramer, D., 45
Kuhn, D., 173

Lamm, H., 273
Larson, L. E., 197
Lautrey, J., 17
Lavin, D., 253
Lee, L. C., 173
Lemaine, G., 16, 135
Leonetti, I., 220
Lerber, E. L., 47, 48, 50, 52
Leskow, S., 182
LeVine, R., 66
Levy, D. M., 42
Lévy, M., 128, 134
Lewin, K., 244
Lewis, M., 32
Liepmann, D., 186
Light, P., 6
Locksley, A., 258

Lombardot, M., 29
Lorence, J., 264
Lorenz, K., 25
Luckmann, T., 242, 243
Lukesch, H., 43
Luquet, G. H., 147
Lurie, E. E., 266, 267

McCartney, K. A., 160
McCuen, J., 253
McDougall, W., 13
McGrew, W. C., 25, 32
McKeon, J., 262
Mackie, D., 133
McMahon, L., 81
MacNeil, M. R., 206
McQuitty, L. L., 184
Maizels, J., 256, 257
Malewska-Peyre, H., 190, 218, 225, 229
Manz, G., 44
Markman, E. M., 117
Matalon, B., 16
Mednick, M. T. S., 254
Merten, D., 201
Milgram, S., 133
Miller, D. C., 266
Miller, S. A., 114
Montagner, H., 24, 26, 27, 29, 31, 32, 36, 37
Moore, W., 261
Morea, P. C., 271
Mortimer, J. T., 264
Moscovici, S., 133
Mugny, G., 1, 6, 7, 16, 120, 126, 127, 128, 129, 130, 132, 133, 134, 135, 136, 137, 139, 140, 141, 148
Myllylä, M., 59

Neave, G., 264
Nebergall, R. E., 196, 209
Neimark, E. D., 173, 181
Nelson, K., 97, 159, 160, 168
Newcomb, T. M., 217
Newman, S. P., 192
Newson, E., 202
Newson, J., 3, 202
Newton, P., 248
Niemi, I., 46, 47, 50
Ninio, A., 95

Ochs, E., 96
Olson, D. R., 110
Ondrack, D. A., 266

Palmonari, A., 1, 2, 9, 234, 236, 266
Pargament, R., 206
Parisi, D., 78
Parker, S., 45

Parsons, T., 13
Patterson, C. J., 117, 119
Peill, E. J., 121
Perret-Clermont, A. N., 2, 120, 127, 129, 130, 132, 136
Piaget, J., 4, 5, 6, 9, 10, 11, 12, 15, 17, 18, 19, 92, 99, 120, 121, 147, 173, 174, 192
Piattelli-Palmarini, M., 15
Pölkki, P., 57
Prado, W., 198
Pulkkinen, L., 55

Ramunni, G., 16
Rasku-Puttonen, H., 53
Raynes, N. V., 231, 234
Redl, F., 243, 244
Renshon, S. A., 186
Restoin, A., 37
Reynolds, V., 25
Richards, M. P. M., 93, 94, 95
Rijsman, J., 136
Rilliet, D., 137
Roberts, K., 265
Robinson, E. J., 92, 108, 109, 111, 112, 113, 114, 115
Robinson, W. P., 52, 92, 108, 109, 111, 112, 113, 114, 115
Rodgers, H. L., 193
Rodriguez, D., 31
Romeder, J. M., 33
Rommetveit, R., 99
Rosenberg, M., 196, 211
Ross, L., 2, 6
Rouchouse, J. C., 25
Rousselet, J., 262, 265
Rutkevich, M. N., 44
Rutter, M., 234, 253
Ryvkina, R. V., 44

Salmaso, P., 168
Sarchielli, G., 248, 262
Sarpellon, G., 231
Sarup, G., 193
Scaife, M., 98
Schaal, B., 32
Schaefer, E. S., 42
Schaffer, H. R., 3, 64, 67, 71, 72, 78, 80, 98, 281
Schank, R. C., 159, 160
Schiff, M., 17
Schmidt, R. W., 273
Schneewind, K., 43
Schooler, C., 43, 44
Schubauer-Leoni, M. L., 121
Schwartz, G., 201
Scollon, R., 96
Scribner, S., 17
Searle, J. R., 72

Sears, R. R., 42
Secord, P. F., 78
Serbin, L., 258
Shatz, M., 72
Shaw, M., 253
Shein, E. H., 263, 268
Sherif, C. W., 8, 9, 190, 192, 193, 195, 196, 197, 199, 200, 202, 208, 209, 212
Sherif, M., 8, 9, 133, 135, 190, 192, 193, 195, 196, 197, 199, 202, 206, 209, 212
Sherwood, V., 2
Shevky, E., 198
Shipman, V. C., 42, 52
Shorter, E., 68
Shuval, J. T., 262
Silbereisen, R. K., 6
Simmons, R. G., 211, 264
Slobin, D. J., 97
Smith, P. K., 25
Smock, C. D., 182
Sonnenschein, S., 111, 112, 117
Speer, J. R., 116
Spitz, R., 25
Srole, L., 257
Staats, A. W., 2, 4, 11
Stanley, J. C., 19
Stayton, D. J., 69, 74, 93
Stenhouse, D., 16
Stern, D., 3
Sternglanz, S., 258
Stewart, J., 17
Strodtbeck, F. L., 42
Swift, B., 249
Szalai, A., 45, 47

Tajfel, H., 211
Takala, A., 42, 43
Takala, M., 24, 42, 43, 47, 57
Teahan, J. E., 274
Thurnher, M., 46
Tinbergen, N., 25
Tittler, B. I., 193
Tizard, J., 231, 234
Tomkiewicz, S., 17
Trevarthen, C., 3, 11
Trommsdorff, G., 273
Trump, J. L., 213
Turner, J., 211

Turner, T., 161

Ullman, V., 27, 29

Vallacher, R. R., 196
Vanhalakka-Ruoho, M., 59
Van Maanen, J., 263, 264
Van Meel, J., 136
Veness, T., 257
Viala, M., 29, 36
Vogt, C., 99
Volterra, V., 102
Von Cranach, M., 78, 82
Vygotsky, L. S., 76, 99

Wallace, M., 271
Waller, M., 5, 6
Walter, H., 43
Walters, G. C., 66
Wanous, J. P., 264, 267
Waterman, A. S., 263
Waterman, C. K., 263
Watts, J. C., 74
Wegner, D. M., 196
Weil, M. A., 192
Weiss, H., 261
Wells, C. G., 113
West, M. A., 248
White, B. J., 206
White, B. L., 74
Whitehurst, G. J., 111, 112, 117
Wilkins, L. T., 257
Williams, R. S., 271
Willmott, P., 44, 47
Wineman, D., 243, 244
Winterbottom, M. R., 42
Wood, D., 81, 82
Wundt, W., 13

Young, M., 44, 47

Zablocki, B. D., 44
Zaleska, M., 190, 218, 225, 229
Zani, B., 64, 78, 234
Zavalloni, M., 217
Zetterberg, H. L., 44
Zigler, E. F., 69